The

Yummy Mummy's
Survival Guide

About the author

Having left Cambridge armed with a science degree, Liz Fraser worked in TV, presenting such shows as BBC1's Holiday and Channel 4's The Virtual Body. After the birth of her second child, she gave up work to become a full-time mother. Six months later, in desperate need of adult conversation and a creative outlet, she returned to work part-time. She is now a freelance writer and lives in Cambridge, in a house not quite as tidy as she'd like, with her husband and three children.

The
Yummy Mummy's
Survival Guide

LIZ FRASER

HarperCollins*Publishers*

HarperCollins*Publishers*
77–85 Fulham Palace Road,
Hammersmith, London W6 8JB

www.harpercollins.co.uk

Published by HarperCollins*Publishers* 2006
4

A catalogue record for this book
is available from the British Library

ISBN 13 978 0 00 721343 6
ISBN 10 0 00 7211343 3

Set in Plantin

Printed in Great Britain by Clays Ltd, St Ives plc

For Harry

OK, I know it's not much, and you've read it already at least once, but it's the gesture that counts. Maybe you could use it to stop the spare room door from banging when the window's open? Oh, and while you're in there, is there any chance you could have a quick look at my laptop – it's gone funny again. Dinner at 6? Love you xx.

Contents

A small note to begin with, just in case you wanted to know

Here's the only breathing exercise in this book: I am not a perfect mum (sharp intake of breath). In fact, I have never met a perfect mum (and another), and the chances are fairly high that you won't turn out to be faultless in every way either (and, exhale). Despite our best efforts at self-improvement, domestic perfection and bum-firming, we are all real, faulty women, and we all come with a certain amount of rubbish-Mum-ness attached. And thank goodness for that, because otherwise it would all be hideously boring, and we'd have nothing to moan about.

My own route into motherhood was fast and furious: while my more sensible university peers went off to make money by getting fast-tracked into one glamorous, exciting career or another, I threw my science degree in the 'I have no idea what to do with you' bin, asked Mr Right to marry me (he said yes, thank goodness), and I found myself on my own fast-track to maternity clothes a year later, at the grand old age of 23.

Gulp.

And then the trouble started: the dreary, mumsy parenting books available to me left me, without exception, feeling like a highly unattractive, undesirable, lardy has-been, condemned to a life of grime, grudge and goo. According to these books, I would spend the rest of my days wearing shapeless, stained clothes and sharing vomit and poo stories with other lardy have-beens. My brain would be locked away in a secure vault to which I would be given the key some twenty or so years later.

Oh help! What had I done? Where were the beautiful, funny, appealing books about motherhood, which would treat me like a thinking woman complete with faults, worries and a shoe obsession, instead of like an impossibly perfect mother? Why couldn't I find a stylish book about motherhood, which I wouldn't have to hide behind a copy of *In Style* on my way to work, and which would tell me how my life would change in the coming year?

And that's where the idea for this book started: I would write it myself.

Alas with a new baby, a sizeable streak of laziness and a Blockbuster video down the road, I didn't get round to it, and it was soon forgotten, along with a million other 'brilliant ideas' I had dreamt up while making playdough sausages.

But now, eight years and three children later, I am coming under increasingly heavy fire from a barrage of questions about pregnancy and motherhood, launched at me by those same old friends, who are finally coming to join me down in the playground. They want honest, practical, relevant information about how to do the Yummy Mummy thing, and still keep their bodies, brains, wardrobes and lives in stylish order, and they seem to think I know...

In a bid to get some peace and quiet, I have written down everything I have learned about pregnancy and what you may experience in the first year of becoming a mother, in the most unpatronising, honest, unfrumpy way I can. Yummy Mummies have complicated, ever-changing lives, and we are required to glide seamlessly between different moods and personalities at the drop of this season's must-have headgear. To reflect this, I've written this book in several different moods, which you can turn to as you need them. You will also find extracts from my diaries, which should cheer you up and offer plenty of reassurance, and there are also strings of pearls of maternal wisdom from gorgeous Yummy Mummies, to whom I aspire daily.

The only thing I ask of you, dear, gorgeous reader, is that you are able to laugh at yourself. The key to surviving motherhood is to have a wicked sense of humour, and never to take yourself too seriously. And that's it. Enjoy it, take it with a pinch of salt where required, and I hope that some of this helps!

Liz xx.

What is a Yummy Mummy?

It's probably best that we get this rather crucial question answered before we go any further, just so that we are all on the same wavelength.

There are loads of different definitions being bandied about these days, so I shall give my own one here, and refer to it throughout the book when I talk about Yummy Mummies.

Yummy Mummy, n.

A mother, of any age, who does not identify with the traditional, dowdy image of motherhood. While she knows her Gap from her Gucci, she is just as happy with a charity shop bargain as an occasional, very necessary splurge, and doesn't want to give up on trying to look lovely just because she is a mother.

A Yummy Mummy is a skilled all-rounder: she tries to keep fit and healthy, loves spending time with her children, knows it's OK to break down and cry and (almost) never forgets to cleanse and moisturise. She can cook, amuse a baby and make work phone calls at the same time but, never one to take herself too seriously, she can laugh when it all goes wrong. A Yummy Mummy tries not to let being a good, loving mother utterly compromise her personal style and outside interests, and is always there to help her friends when they need her. Often juggling family and a job, she finds being both a mother and an independent woman very hard at times, but tries her best to make it work for her family, and for herself.

A Yummy Mummy is the ultimate modern woman.

PART ONE

Before It All Starts

Prepare, Prepare: What You Should Definitely Do *Before* Getting Pregnant (or what you should have done months ago, but could start now)

Growing a baby is like any other form of DIY: preparation is key. How you react to this first section depends entirely on your current situation (and on your sense of humour). If you are not pregnant yet, and you bought this book because you are somewhat curious about what lies around the next Big Corner, or you hope you might get pregnant *soon*, this is very good news: you still have a few months to play with before the big OFF, and there's plenty of opportunity to lay down some solid foundations.

If your bun is already rising in the oven, and you are merrily cruising down the road to Yummy Mummyhood, then some of what you read may sound a tad gloomy and depressing, and you'll be kicking yourself every paragraph or so. (As maternal luck would have it, one of the manoeuvres pregnant women can still do is kick themselves. Where's the justice?) Please try not to get too cross, and take heart from the fact that much of this preparation is never done by millions of perfectly gorgeous and healthy mothers every year.

For everyone else, like me, here are some things which, if you do them for about six months before you become pregnant, should reward you with an easier and healthier pregnancy, and will make life after the birth a lot less, errr, wobbly.

1. **Get Fit**

As the perfectly formed people at Nike tell us, ***JUST DO IT***. Even bold, capitals, italics and a forceful-looking font don't convey the importance of this Top Tip. Obviously, if you've never seen a pair of trainers before, then now is not a good time to start marathon running. But, being the self-respecting woman that you are, you probably look after your body well, and are reasonably fit already. This is excellent news, and a great position to start from.

Pregnancy plays the *most* havoc with your **stomach**, so if you can get your abs strong and toned before your pregnancy, you'll carry the baby better and you will get back into shape much more easily. I do speak from experience here: I was least fit before my first baby, and have become fitter and stronger in between each of the others. (Something to do with a growing fear that I've been lucky so far, and everything is about to fall apart and flab out all over the place!) My body coped and recovered much better the stronger my tummy muscles were *before* I started expanding, and it made getting back into some decent clothes much easier. Pain, gain, blah, blah.

Babies get very heavy towards the end, and having **strong legs** helps with the whole 'lugging yourself up flights of stairs' problem. The same goes for your **back**: strong back muscles will make carrying the baby much easier and less painful.

Something else to start toning up is your pelvic floor muscles. Pelvic what? Ha! Now we're really getting somewhere. Another of those 'never heard of them before I was pregnant; will think of them for the rest of my life afterwards' things, your pelvic floor muscles are the ones which allow you to stop weeing halfway through weeing, if you see what I mean. In a nutshell, they are completely trashed when you give birth, and unless you sit at your desk squeezing them in and holding for a count of three while your computer re-boots, you will never get on a trampoline again without incontinence pants.

And Agent Provocateur don't make those, in case you're wondering…
Strengthen your pelvic floors now, and you'll be able to jog, jump and
sneeze while your best undies stay Martini-dry.

2. Clean Yourself Out

If you've ever tried to detox then you'll know what a joyous, exciting time you're in for, but, equally, you will know how beneficial it
can be. Your baby is going to grow inside you, and if *you're* clogged
up with toxins then your baby will probably clog up pretty soon
too, because anything which is in *your* blood will get into your
growing baby's blood too. It takes a while to flush all the poisons
out of your system, so starting the clean-up well before you become
pregnant is a good idea.

☆ **Stop smoking.** Yummy Mummies don't smoke.
☆ **Cut down on coffee.** Coffee may taste great and be served in
   rather nice cafés absolutely everywhere, but it's still a strong stim-
   ulant, and there has been talk that it doesn't do growing babies
   much good. This may be why many women feel sick at the very
   smell of coffee in the early weeks. Clever old biology. The same
   goes for tea, if you can bear to give that up as well, but as with
   all things, use your head: the odd cup is almost certainly fine,
   especially if it cheers you up.
☆ **Drink less alcohol.** (Unless you drink tons, in which case, drink
   a lot less.) Pickled babies are not cool or Yummy at all.
☆ **Drugs.** Don't really need to say it, do I? You're intelligent – you
   work it out.
☆ **Don't panic if you haven't done any of this**, and you are several
   months down the line already: you are almost certainly in the
   majority, but starting now is better than not bothering at all.

3. Become a Health Freak

Your growing baby is entirely selfish, and will have no concern
for your wellbeing at all. It will drain all the goodness out of your

body, leaving you with the dregs, the cheeky young thing. Because pregnancy puts such a huge strain on your body, the healthier you are before you start, the better you will feel, the better your chances of having a healthy, strong baby, and the more quickly you'll recover afterwards. And it's after the baby is born that you need more reserves and stamina than ever… So, eat tons of fresh fruit and veg, up the iron intake (it makes you less tired), drink lots of water, get plenty of fresh air and all that other healthy stuff you know about already. You won't regret it.

4. Take Folic Acid
'Top Scientists' have found very good evidence that taking 400mg of this stuff for the first three months of pregnancy can significantly reduce the risk of your baby developing spina bifida. They now recommend that you get your levels up before you're pregnant, and that you take it throughout your pregnancy. Not a lot to ask really.

5. Take a Special Multivitamin
Only take a multivitamin which is specifically designed for pregnancy. Certain vitamins are potentially harmful to the foetus if levels get too high, and the pregnancy multivits have just the right amount of everything. Bless those Top Scientists.

Some Good News
One of the best things about getting pregnant for the first time is that it shocks you into being more healthy almost overnight, and once you've learned some new habits, and have managed to give up the three vodka and tonics and a kebab on the way home from work, you might just hang on to them for the rest of your life. It may feel like a brutal change of diet and lifestyle to start with, but there are great benefits. There's a good reason why pregnant ladies are said to 'glow' halfway through the pregnancy – *anyone* who pays as much careful attention to eating well and avoiding all toxins would glow after a couple of months! See your clean-up act as the

best beauty routine ever, and it might not feel so hard. In fact, for many of you it won't be hard at all, as your new body just doesn't *feel* like ingesting tons of toxins every day. Anyway, you'll be back on the double tall lattes before your baby can say 'Mummy, are you sure you wouldn't rather have an organic peppermint tea?'

Common Concerns of Future Yummy Mummies

This section is for you if you have ever worried about what it might be like to become a **MOTHER** (in other words, if you're just like every woman I've ever met). Oh, how we ladies love to worry! The list of concerns and questions all future Yummy Mummies carry around in their heads is breathtaking, and it makes one fret for the future of the human race: will anything make all you potentially fantastic mothers take the plunge and actually *procreate*? Will any reassuring words overcome your dread of turning into a fat, boring Frumpy Mummy, who fails miserably at every aspect of baby care, and who never sees the inside of a fancy restaurant again?

I seem to spend half of my free time pacifying freaked-out child-less friends who are terrified of committing to their perceived life of drudgery, lard and frumpiness. 'Hang on!' I cry. 'Are you saying *I'm* lardy and frumpy? Did *I* know what I was doing before I started? Do I know *now*?' No, no and no.

However, I have learned quite a few things about what it feels like to become a Yummy Mummy, and I'll do my best to ease at least *some* of the stress. Where I fail, watching anything with Paul Bettany in it should relieve any furrowed brows.

Here are some of the most common worries my friends seem to have, and some mildly helpful advice:

I don't feel very maternal – maybe I'll be an awful mother
This is a disaster. You will never be a good mother, and you should book in for a hysterectomy immediately. You probably shouldn't have pets either. Or houseplants.

I'm lying, of course: very few women feel very maternal before they have a baby, and most go on to become fantastic mums. (Many don't even feel that maternal *after* the birth, but it's not something people like to talk about. I like to talk about it a lot, and so I do in Part Five).

It's not even clear what feeling 'maternal' means, anyway. In a similar way to how much libido a woman has, so women have varying degrees of maternal urges, and there's nothing to say that you should be consumed with the desire to foster every child on the planet before having a baby yourself.

'Feeling Maternal' could mean any, or none, of the following:

☆ Realising that babies and children exist.
☆ Being able to sit in the same room as a child without feeling annoyed or put off your food.
☆ Finding children quite cute.
☆ Saying 'Ahhhhhhh' when you watch a nappy advert.
☆ Starting to cry at the mere mention that somebody you know, or even somebody you don't know, has had a baby.
☆ Buying baby clothes when you haven't even found a prospective father yet (and this is a sure-fire way never to find one, unless you keep it very secret).
☆ Genuinely liking the smell of newborn babies, rather than just *saying* you do.
☆ Being able to wipe somebody else's child's snotty nose without retching (I still haven't reached this point yet).

Wherever you sit on this scale *before* you have a baby, you will almost certainly sit somewhere else afterwards, and not necessarily at the more maternal end. I didn't feel the overwhelming urge to have babies before I became pregnant for the first time, and I was quite able to pass babies in the street without drooling. In fact, I was barely aware of their *existence* until I was at least five months pregnant, and that was mainly because I was checking out groovy pram models.

Happily, something inside my brain changed the moment I held my first baby, and I have been unable to hear a baby crying or see a child in distress since without being overcome with the compulsion to cheer the poor thing up. It's just Yummy Mummy Nature doing her bit, and luckily it works for the majority of women. I've also had periods of feeling very un-maternal, for reasons I'm yet to understand, but these pass and I get back to being sickeningly in love with all three of mine very quickly.

Don't worry if you don't think you feel maternal enough: either you will become more maternal when your baby arrives, or you will remain as you are and do a perfectly good job of looking after your baby anyway. Worrying about it now is pointless: you just have to wait and see what happens, and stop telling yourself that you're not kitted out to be a mother. If you've got a heart, a womb, some self-respect and a sense of humour then you're good to go.

I don't want to get fat

This seems to be one of the biggest off-putters for my child-free friends. I can't believe how many pre-pregnant, gorgeous women freak out about this. Why should you get fat? If you're not fat now, and if you care about how you look, and if you don't want to become fat, then why should pregnancy make you fat? It's a bit like saying: 'I really want to go to Antigua this summer, but I'm worried I'll get sunburn.' Pack some sunblock then, stay in the shade and wear a wide-brimmed hat. Bingo – no sunburn!

Seriously, though, worrying about becoming fat during pregnancy is normal, because it happens to quite a lot of previously slim-line ladies. But the news is very good: if you are careful about what you eat, if you continue to exercise and if you don't treat pregnancy as an excuse to eat all the pies, then you will almost certainly not get fat. A little rounder-of-hip perhaps, but not *fat*. (See **You're Eating for *How* Many?** in Part Three.)

What about the rest of my body? Won't it be ruined?

No, it won't. Lots of bits of your body *will* change, not necessarily for the better, but with a lot of effort most of this is perfectly fixable. If you are really worried about what will happen to your lovely body when you become a Yummy Mummy, then here are some honest truths:

☆ You *might* get stretch marks, but many large mothers don't, many skinny, childless women (and men!) do, and there are ways of reducing the damage, should you be genetically challenged in this department.

☆ Your breasts will first become much bigger, and then much, much smaller and less pert. There's always surgery, or you could, or probably should, just learn to like them that way.

☆ You *might* get varicose veins, but rarely after a first pregnancy, and your genetic makeup has more of a role to play than any growing baby does.

☆ Your tummy will become more wobbly for a while, but this is absolutely curable with enough crunching and squeezing, if wobbly's not your thing.

☆ *But:* You get a child at the end of it all, and no amount of wobble or droop can outweigh the positives of having a baby. Some perspective, please!

What if I mess it all up?

This is a hard one to answer, because I suppose you *might* mess it all up; you *might* be the worst mother ever known; you *might* leave your new baby in a motorway filling station by mistake because you were busy trying to open a packet of M&Ms and got distracted; your marriage *might* fall apart because of the sudden droopiness of your boobs; and your children *might* hate you forever and turn to a life of drugs and crime. You *might* be forced to spend the rest of your life with 'The Terrible Mother Who Messed It All Up' tattooed across your forehead.

Or, you might just surprise yourself and cope very well. That's the thrill of it – you have no idea how it is going to go, things change every minute and you just have to fly by the seat of your still-gorgeous pants and hope for the best. You may have to readjust what your idea of 'the best' is, to fit in with the realities of looking after a baby and keeping your sanity, but you are more than likely to do a fantastic job and not mess anything up at all.

What about my career?

This is a very tricky one, and, depending on what you do for a living, this could be more or less of a real worry for you.

Some types of work just don't allow for Yummy Mummyhood at all, because they require your presence fourteen hours a day, 365 days a year (if, say, you are the Prime Minister), or because there are physical factors to take into consideration, like being an astronaut or something.

Assuming you are neither an astronaut nor the Prime Minister, then **having a baby should *not* mean the end of your career,** and any employer who suggests it does should be hung, drawn and quartered. Or something else which isn't very nice. The only effect that becoming a mother will have on your career is that everything you do will be enormously more difficult and complicated forever: there will be logistical and practical hurdles involving childcare, illness and just getting out of the house on time, and every day will now carry a huge emotional burden.

If you do go back to work, three things will be different:

☆ You will have to work harder than everybody else to prove that you are not a waste of company time and money.
☆ You will feel guilty because you are not with your baby.
☆ Your career progression will probably slow down.

If you can handle all of that, and can accept having to take a step back – or sideways – for a while, then some of the worry will be eased.

The real rub is that you, like most other women these days, have probably decided to think about having a baby at exactly the point in your career when things could really take off. You have worked hard throughout your twenties to reach a certain rung on the career ladder, and the last thing you want to do is jump off the ladder, only to be begrudgingly allowed back on somewhere near the bottom again.

This is fair enough. But a Yummy Mummy knows that having a baby is something important that she wants to do in her life, and she will find a way to make it work for her, somehow.

It all comes down to one question: **which is more important to you – furthering your career now, or having a family now?** Only *you* can answer that, and deep down you know the answer already. In this country we can, at last, have a career *and* a young family without drowning in other people's scorn and too bloody right. But this long-overdue progress can't solve the central issue: **you can't do both of them 100% of the time or give them both 100% of your energy and care.** You just have to decide where the balance lies for you.

The only thing which is *not* OK is doing something you are not happy with because you feel pressured, worried or guilty, or because somebody forces you to. You do what you gotta do, and all will be wonderful.

I'm just not that organised!

No you're not, and why should you be? I wasn't, no mum I ever met was always as frighteningly organised as she is now, but by some as-yet-unexplained process you will become highly skilled at getting a hundred times more stuff done in a much more efficient and effective way than you can at the moment. You'll still forget half of what you need to remember, but you *will* become more organised.

Chrissie Rucker, founder of The White Company
Don't worry if you are not a very organised person yet – I was never organised at all, but having a baby changes all of that. You learn very quickly how to keep on top of things, and you develop your own system of doing things which works for you.

Isn't it selfish to be a Yummy Mummy?

No.

Real Yummy Mummies dedicate huge amounts of their time and emotional energy to loving and caring for their children – but always reserve some time to make *themselves* feel special too, which generally involves bottles of sweet-smelling lotions and gorgeous things to hang in their wardrobes.

Real Yummy Mummies would rather spend time with their children than anything else – but realise that spending *no* time away from them is very unhealthy and can lead to lifeless hair and a deeply wrinkled brow.

If you are simply too selfish to look after your children properly then you are a Rotten Mummy, not a Yummy Mummy, and you don't need a book, just a good telling off.

I'm too embarrassed about people poking around 'down there'

Not much I can say to this one, except 'Oh grow up.' Doctors have seen it all before, and they really don't (or shouldn't) get a kick out of examining your cervix. Your vagina looks like the millions of other vaginas your midwife has already inspected, and there's almost nothing which can embarrass them.

That said, there does seem to be an unfeasible amount of prodding, poking and measuring involved throughout pregnancy, and also well after the birth, and even the least prudish and most patient of you will be pushed to the limit. I never got used it, and I still *hate* being asked to 'lie down on the bed and bend your knees up'. Except by my husband. Unfortunately it's just part of being a woman, and the only way to deal with it is to stop thinking of yourself as a person and throw yourself into the glamorous role of 'car going in for a service'. If you can be an Aston Martin rather than a Ford Mondeo that will also help.

I'm scared of all the pain

This is a very good sign. It shows you are a normal, healthy, sensible woman who knows that squeezing a hard object the size of a basketball through your very small and delicate parts will hurt like hell. It also shows that you have put some considerable thought into the 'motherhood' issue, and have already reached the critical stumbling block. Good. Now you progress past this point by realising the following:

☆ Giving birth is the most painful thing you should ever experience. It is agonisingly, excruciating, faint-inducingly painful.
☆ Once you have done it, no other pain will ever seem as bad (until you do it again).
☆ Doesn't the fact that some women go through it more than once show it can't be *that* bad? Actually it is that bad, but Mother Nature has solved this by ensuring that…
☆ You will forget how awful childbirth is almost immediately.
☆ Not all women find childbirth terribly painful.
☆ The drugs work. No pain; lots of gain.
☆ Put it in perspective: when the result of this pain is your own baby, who will grow into a child, an adult and then the bearer of your grandchildren, and will fill your life with more joy and love than you can imagine yet, what's twelve hours of pain, really? I would go through a month of pain to get the children I have now. Ahhhhh.
☆ The pain stops abruptly once the baby is out. Most discomforts and pains linger on for ages and gradually just peter out. Not childbirth: it's excruciating one minute, and then it's completely gone the next. And *that* feels fantastic!
☆ Going through childbirth gives you the automatic and unquestionable right to have the tapless end of the bath, never take the bins out and have a foot tickle every night for the rest of your life. If he does question this right, suggest you shave his testicles with a cheese-grater, and see how fast he moves.

What if things go wrong between me and my partner?
Not the most optimistic way to approach motherhood, but if you *will* examine every depressing possibility then I guess I would agree that having a baby puts a vast amount of strain on the relationship you have with your husband, or partner, or whatever we're calling him or her. Whatever your relationship is now, it will be completely different once you have a baby, and even well before that moment actually comes. The only way of succeeding is to **TALK about EVERY-THING** and to know where you stand before you get too far down a road you're not happy with. There is more about this in **New Relationships** in Part Eleven, but, until then, perhaps telling your

partner about your concerns is a good idea, as is setting out to make it work instead of preparing for it to fail.

I'm too old/ I'm too young

Well at least you can't be worrying about both of these!

There is no 'good time' to have a baby – what suits some people doesn't suit others. I did it very young, which means I had tons of energy (never underestimate how important this is), my body didn't suffer very much, by the time I was thirty I had all my child-bearing days all over with, (I think, but I still have all the baby clothes in the attic) and I will be able to wear my daughters' far more fashionable clothes very soon. BUT, I missed out on my carefree, childless twenties, I didn't manage to get my career going as I might have liked, my husband and I had very few years alone together, and I now have to do the career and kids things at the same time.

Older mums have the advantages of enjoying a successful career first, often having more money, being more self-confident and sure of what they want and wanting the time away from work to enjoy being a mum. BUT, it is harder to get pregnant as you get older (tick-tock, tick-tock); you will find the exhaustion harder to cope with; your body will probably suffer more and be harder to get back into shape; you will find all those years of independence and smart, child-free living very hard to leave behind; and you may find it harder to get back to work at the same level in your late thirties or early forties.

Both ways are good and both are bad. I would just urge as many women as possible to remember the biological clock. Science is great and everything, and there have been some huge advances in fertility treatments, but the wobbly bottom line is that, in the same way that 8 inch stilettos are not designed for rock climbing, so we are not designed to have babies in our fifties. We can still do it, but it's a heck of a lot harder. Just wanted to get that off my pert-ish chest.

PART TWO

Pregnancy –
The Early Days...

On your marks, get set...what?

Here's where our little journey into Yummy Mummyhood kicks off, and I start waffling about nipples, hormones, pelvic floor muscles and elasticated waists. Once we've started, there's no turning back (which is one of the key concepts to grasp when you're going to have a baby), so if you need a little Dutch Courage, go get it now, while you still can.

Ready now? Let's go.

The first few weeks of your pregnancy can be the most exhilarating, debilitating, confusing and terrifying weeks you have ever experienced. Yippee. With your emotions bouncing around like Zebedee on speed, your body starting to do the most peculiar and unpleasant things, and your list of worries growing as fast as your certainty that this was a Good Plan is shrinking, you can be left wondering whether you really are only pregnant, or whether you have been transported to a parallel, less pleasant universe.

Things will get a lot easier, so if you can just get through the initial shock, everything will be cool...

Getting Pregnant – A Brief Biology Re-cap

What's the best way to conceive?

Have sex.

That really is all there is to be said on the matter, and anyone who gets themselves bogged down with sexual positions, moon phases, eating certain fertility-boosting foods, the right music, positive mental vibes or other mumbo-jumbo is wasting a lot of shagging energy. In my humble opinion. If you have sex, you might become pregnant and that's the end of it. Having difficulty conceiving is no laughing matter at all, and it's one of life's cruellest tests. Unfortunately life is how it is, and some people are just more fertile than others. How you decide to go about raising your chances is up to you, and there is a lot of detailed information out there on the subject. For now, here are some tips which might help you out a little:

☆ **The more you worry about it, the less likely you are to get pregnant**. I don't know why it is, but this really seems to be true. Look at all the women who try for years with no luck, and the second they adopt a baby they find themselves expecting twins. Those who want a baby can try desperately for ages in vain, while the reckless, highly fertile singleton who just fancies a quickie in the stationery cupboard is pregnant in less time than it would have taken to actually *get* the printer cartridge she pretended to be fetching. It's unbelievable and very unfair, but the mind is a powerful thing. So, if you can, try not to be desperate for a baby, and you might find yourself knocked up in no time. Well, a few minutes maybe.

☆ **Forget predictor kits**. These are supposed to tell you when the most likely time to conceive is, but they feel like a big con to me. The manufacturers are preying on our nervous, befuddled disposition and our desperate need for anything which seems like it might help. I took several of these tests, for exactly that reason, but I always felt that *I knew*, from my own cycle length and finger-counting, when the most likely time to conceive was, and that I was just paying a lot of money for some confirmation of this. Again, it's a very costly way of being told something you probably know anyway. Shagging frequently is cheaper and much more fun, and makes the event a lot less like a military operation.

☆ **Don't have sex for a few days before your most fertile spell**. I know this sounds very cruel, but I have heard that saving up a bit more sperm and then delivering it all in one go (so to speak) can boost your chances of getting one determined little bugger who makes it all the way.

☆ **Try to enjoy it**. We've all done it, or know someone who has: we've looked at the calendar, checked our watches and run downstairs shouting, 'Switch the footie off – we have to have sex NOW!' This is not very sexy, and the moment having sex becomes nothing more than an exercise in getting pregnant is the moment it stops being fun. Once this has happened, it's hard to go back.

☆ **Don't tell anybody you are trying to get pregnant**. A fatal mistake, because once the pressure is on, the likelihood of conceiving will drop through the floor. Act like all those sensible celebrities who 'have no plans to start a family just yet', but who have decorated the nursery and already own six pairs of baby Nikes. This is also a good protective measure for your partner, because if you *do* having trouble conceiving, everybody will assume there's something wrong with his John Thomas, and that can't boost a man's self-esteem.

The Thin Blue Line: *That* Moment

I love a good 'apparently' as much as the next Yummy Mummy, but this one really takes the Farley's Rusk. *Apparently*, some women can go to full term without ever noticing they are pregnant. *Apparently*, they just feel a bit bloated, and then one day they go to the loo, experience an 'odd' sensation and wham! a fully developed baby drops into the bowl. Apparently.

To counteract this strange group of women who house a black hole in their abdomen is another unlikely type who, *apparently*, know they are pregnant the second a sperm arrives, gasping, at an ovum. These same ladies can usually tell you the sex, weight and IQ of the unborn child as well.

For the rest of us (who also don't believe that a swan can break your arm or that you can *really* think yourself slim), learning that we are pregnant is life-changing news, confirmed by a strip of blue ink about a centimetre long and a millimetre wide which smells of wee. Cruelly, this line is almost impossible to see if you are desperate for a baby, and is impossible to miss if you're hoping that you're just a bit late because of the recent extra stress at work.

Taking a pregnancy test isn't like waiting for the lottery result, or standing on the scales after a week's skiing and fondue-eating. **It's a huge deal.** If you've ever stood in the loo with a thong around your ankles, holding a white plastic pen-like object to the light and straining your eyes in the desperate hope for a trace, *any trace at all*, of something which could possibly pass for a blue or even a blue-*ish* streak while time stands still and your bottom freezes, then you'll understand what I mean. I remember asking my husband after several negative tests if he was absolutely *sure* he couldn't see anything there, and he suggested I go and have my eyes checked instead of my hormone levels.

Before taking a pregnancy test, there are some tell-tale signs of possible pregnancy to look out for, but not everyone gets any of these, so don't worry if you feel perfectly normal – you may well be pregnant, but just be one of the very lucky few who are in for an easy ride...here's hoping!

- ☆ **Missed period.** Duh. No, really?
- ☆ **Extreme tiredness.** I really do mean *extreme* here: it's not just 'more tired than normal', but an overwhelming, unbeatable exhaustion unlike any other, which leaves you falling asleep in meetings, feeling like a lead weight and crawling into bed at 7.30. It does pass though!
- ☆ **Weeing between ad-breaks.** If you can't make it until the next commercial break for a trip to the loo, go back and check your dates again.
- ☆ **Tender breasts and nipples.** Not necessarily *sore*, but much more sensitive than normal, in a bad way. Fondling is not welcomed, and going bra-less is impossible.

☆ **Feeling bloated**. As most of us feel like this at some point in the month it's not such a good indicator, but if it's much more than usual and combined with tenderness in your abdomen, then there could be a teeny, weeny bun in there.

☆ **Feeling or being sick**. (Unless you drank two bottles of wine the night before, in which case it's just a bad hangover.) This sickness is not restricted to the morning, so if you're talking to God on the big white telephone every evening, something might be afoot.

If you've experienced any, all or none of these things and you think you *might* be pregnant, it's probably time for a test to confirm things. Pregnancy tests are unbelievably accurate, and can detect the tiniest increases in hormone levels, so they are a very good way of getting an answer. But, before you rush to Boots, here are some survival tips for taking pregnancy tests:

☆ **Don't do too many.** They are very expensive, and you usually have to take several, because it's the wrong time of the month, you drop it in the toilet (I've done that *four* times!) or you just refuse to believe the result. I've spent a small fortune on them over my three pregnancies, and, looking back, I wasted a lot of money. If you can, try to wait a few days between tests (the packet should tell you exactly how many), and if you still have any doubts ask for a free test from your kind GP.

☆ **Get it over with.** Waiting for the best moment to do a test is futile: you will be so wound up with nerves that you'll mess it up and have to do another one. Get up, wee, look, and then cry either way.

☆ **Don't worry about doing it right.** If you are, you are: whether you've had a glass of water first, or have drunk too much coffee, or weed on it for eight seconds instead of five, if you're pregnant the test will be positive. Almost definitely. But do get confirmation if you want to be sure.

When that moment happens, and the little window signals the end of your life as you know it, you cannot predict how you will react. Some of my friends fainted (a tad over-dramatic I'd say), others cried or laughed or screamed with delight (or woe – they're never quite clear on why they screamed…). I tended to be quite quiet, which always surprised me, as I imagined I would at least whoop a *little*. Perhaps it was just the fact that I was still naked from the waist down.

Tired, Tired, Tired

We've all been tired. We've been tired after partying too hard, working too hard or making babies too hard.

When you are pregnant, however, you will experience a new kind of tiredness – actually a kind of total, numbing exhaustion – which is so intense and overpowering that you might mistake it for certain, impending death. This sudden, debilitating tiredness was always my first clue that I was pregnant, and every time it left me baffled: how can something so tiny reduce a grown woman to a useless heap? When you're seven months down the line and hauling about a considerable amount of bulk around with you, feeling exhausted will seem perfectly understandable. But not in the first few *weeks!* There's nothing *there!* You can't see anything, feel anything, or, worse still, tell anyone yet, so you have to suffer in complete silence.

Survival Tips

☆ **Lie.** If you are not ready to tell anyone yet, then you will need to have some fantastic 'Oh, yeah, I was at *another* amazing party last night' stories lined up if you are to explain why the bags under your eyes are bigger than the ones you come back carrying after an extended lunch-break, and why you are suddenly falling asleep at your desk several times before morning coffee (which you are suddenly not drinking…)

☆ **Don't fight it.** This is not the kind of tiredness that can be out-done by regular double-espressos. During pregnancy, your body is very good at letting you know what's needed, and the intensity of tiredness in the early stages can only mean that you should get as much sleep as possible. I went to sleep well before anything decent was on telly for the whole of this miserable period, and it was a very wise move, if very boring. Maybe Nature is just preparing you for the decades of sleepless nights to come...

☆ **Indulge in some pampering.** Falling asleep because you're tired is one thing, but dozing off because you are so relaxed that your legs can't move any more is quite another. Treat yourself, and these weeks will glide by in an aromatherapeutic haze. Ahhhhhhh.

☆ **Take some exercise.** Not only is this a stage when you still *can*, but it's also a good way of feeling energised, looking better as the blood gets into your grey cheeks at last, and forgetting how rough you may be feeling. Don't do anything super-strenuous or new: your body is a bit confused, so stick to what it can already handle.

☆ **Remind yourself daily that it won't last long.** This early tiredness usually passes within a month or so, so get the rest you need, and look forward to better times around the corner.

Breaking the News

1. To the father (who I shall assume is also your partner)

This is the fun part. As the holder of some earth-shattering news, you are in a position of considerable power. So what do you do? Tell him straight away? Over the phone? After work? By text? (Never by text. It's absolutely not the done thing).

I developed my own little routine for breaking my exciting news: I kept it to myself all day, while the enormity of it sank in, and I then took my husband to a bar after work, ordered him a double whiskey and myself a gin and tonic, and told him straight out. The first time he was surprised and delighted, the second time he looked less surprised but equally delighted, and when it came to announcement number three, in the very same bar, he just asked me when it was due before the drinks had arrived. Spoilsport.

2. To your parents

This is a lot less fun, or at least it was for me, and I've heard similar stories of disappointment from other friends. Telling your parents you are expecting should be a perfect, bonding, happy-families kind of moment, where time slows down, everything goes a little out of focus and somebody starts to play the harp. In reality, breaking the news to the future grandparents can leave you feeling somewhat short-changed.

I've heard of responses ranging from 'Oh at last. We were beginning to wonder', to 'Already! But it's only been three years', and even the astounding, but absolutely true, 'Are you *very* sure? Hold on, I have to drain the potatoes. Can I call you back after dinner?'

No doubt your own parents and in-laws will be as beside themselves with excitement as you are, but it's good to be prepared for a less-than-ideal reaction. Perhaps the idea of becoming grandparents is too much to take in, and they just say whatever pops into their heads first. Or perhaps they really are that tactless.

3. To your friends

Oooooh, lots and lots of fun. Friends are so great at this kind of thing because, being friends, they know exactly what they should say to make you feel fantastic, and they deliver every time. This kind of news is usually cause for a party and lots of gorgeous presents, so pick a time when your diary is looking free.

When Should We Tell?

Because the first few months of pregnancy can be a bit risky, and miscarriages are most common within the first twelve weeks, you might want to try and hold off breaking the news until you have passed this milestone. Another advantage of holding off as long as possible is that friends don't get bored of the whole thing by the time you're only halfway there. Nine months is a heck of a long time for someone to be excited about something which only affects them at a distance. Waiting until you first start to show (usually at around four months) means that before they know it you're into the final stage and ready to go. Much more exciting.

That said, if you tell your friends and family the moment you know, they will be able to help you through this difficult, vomitty, sore-boobs, random-tears stage, and if things *do* go sadly wrong after all that, as they do sometimes, you will have a lot of much-needed support.

Work: Mum's the Word? When to Tell, What to Expect

How you play your cards when it comes to spilling the beans to your employer is up to you. Maybe you have a fantastic relationship with them, and they are super family-friendly, in which case you'll probably walk away with a bunch of flowers and your first pair of baby booties. If, on the other hand, you are instrumental in a huge company buyout, which is due to complete three weeks before your due date, then you should expect less jubilation.

I had one bad experience of this, which happened during the final round of auditions for a career-making presenting job. I was newly pregnant for the second time, and I decided that the honourable thing to do was to let them know, because Saturday morning kids' TV wasn't, and still isn't, exactly awash with pregnant presenters. When I didn't get the job I spent the next few months fuming at the injustice, and quite convinced that I missed out because of my expanding waistline. (I now realise it was because I was rubbish, but it was hard to see that at the time!)

Once bitten, twice very devious, and the next time I was in a similar position I decided to keep schtum. I *still* didn't get the gig, but at least this time I knew it was because I wasn't right for the job, and not because I was gestating. There are, however, some **legal and practical guidelines** to be aware of:

☆ **You cannot be dismissed (sacked, fired, booted out, shown the door) for being pregnant.**
☆ **To qualify for statutory maternity pay** you must tell your employer that you are pregnant by the fifteenth week before you are due, *and* tell them when you intend to take your maternity leave.

★ **You don't *have* to tell your boss that you are pregnant** (but he or she will probably notice eventually).

★ **You can take time off for antenatal appointments** and classes without missing out on any pay..

★ **You don't have to tell a potential employer** at a job interview, and if you do, they can't discriminate against you. (Even though they probably will, but will claim it's because you are overqualified, underqualified, or some other nonsense like that.)

The details of your maternity rights are far too dull for this beautiful book, but if you want all the useful facts then go to www.tiger.gov.uk.

Olivia, mother of Clemmie, eight months

I had to take a bunch of journalists on a flight to Scotland at nine weeks pregnant, and I couldn't let on that I felt like throwing up the whole time. I had to concentrate so hard on overcoming the constant feeling of nausea, and I sucked Murray Mints the entire day. Twelve hours later, after I'd dispensed with the press packs and waved everyone a jolly goodbye, I dashed back to the car and immediately threw up.

Hello Boys! Some Physical Changes You (and Others) Might Notice

The starting gun will still be smoking when your body starts to change all over the place, and the rate at which this happens can be alarming. One of the good side-effects of pregnancy is that your breasts get bigger: even if you have practically no breasts at all you will develop something worthy of a decent 'Phwoooaaar!' if you happen to pass a building site. This is just one of the changes you'll notice within weeks of fertilisation, along with the following:

★ Your boobs become tender and harder (oh great) before getting noticeably bigger (great!).

☆ The skin around your nipples gets darker (this part is called the areola, if you really want to know).

☆ You might get light-headed easily.

☆ It gets harder to pull your abdomen in successfully and pretend you have a washboard stomach: it's like having permanently bad premenstrual fluid retention, except this time it doesn't go away – it just gets worse.

☆ You have trouble sleeping, despite being exhausted.

☆ You start having very complicated, frantic dreams, in which you already have a baby but you keep doing all sorts of dreadful things to it, such as dropping it off the top floor of Selfridges, leaving it at a bus stop, forgetting you put it in the bath while you went out for a meal, only to find…well, it's not pretty, but it's just a normal reaction to your huge news.

☆ You might start to feel sick, or even be sick (see **Morning Sickness** below).

Morning Sickness: If Only it Were That Simple...

What a misnomer! Firstly, as millions of women every year discover, it does *not* only occur in the morning, and secondly, it does not always involve being sick. The (presumably male) genius who came up with the term 'morning sickness' should have spent a month or two in *our* house during the first trimester of my pregnancies, and then maybe we'd have had something more realistic to work with: 24-Hour Nausea, Early Evening Retch, or Twelve-Week Hell, for example.

From what I've read, this 'feeling really sick', which you are very likely to experience to *some* degree in the first few months, seems to have something to do with hormones, as usual, and the reasons it seems worse in the *morning* are, apparently:

☆ The levels of these wretched hormones are higher in the morning.

☆ Your stomach is empty, so you feel sicker.

☆ It's Nature's clever way of saying 'Put that third pain au chocolat down! You're about to start expanding wildly, so just suck on a lemon drop instead.'

I suffered from evening sickness, which confounds all these theories. I was fine all day until about three or four in the afternoon, and from then on it was just a case of surviving until my husband came back from work (he had to negotiate shorter hours just to get me through those weeks). I would immediately collapse into bed and try to fall asleep, just so that I could forget how awful I was feeling. Oh, happy days.

The other misleading thing about 'morning sickness' is that it sounds as though you are actually going to be sick. If only. In fact, one of the things I found hardest to bear was that I *wasn't* sick. Ever. I always felt that if I could only *be* sick, I would somehow feel relieved and better, but I never was. It was just hour after hour of *feeling* sick, like terrible sea-sickness, except that, being pregnant, I didn't want to take any anti-sickness tablets, because of the potential health risks. I even *made* myself sick a couple of times, just to get some relief, and although I did feel better for a while afterwards, it wasn't for long and it's probably not a very good idea.

Common Concerns

I'm just being pathetic

No you're not. Feeling nauseous and being sick for week after week is physically and mentally crippling, and for many of my friends it was the worst part of the whole pregnancy. For some it was even worse than the actual birth part, so don't ever kid yourself that you should just pull your socks up and stop being such a whinger: you're pregnant, so whinge away! Anyone who hasn't eaten properly for six weeks, feels as though they are on the high seas with Ellen MacArthur, and is trying to come to terms with the mind-blowing fact that there's a human being growing inside her is entitled, and absolutely *bound*, to feel well below par and to want some sympathy. Morning sickness is not just a mildly unpleasant inconvenience – it can be almost unbearable, so give yourself a break and spend some extra time trying to look after yourself.

I'm not eating enough because I feel so sick. Is it bad for the baby?
Miraculously, if you are managing to eat and drink anything at all, your baby will carry on as if nothing is wrong. That's where your reserves come in handy: the baby takes all the nutrients it needs from what you have stored up over the last few years, and it can survive very well off those while you walk around like a nauseous zombie for a few months. But if you can't keep any food or liquid down then you must get medical help. There is a condition called Hyperemesis Gravidarum which causes this sort of complete food rejection, and you can get more information at www.hyperemesis.org. A small number of women end up in hospital for a while if the sickness gets really bad, so keep an eye on things.

So what can I do to make it better?
Short of spending a night (or several) with Gael Garcia Bernal or receiving a lifetime's supply of Crème de la Mer products, I really have no idea, because there are as many supposed remedies for the condition as there are positions for getting yourself knocked up in the first place. As that is so obviously *not* the answer you were after, here are some suggestions from my Yummy Mummy friends which are all *supposed* to help:

☆ Eat more ginger – crystallised, or in tea or capsules – or slowly nibble ginger biscuits.
☆ Eat small amounts regularly, so your stomach never becomes empty.
☆ Sip water frequently.
☆ Get more sleep and rest.
☆ Cut out coffee and alcohol.
☆ Only turn left, except on Wednesdays when there is a full moon (no, not that one).
☆ Smell fresh mint.
☆ Get as much fresh air as possible.
☆ Press your pressure points: $1\frac{1}{2}$ inches from your wrist on the underneath of your forearm, in the centre. Try it – it just might work!

☆ Take extra vitamin B6, or eat more nuts, bananas, avocados and whole grains, which contain it.
☆ Try yeasty foods, such as Marmite, bagels, dry fruits and beer (sparingly!).
☆ Eat more iron-rich foods, such as beef, sardines, eggs and leafy greens.

I tried all of these to almost no avail. The things which made *me* feel a little better were brushing my teeth about fifteen times a day, smelling fresh coffee and drinking diet lemonade.

Sonia, mother of Freya, two, and Louis, eight months

It sounds mad, but I had to drink a can of ice-cold Coke the minute I woke up, and I was absolutely fine all day after that. After about eight weeks all the symptoms disappeared, but I still have my morning fix!

I've recently discovered all kinds of 'natural' remedies available on the Web, which all have glowing reports from absolutely-not-nauseous-at-all-any-more mothers. These include naturally coloured lollipops, glamorously named 'Preggy Pops' (wouldn't you just love to have sat in on *that* meeting?), wristbands that apply pressure to your wrists and apparently relieve nausea that way, and even specially compiled recordings of soothing sea noises for pregnant ears. This last idea seems somewhat insulting to our intelligence: pregnancy may leave you a bit befuddled for a while, but surely it doesn't render you gullible enough to shell out a tenner for some whale songs and wave noises in the belief that they will ease the queasiness? I suppose if the nausea gets completely unbearable then you will probably be ready to try almost anything. Even whale songs will seem worth a try. **Do not, however, take any anti-sickness pills** without asking your doctor. There are many available, and not all are suitable during pregnancy.

One final thing you should be prepared for, as I wasn't the first time, is that it *doesn't* last for 12 weeks and then stop. Or, at least, it *might*, but it almost certainly won't. Everyone I have talked to has had a different experience. Things always settled down for me at around this time, but for every textbook case there's one lucky lady who never gets sick at all, and another one who throws up three times a day for nine months. *C'est la vie!*

Oh, and it does tend to get a little bit worse with multiple babies and with each successive pregnancy, so count yourself lucky you're not on baby number six yet!

More Worries

More? How much can one woman worry about?

I'm afraid sections dealing with worries, concerns, fears and feelings of utter doom and gloom will crop up time and time again throughout this book. This is not because I am the world's greatest pessimist, or because I am trying to wind you up into a panic, but because *you* will experience many of these worries over the course of becoming a Yummy Mummy, and I couldn't possibly fit them all into one part. Anyway, if I did manage, you would take one look at it and run to the nearest department store for some cosmetics or footwear-related escapism, never to emerge. Fun, but very expensive, and anyway, denial is not very helpful at all, no matter how high its heels are. Better to tackle the issues head-on, and be prepared.

Most of *my* worries in the early months of my pregnancies focused on all the evils I had done to my body in the *past*, rather than what awaited it in the immediate future. Could a baby grow inside a body which was previously best known for its pint-downing ability? What about that magic mushroom I was offered in Indonesia ten years ago? Maybe just being in the same *tent* had an effect on my brain, which would surely be passed on. And what about the genes from the rest of my unsuitable family? Mum used to smoke, my dad's great-great-great-grandmother had a heart attack, my husband used to live next to an asbestos factory, there's a phone mast at the end of our road, and I don't drink green tea. Oh God, oh

God! This baby is doomed to grow into a hallucinating piss-head, with heart trouble and a carcinogen-filled brain. What have I *done*?

As far as I can make out from other Yummy Mummies, this sort of irrational panicking is perfectly normal.

Heather, mother of Alex, three, and Katie, six months

We went to a wedding when I was eight weeks pregnant, although I didn't know at the time. I got hammered, and I put all the throwing up down to the ten glasses of champagne I had quaffed during the reception. When it turned out I was pregnant, I was convinced my baby would be a pickled onion rather than the healthy child she was. It was worrying, though.

Cheering Yourself Up

If you are feeling worried and scared about what is happening to you, and about the whole 'becoming a parent' thing, then read this bit as many times as you need to over the next nine months:

☆ **Becoming a mother is the best thing you will ever do.** (Read that bit again a few more times now, if you like.)

☆ **Becoming a mother changes the way you feel about *everything*,** and if you are not sure about it now, you will be absolutely sure about it, and know you have done the right thing, when the baby comes. You will manage just fine.

☆ **You *will* get your figure back,** and you will look wonderful and sexy again.

☆ **Being a Yummy Mummy does *not* mean you change who you are,** and you will still be able to go out, have a job, go shopping, travel and see your friends. A little less than before, but you can still do it.

☆ **You will get Mothers' Day treats** (yippee!).

☆ **You will be able to board flights first.**

☆ **You get balloons** when you go to restaurants with your baby.

☆ **Yummy Mummies are the luckiest people alive today**, because being somebody's mother is the happiest feeling in the world, and we *still* get to look fab and have a job. How good is *that*?

And, finally, with the 'mush factor' turned up to the max, just remember:

☆ **Your baby will grow up to be the best friend you'll ever know**, and you'll have many, many years of happiness, laughter, love and fun to look forward to together. Your baby will make your life better in more ways than you can imagine now, and you will wonder how you could ever have worried about it all. Awwww, sweeet.

Anya Hindmarch, designer

Being a mother is very hard. You are getting up in the middle of the night, clearing up sick and giving most of your attention, love and resources to someone who is brand new in your life and hasn't even earned it. It doesn't really add up on paper but somehow it is the ultimate privilege to watch this little person grow and be allowed to enjoy steering them and teaching them everything you know.

PART THREE

The Middle Bit

In theory, after about 12 weeks you enter a new, easier, more Yummy and less vomitty phase, known as the second trimester. I call it the Middle Bit, because that's just a lot clearer, as I'm sure you'll agree. The middle bit brings clearly visible physical changes, and it heralds the beginning of your pregnancy 'proper', as opposed to some invisible affliction which makes you tired and grumpy. *Now* we can all see why!

It's during this stage that you will finally start to feel pregnant, and it can be very odd realising there really is a baby in there, and you really *are* going to be a mum fairly soon. Scary stuff, but something you'll get used to in about ten years' time. This part deals with some of the key physical and mental hurdles you will stumble ungraciously over, and hopes to make the transition into Properly Pregnant Lady a little smoother.

Physical Changes

15 October. 8 p.m. Hotel room in Manchester.
Seven months pregnant.
We are near the end of filming a very boring maths series for schools. My bump has grown so much over the course of the three-week

shoot that we have had to resort to all sorts of clever trickery to conceal it: sitting down, holding objects at bump-level, shooting from the waist up and so on. Today wasn't even subtle: they just stuck me behind the sofa instead of on it, and had me casually leaning over from the back. At one point I heard the floor manager complaining to the director that we needed to 'find some way of disguising the situation'. I am not a situation. I am a pregnant lady who is not feeling very glam, and could do with someone telling her how gorgeous she is, and not that she is now so offensive to the eye that she needs to be hidden behind items of furniture!

The worst thing is that I am starting to feel guilty about being pregnant: that I am ruining their show because of my big tummy. I should be proud, not ashamed. I felt tons better after going to the gym this evening and I managed to have a chicken salad and a yoghurt for dinner, instead of the banoffee pie and large glass of wine I actually wanted. Good girl. Now to try and sleep despite all the heartburn and a bump which means I can't get comfortable, ever. Good night.

You will have noticed by now that pregnancy doesn't just affect your tummy and breasts. Sure, these are the areas it hits hardest, but the whole of your body, including your brain, God-dammit, will feel the effect in some way, and each day will hail the arrival of a new change for you to get used to. Well, at least it's not boring…

1. Hair

Ahh, some good news here. It is very common for pregnant women to have thicker, more glossy hair for the last two trimesters. This is partly thanks to your hormones, which stop hair falling out so fast, and also partly because you have stopped murdering it with chemicals and treatments now that you are up the duff. If you already had thick hair then you might look like a backcombed toilet-brush, albeit a glossy one, so work out a style which works for all the new volume. If your hair becomes more oily, use a milder cleansing shampoo and don't rub with your fingertips – this will stop it getting even oilier. For dry haystack hair, use a moisturising treatment every two weeks and leave overnight for a more intense effect.

Top Tips for Pregnant Hair from Daniel Galvin Senior, and Lino Carbosiero, Artistic Consultant at Daniel Galvin, London

You are more than safe to carry on having your hair coloured during pregnancy: there is no evidence that it can cause any harm to you or your baby, but if you are worried, then leave it.

Semi-permanent colours contain no ammonia or peroxide, which you might feel happier about. Vegetable dyes are also a fantastic, gentler option.

Having your highlights done regularly will keep you looking groomed and fresh throughout your pregnancy. It's also a good way to relax for a few hours.

Keeping colours lighter towards the hairline opens up the face, looks more natural, and can make you look thinner.

Maintain your routine with your stylist throughout your pregnancy, so he or she can help you through any changes in condition and style.

If your face becomes bigger, avoid short hair styles: this just makes your face look even rounder.

Try softening the shape around the front of your face by going for a soft fringe, or gentle layering from the chin downwards.

We recommend to all our pregnant clients that they get their hair washed and blow-dried before they go into labour. It doesn't take long, but it will make you look sensational, and can really boost your mood. Lino's wife swears it helped her to get through it all!

NB: DO NOT GO FOR A RADICAL RESTYLE WHILE YOU ARE PREGNANT! Firstly, your face will change shape (see over) so what suits you now might look awful within six months, and secondly, you are just a confused pregnant lady who thinks a change will make her feel better about the whole thing. It won't. It will lead to tears and a disastrous barnet.

2. Nails
Like hair, your nails can look particularly lovely during this stage, and they can grow much more quickly. Unfortunately this can mean they become thinner and more brittle, but it's a perfect excuse to have regular manicures.

3. Eyes
I had a very weird side-effect between about five and eight months pregnant with my third baby: my eyes became dry and itchy, and it looked as though the corneas were swollen and detached. Very gross, and quite worrying for a while. A check with an eye specialist concluded I had a 'previously unseen and possibly pregnancy-related swelling of the cornea', which I took to mean: 'I haven't got a clue but you're not dying and it will probably go away eventually', and I was discharged (sorry, unfortunate word for our subject). I only mention it to demonstrate the kind of bizarre changes you can come across.

4. Bottom and Thighs
The Middle Bit is when things start to change in these regions, and if you've been a bit smug so far, you might have to eat your words now. Despite your best efforts, your legs and bum will get a bit bigger now, because your amazingly intelligent but fashion-unaware body is programmed to retain some extra fat stores for after the birth.

5. Arms
Arms? Yep, even these can put a bit of worst-case-scenario-preparation flab on them, but if you are doing your weights in the gym then any emerging bingo wings can be sorted out quite easily.

6. Face

This was my worst bit. Seriously. I didn't mind the legs or stomach, or even the occasional swollen ankle. But in all of my pregnancies my face got bigger, and I hated it. Sadly, it is very common: you've probably seen pictures of famous Yummy Mummies getting fuller in the face as their pregnancies progress, and it isn't because the camera starts to add more pounds too – it's because they really are getting bigger there. There is nothing you can do about this new look, except to try and like it. Most women actually look better with a rounder face, but we are too used to thinking of chiselled jaw-lines and defined cheekbones as desirable to adjust easily.

7. The Linea Nigra

There it is!! This is a faint brown line from your tummy button to your pubes, which usually appears at around three months. I was obsessed about the lack of mine for weeks before it showed itself, because I thought I should have one, and I wanted to see some proof that I was doing this pregnancy properly. As soon as I saw it I wished it would go away of course, but I was still happy that I had managed to make one! How dark this line becomes depends on how much melanin your body makes, and it should fade over a year or so, if you're lucky.

8. Milk production

Eeeek. At about twenty weeks (or so – everyone's different, remember) your boobs will receive a message from Mission Control, telling them to get their milk production sorted out quick smart, because pretty soon there will be a baby to feed, and they should allow for technical glitches and printing errors.

So they do. And it's very, very weird. Like squeezing spots or picking dry skin off your heels, squeezing milk out of your nipples is a bit gross, but very satisfying. What comes out to start with isn't actually milk, but a thick yellow goo called colostrum. Bath-times have never been so much fun.

If this is all getting too much for now, then I'll move on. I just thought you should be prepared for the moment you turn into a dairy cow.

9. Heartburn

If you are experiencing this already, then you are in for quite a rough ride, as heartburn only gets worse as the baby gets bigger. I got it terribly, and couldn't sleep without drinking milk and downing the Rennies. Antacids aren't thought to be dangerous for the baby, but ask your doctor or midwife about how many and which to take.

10. Insomnia

There's a lot going on in your mind, and as the baby starts to move about and get more cumbersome, sleeping becomes very tricky. So unfair, given how much you need to stock up on the stuff – where's the evolutionary advantage of insomnia then, Darwin?

11. Uncomfortable bump

Now that you are finally getting BIG, you will notice knock-on effects such as back pain, aching tummy muscles (if you still have any), and trouble getting comfortable, especially at night. This is a good time to start sleeping with a pillow between your legs, because it makes the bump pull down less, and if you can pretend that it's Johnny Depp and not a pillow at all, then you won't mind all the insomnia. Sorted.

12. Cravings

I hate to burst a somewhat amusing and traditional bubble, but cravings are a hugely over-emphasised part of early pregnancy. Gherkins with cream, charcoal and raw onions are all the stuff of hearsay and fantasy, because the truth is a whole lot less exciting. Sorry.

Here are some cravings I *can* vouch for, as related to me by several Mummy friends: fresh fruit smoothies, sweet and sour Chinese food, iceberg lettuce, roll-mop herrings, vinegar (my mum used to drink it, which may explain a few thing about me…), strawberries (one lady could smell them from 800 metres away!), strong curry, ice-cream and black olives.

I never craved anything, apart from a flatter stomach, but I did go off things I had previously adored: Marmite made me retch, hot chocolate (which I had previously guzzled in pints) suddenly smelled like rotten cider, and I couldn't eat lettuce at all. Disaster! I had no problem with coffee, which is supposed to make all pregnant women feel sick, and even alcohol never lost its appeal. Here's hoping you experience some wacky cravings to tell your children and Yummy Mummy friends about. It's kind of expected…

13. Skin

Despite what your partner may try to tell you, the skin is the biggest organ in the human body. (Worth remembering for times when a severe put-down is required – any time he tries to have sex with you when you are in a bad mood for example.) It's really no surprise, then, that an event as physically demanding as pregnancy will have some effect on your skin. You may even get more skin problems *after* the birth than during the pregnancy itself.

In my case, the biggest skin problem was hyper-pigmentation.

Hyper-what?

Pigmentation. What started as sweet-looking freckles around my nose and dotted across my forehead (very Milly Molly Mandy; very cute), grew into patches of darker skin all over the place. Suddenly, this stopped being cute and started to be unsightly.

Early attempts to cover this up with foundation were successful, but as the months progressed the dark patches became so notice-able in the middle of my face that no amount of slap and powder would hide them properly, and they began to make me miserable. The final straw came when my peach-skinned three-year-old asked, in that levelling way only three-year-olds can get away with: 'Mummy, what are those horrid brown marks on your face? Did the baby make them?' Grrrr.

Time for some science. Ahem!

Skin discolouration, or pigmentation, is the result of increased local melanin production. Melanin is the skin pigment which protects us from the effects of strong sunlight (you knew that), but often, due to environmental or internal influences (I'd say pregnancy is probably a fairly hefty internal influence), the skin produces more melanin than it needs. During pregnancy, our good old friends oestrogen and progesterone are thought to cause greater stimulation of the pigment, resulting in hyper-pigmented skin spots. (You didn't know *that*!)

Luckily for you, cosmetics and pharmaceutical companies have been quick to cash in on the increasing awareness of this problem, and the number of 'skin-lightening' and 'blanching' products, which aim (and claim) to remove, or at least lessen, pigmented areas, is rising.

These either stop the melanin being produced or act as super-exfoliators, penetrating the skin, removing the old cells and increasing the production of new, unpigmented ones.

I peeled, masked and creamed religiously for six months after the birth, and I am pleased to report a dramatic improvement. Whether this would have happened anyway, I'll never know, but just doing *something* about it felt better than sitting the ugliness out.

Before you rush out to fill your rather lovely Anya Hindmarch tote with acids and peels, here is some life-changing advice from one of the UK's best dermatologists: photocopy it and stick it to your bathroom mirror.

> A good sunscreen is a woman's most important weapon against skin pigmentation. You should wear it every day, even in winter or on overcast days, and you should apply two coats half an hour before you go out. There's no point treating your pigmentation marks unless you also use a sunscreen of at least factor sixty every day. Finally, always wear a hat and try to stay in the shade.

You heard the man! I never leave the house without at least one coat of factor sixty all over my face these days, my hat collection has almost outgrown my bedroom, and the same is now true of sunglasses, but can a girl ever own too many?

Some skin lightening products you might like to try:

☆ **Dermalogica: Skin Brightening System.**
☆ **Elizabeth Arden: Visible Whitening Pure Intensive Capsules.**
☆ **Lancome: Blanc Expert range**, and **Absolute Radiance Anti-Dark Spot Concentrate.**
☆ **Guinot: Lightening Serum, Lightening Mask,** and **Lightening Cream** reduce melanin synthesis and lighten the skin.

And some excellent cover-up products to hide the damage:

☆ **Stila: Illuminating Liquid Foundation**, and **Face Concealer**, which blends brilliantly, allowing you to wear it on its own.
☆ **Jo Malone Finishing Fluid.** Smells divine, goes on like cream, and leaves even my skin looking remarkably even-toned. This is fabulous stuff.
☆ **Bobbi Brown: Foundation Stick** gives very good coverage, and it's a great pop-in-your-handbag product.

14. Alien

Somewhere around the fourth month you will be convinced you have turned into Sigourney Weaver. Not because you suddenly grow six inches taller, develop dramatic cheekbones and achieve a perfect smile, but because a creature will start moving around inside you.

This is one of the weirdest, best and worst things about pregnancy: weirdest because – well, how weird can it get? There's a human being moving inside you! The best because it connects you so strongly with your baby, and worst because it can get very uncomfortable and sore if there's a mini David Beckham in there.

The first time you feel your baby move seems more like trapped air bubbles jiggling about in your tummy than a foot or hand doing anything interesting, and you may not notice anything for quite a while. As these sensations grow into more noticeable jiggles, you might wonder what you've been eating recently, until finally, one day when you're least expecting it, you will feel a kick!

This is a fantastic moment, and the only shame is that your

partner can't share what you feel. This is the moment you *finally* believe you are pregnant.

As the weeks go by, these movements will get very strong, and towards the end there can be all kinds of bones, limbs, digits and other unidentifiable body parts jutting out under your ribcage, out of your tummy button or near your pelvis. I used to love all of this, but I know lots of mums who found it far too peculiar. I would spend hours in the bath talking to my internal gymnast, massaging a protruding bottom, or tickling a cheeky foot. It sounds crazy, but it sure beats depressing yourself about how big your legs are getting near the top!

TOP TIP: *If you think your baby has suddenly stopped moving about as much as normal, keep an eye on it, and if you are worried then call your midwife. Hospitals are usually happy to monitor your bump for a while, just to check everything is normal. Don't panic immediately though: babies do sleep occasionally, you know, and you will feel like a real clot when you rush in, only to monitor a baby having a well-earned nap.*

15. Stretch marks

Ready? These are a complete misnomer, because stretch marks are not caused by stretching at all. You can get them without being pregnant, whether you are fat or thin, as a teenager or even if you are a man. Ha! Some think they can even be caused by stress. Stretch marks can look like thin red lines or patches. They sometimes turn white with time, and in bad cases they can actually be raised from the surrounding skin.

The bad news: There is almost nothing you can do to prevent them from appearing. It's in your genes, so start praying you've got some good ones. Oh, and they are permanent.

The good news: Lots of pregnant women never get any, and they do fade with time, so 'permanent' doesn't mean permanently very visible.

Can I do anything to prevent these ugly marks?

Oils and Lotions. Whether these have any significant effect is still up for debate, but there are lots of lovely lotions, oils and creams which are definitely worth a try – and feel wonderful too.

☆ **Mama Mio Superstretch Tummy Rub:** This very stylish brand promises stretch mark-free tummies up and down the country.
☆ **Pure Vitamin E oil mixed with wheatgerm oil.**
☆ **Jo Malone's Vitamin E Gel:** This is used in her heavenly facials, but clients started to report back on its fantastic stretch-mark-preventing potential.
☆ **Clarins 'Tonic' Body Treatment Oil:** A legendary oil which tones, firms and moisturises. I've seen it in lots of my Yummy Mummy friends' bathroom cabinets. I do like to snoop, you know.
☆ **Clarins Bust Lotion and Bust Gel:** Because you can't forget the marks which might appear here as well.
☆ **This Works Stretch Mark Oil:** It does, apparently.
☆ **Vichy Complete Action Anti-Stretch Mark Cream:** Helps to prevent new ones, and reduce the appearance of existing ones.

Exercise. If you keep the exercise up, your skin should stay more toned and the risk of stretch marks might be reduced. *Might,* but even a 'might' is worth a few extra visits to the gym.

Looking Good: Gorgeous Clothes for the Suddenly Large of Girth

> ### 18 December. 5 p.m. Seven months pregnant.
> *I've been trying on outfits for an hour, and I am now so depressed and disgusted that I don't think I'll manage to drag myself out at all. I look like a dairy cow – I have to stop looking in this mirror.*
>
> *And my shoes don't bloody fit because my feet are swollen! Why can Sarah Jessica Parker look so fabulous with a great big belly? Oh yes, Oscar de la Renta. Well, Zara will have to work the same magic for me.*

Once upon a very unfashionable time, all pregnant women dressed badly. This was partly because there were no gorgeous maternity ranges available, and partly because Yummy Mummies hadn't been invented yet. Happily, times have changed, and we all know that pregnant ladies can look fabulous: just look at Anna Friel and Victoria Beckham.

Of course everyone has a different opinion of what constitutes an attractive woman: some like their ladies curvy, others prefer the androgynous nymph; curls do it for some, poker-straight for others. Tall, short, blonde, brunette, muscular, willowy, bold, reclusive, pale, tanned, made-up or natural, we come in a glittering array of shapes and forms, and manage to look sexy and feminine in all of them. We are clever, aren't we?

But whatever your personal ideal, one thing makes a woman *look* like a woman, and *feel* like a woman. It's such an important biological characteristic that even babies can tell the difference between a man and a woman by it. No, it's not the presence of breasts: it's the hourglass figure created by having *a defined waist.*

Ah! A *waist*! A flat, trim, nipped-in waist. Hips are fairly crucial to the female form too, but unless your waist is smaller than your hips, it's very hard to look feminine, and it's harder still to *feel* beautiful. Social anthropologists reckon a 'magic ratio' of waist to hips of 7:10 is evolutionarily significant: it signals sexual appeal at a primal level, as it indicates good child-bearing potential. You mean men think *that* hard?

Those geniuses among you will already have guessed where I'm going here: when you are pregnant, your waist disappears for a while, and then reappears as your bump starts to come *out* – a LONG way after a certain point, and it is not the most flattering shape when it comes to modern fashions and ideas of femininity, and looking good in these circumstances takes some effort.

The First Signs of a Change
I always imagined that the Absolutely Enormous phase towards the end would be the worst time of pregnancy, in terms of how I looked and felt, but actually many of my friends agree with me that the

moment your waist disappears is one of the big pregnancy lows. At least when it's *out*, it's out, and you can pretend to glow and blossom into your new shape. But when it's just not there at all you look neither slim nor pregnant. I wanted to wear a badge explaining: 'I know I don't really look it yet, but the reason I'm a bit shapeless is that I'm four months pregnant and my waistline is in temporary hiding. Please stop staring at me and pretend that I look lovely.'

Unfortunately, there's very little that clothing can do to help. Developing an addiction to Juicy Couture trousers is not so much a fashion statement as a 'missing waist' concealer, and it works, and I'd advise any bloated-feeling Yummy Mummy-to-be to do the same. Don't do what I did though: I lived in some very unattractive tracksuit trousers for a month or so, and all this did was to make me feel incredibly fat and ugly. By my third pregnancy I'd learned that 'comfy' doesn't mean shapeless and without-any-style-at-all. Wearing some stylish, comfy trousers at this not-quite-pregnant-enough-yet stage makes you feel much better about your condition.

Pregnancy Wardrobe Phase One: Before It Really Shows

☆ Wear comfy (but gorgeous) trousers, which fit your legs well but have a forgiving waist: stretch fabric, low-slung and elasticated all work at this stage.
☆ Make sure your top half is longer than waist-length.
☆ Three-quarter-length jackets come into their own now.
☆ Tie a hoody or a jumper around your waist and pretend the bulk is from that.
☆ Wear a really long, skinny scarf which hangs loosely down to your waist: it hides what's behind. But don't wear belts or tie scarves around your waist – it just accentuates the enlargement.
☆ Long cardigans (worn open) can hide your curveless middle zone.
☆ Dresses can be a good plan, as the whole 'waist' issue is lessened, but avoid anything tight, obviously. Keep that for later.
☆ Floaty and feminine is a look which works; structured and fitted isn't. Avoid über-floaty though, as this can easily turn into 'shapeless heap' which helps no one. You need *some* structure.

☆ Don't buy maternity clothes yet. You want to enjoy these last months of wearing semi-normal clothes while you can, and you may not even need them, if you are lucky and clever with your wardrobe. And anyway, you won't *believe* how big you are going to get, and you will almost certainly buy everything a size or two too small. I had to take everything back the first time, because I grew out of them at seven months. Darn!

☆ Accentuate the positive: legs, bust, neck, shoulders, arms – wherever you look best is what we want to see most of.

Later On (When You Are Really Showing)

For me this tended to happen at about six months. Until this point I was always certain that I wouldn't get *that* much bigger, being what I considered to be enormous already. Everyone convinces themselves of this, because thinking any other way is just too depressing. But a moment passes at around six months in your first pregnancy (and at about three months in subsequent ones) when your stomach will start its journey outwards, and this signals the end of Pregnancy Wardrobe Phase One.

Now that your bump has become clearly visible, you enter the next phase of wardrobe confusion. Instead of cunningly concealing a slightly tubby midriff, the best way forward is to **embrace your bump and make a feature of it**. A protruding, pregnant waist is not at *all* the same as a fat stomach: the latter comes with all the trimmings of a fat everything else, usually, and making an effort to lessen the impact is probably a good idea. But when you're pregnant, 90% of your body is almost as trim as it was before, and you just have an unamusingly large middle zone. Trying to hide it is the female equivalent of sweeping long straggles of wispy hair over a man's bald patch: it looks worse than it did before, and fools nobody.

Pregnancy Survival Wardrobe Phase Two

☆ **Stay in regular clothes for as long as possible.** If you're lucky, you will be able to wear non-maternity bottom halves right up to the birth, by tucking the waist *under* your bump and wearing trousers as hipsters. But remember that clothes will sit differently now, so make sure they still look good.

☆ **Long skirts can make you look dumpier** and more box-like, because they don't show your legs. Minis have the advantage of slim-leg exposure, which takes the eye away from the waist, but they are only for the brave (or tasteless – I never went along with the 'pregnant hooker' look, but perhaps you can pull it off better than me.) Mid-length will slim you out if your calves and ankles are still trim, as they might be if you are still exercising well and putting your feet up whenever possible.

☆ **Don't move into your partner's clothes** just because they are bigger. They *are* bigger, but they are not cut for your shape or size, and the old 'looking like a sack' adage will apply to you.

☆ **Don't over-complicate matters.** Keep it simple: bold patterns and prints may be in, but you should stick to understated and muted for now, unless you are as self-confident as Trinny or Susannah.

☆ **Invest in some hip maternity clothes** to see you through this last bit in style. *Now* you can go for the maternity wear if you need to (see below), but remember you will get bigger than you think. Think bigger, bigger, bigger.

☆ **Black works.**

☆ **Try support tights.** These make Bridget Jones's knickers look like something from a Victoria's Secrets catalogue, but they do apparently have some amazing health benefits for your legs: they can reduce varicose veins and can even keep your legs trimmer and more shapely. I never wore them, mainly because I never wore skirts much, but I have heard some very favourable reports from other Yummy Mummies who swore by them. Or was it *at* them? Not sure.

☆ **Sexy underwear is absolutely essential.** I sparked off quite a debate in Cambridge when I happened to mention in one of my parenting columns that I still possess, and wear, thongs. '*Thongs?* A mother wearing a *thong?* A *pregnant* mother wearing a thong? Disgraceful!' cried the forward-thinking inhabitants of this highly educated city. Perhaps some learned professor could explain the psychology behind the theory that 'all women who are pregnant should make themselves feel worse by wearing Big Pants'. It's complete tosh. Quite apart from the fact that increasing numbers of medical professionals will be looking around down there, and so making an effort is only polite, *you* will feel better if you stick to sexy lingerie.

☆ **All hail Diane Von Furstenberg**, who invented the wrap dress. Now *here's* a style which works throughout pregnancy, provided it fits well. Whether it's a crossover shirt, jumper, dress, or a long-sleeved T, wrap yourself in one of these and cruise to the finish-line looking sexy.

☆ **Leggings.** You're getting into dangerous territory here, and you should try to avoid these unless you want to look like a maternity-wear model in the mid-Eighties. I wore them, and hated myself every day. The same can be said for…

☆ …**dungarees.** (Unless you are as hip as Sarah Jessica Parker, in which case you can look fabulous in the frumpiest of maternity frocks.) Dungarees are actually having a bit of a revival at the time of writing, but fashions come and fashions go, and this is one item which needs some careful research.

Top Wardrobe Tips From Vanessa and Baukjen, designers of hip maternity label Isabella Oliver

Soft, drapey jerseys, and anything that stretches, are the best fabrics and cuts to cover your bump. They are always comfortable and will grow and move with you, while still looking feminine and sexy.

Buy as many little black jersey dresses as possible for pulled together, versatile looks which are always feminine. They are easy to wear for work, or dressed up for an evening out with sparkly accessories and sexy heels.

You shouldn't have to change your style just because you are pregnant. The same rules of dressing still apply – there is no reason to start wearing oversized, tent-like clothes or pinafores just because you are pregnant.

Splurge on handbags, shoes, scarves and jewellery. Make the most of your classic, versatile wardrobe by changing your accessories to fit the occasion. It is so easy to change your daytime and evening look by simply putting a few strands of chunky beads around your neck or by adding a pair of dramatic, sparkly earrings. The possibilities are endless!

☆ **Mind the Gap.** If your tops aren't long enough you will have a gaping hole between the bottom of your top and the top of your bottoms, which can only be filled by a swollen, veiny tummy. You will also look much bigger because everything will hang straight from your boobs down, with no curves or shaping. Tops have to cover your bump and fit well.

☆ **Shoes.** Here's where you can add some essential sex-appeal. Living in trainers for four months is very comfortable, but it's highly unglamorous. Do what the sexiest Yummy Mummies do and stick to something pretty for as long as you feel comfortable (and stable!) and keep trainers as part of a low-key, funky street look, rather than a 'dishevelled blob who crawled off the sofa to fetch a pint of milk' outfit.

☆ **Accentuate your neck and shoulders** with pretty necklines. That's 'pretty', not 'plunging', unless you want to show off your newly impressive cleavage.

☆ **Use accessories** to draw attention away from your waist. Scarves, earrings, hats and brooches all work, but not all at the same time: less is always more on the accessories front.

☆ **Avoid large areas of uniform colour.** Breaking things up a bit, especially across your chest, will make you look smaller.

☆ **Stand and walk tall**, and pretend you don't feel pregnant. This *really* works, and you will look 1,000 times better immediately.

Shoe Warning!

Don't even think about buying expensive (but obviously gorgeous) shoes when you are heavily pregnant, especially if it's in the summer months. I made the huge mistake of indulging in some 'shoes are the only answer to my hideousness' retail therapy care of Anya Hindmarch when I was eight months pregnant with number three, and walked away beaming with a pair of almost edible kitten heels.

Alas, when it came to the Big Summer Wedding three months (and one baby) later, I discovered that they were a size too big. Needless to say, I wore them anyway, with several layers of insoles, but to be honest I just looked ridiculous, they came off with every step, and I ended up barefoot on the dancefloor. Silly girl.

Maternity Clothes You Might Like to Buy

The excellent news for all you future Yummy Mummies is that maternity wear has become as stylish as normal gear, with everyone from Juicy Couture to Elle MacPherson launching maternity ranges. Not only that, but many high-street brands have been quick to get in on the act, and now make utterly fashionable, very affordable maternity wear. You don't need a budget like Liv Tyler to look as glamorous as she did when she was pregnant, so get yourself down to one of the stores listed on pages 51–52 and get some figure-flaunting, sexy outfits.

Is it worth it?

If you're only going to be in them for a few months, after which you'll want to burn the lot, is it worth spending money on nice maternity clothes?

Yes! Yes! Yes!

As every woman knows, it's not how you look, it's how you *feel*. Although obviously if you *look* terrible you will also *feel* terrible but it's safe to say that you need every bit of help at this time to feel good in your new body, and investing in some pretty maternity gear is one huge leg-up. Good maternity clothes can improve your look dramatically, because they are specially cut to fit your peculiar new shape, which makes them much more flattering: normal tops are always too short and tight, skirts are too short in the front and look ridiculous and so on. As well as this, anything non-maternity you wear in these last months will stretch so much that it will never go back to normal, and you'll regret ruining half of your wardrobe.

1. Underwear

You need a good, supportive bra for the extra volume (and hence extra weight) and if you are going to breastfeed then you might as well make it a nursing bra while you're at it. Don't buy a plain white tit-sling: buy the most beautiful one you can find, even if it's slightly squeezing the budget. Bits of this bra *will* appear in public when you start feeding, and you should be very proud to have it on display. Elle MacPherson has a lovely range, as do faithful M&S.

2. Vests

Maternity ones have better boob support than your normal ones, which is essential for you, and they are cut longer to fit snugly over your bump, which is essential for everyone who has to look at you. I bought four from Top Shop and used them until they fell apart, which was about three months before I did.

3. Jeans or Trousers

I feel a bit hypocritical telling you to buy a pair of maternity trousers, because I didn't for my first two pregnancies. I found the stretchy panel over the bump part just soooo unattractive that I stuck to my regular jeans and tucked them under my bump. However, during my last pregnancy, I discovered the truly gorgeous Earl Jean maternity range, which succeeded in making me neither look nor feel particularly pregnant at all, and anything which can do *that* is worth serious consideration. I've since noticed several pregnant friends looking great in H&M and Next maternity jeans, so have a look and see what feels good.

4. Workwear

If you need to look suit-smart at work, investing in a proper maternity one could be a great investment, unless you are one of the 2% of (lying) pregnant women who manage to fit into all their normal clothes until the birth.

If you work in an office where shirts are the norm, it's worth buying a maternity one, because they will fit *much* better and you'll avoid the button-popping look over the waist and bust-line. You might even consider getting a smart, properly fitted maternity skirt if your ankles are still worth seeing, and if not, then stretchy boot-leg black trousers will see you most of the way through. Check out Formes, Séraphine, Tête-à-Tête, Upfront and Top Shop B maternity range for some good work gear.

5. Eveningwear

You *will* be invited to a stylish function when you are absolutely humungous – it's Mrs Murphy's Law – so be prepared. It may feel like a huge waste of money, but buying a glam maternity dress which will make you the most attractive, sensual woman in the room is worth it. If you are not brave enough to do the top-to-toe clingy black dress *à la* Victoria Beckham, then go for something a little more conservative but equally stunning. You can't pretend you don't have a massive stomach, but you *can* pretend that you *feel* sexy. Cunning.

That's about it to be honest. Above all, have fun with your temporary wardrobe. Hiding away for three months because you have nothing beautiful to wear is absolutely not acceptable: you are a gorgeous Yummy Mummy-to-be, so show the world what you're made of and strut!

Where to Buy Your Yummy Maternity Clothes

Good Value: Shops

☆ **Top Shop:** Already everybody's favourite shop, but it just got a little bit better for mummies-to-be. Great!

☆ **Dorothy Perkins:** Good for staples like vests and definitely affordable.

☆ **H&M Mama:** You wouldn't expect this range to be anything less than fashionable, beautiful and well within budget and it doesn't disappoint at all.

☆ **Gap:** No maternity range yet – watch this space! - but their generous sizing means you can get away with non-maternity stuff for a long time, and it's all very preppy and cool.

☆ **Formes:** Now *here's* one of the most stylish places to buy maternity wear. A tad more expensive but gorgeous, gorgeous, gorgeous!

Good Value: Online

This is a great way to shop if you feel so queasy or fat that you can't face trawling through the shops. Many websites are beautifully designed, so you can stock up your new wardrobe feeling confident and lovely. Just go easy on the 'buy' button: you'll only need most of this stuff for a couple of months, so *four* pairs of maternity jeans is probably overdoing it a bit.

☆ **Blooming Marvellous:** Plenty of choice and it'll see you through the 'big' months looking fine.

☆ **JoJo Maman Bébé:** *Très chic* basics and dresses.

☆ **Isabella Oliver:** Beautifully designed flattering wardrobe essentials for you to look fabulous throughout.

* **Bumps Maternity Wear:** Pretty lingerie and also baby clothes.
* **Maternity Exchange:** For fabulous second-hand designer labels (which, don't forget, won't have been worn for more than a couple of months).
* **Homme Mummy:** The Essential Maternity Wardrobe is a fabulous capsule wardrobe of stylish maternity basics – looks great, saves time!

Budget Blowers: Shops

* **9London:** Extremely exclusive. Breaks the bank, but the Yummiest Mummies shop in there so may be worth the overdraft. And it smells lovely.
* **Diane Von Furstenberg Maternity:** Well, the queen of the wrap has now launched an equally marvellous maternity range, so you don't have to stretch your normal dresses and tops any more!
* **Bumpsville:** This is really special stuff, and a couple of basics from here will be worth the minor splurge.
* **Blossom Mother and Child:** Already visited by Kate Winslet, Thandie Newton and other A-listers, Blossom stocks regular designer labels which you'll still fit, as well as their own gorgeous maternity one.

Budget Blowers: Online

* **Séraphine:** Prettiest, most feminine maternity clothing I've ever seen. Well what did I expect? It's French.
* **Arabella B:** Excellent denim collection.
* **Push:** The most un-glamorous name imaginable, but the collection is as sexy as it gets, and Push has a huge celebrity following so you'll be logging on soon.
* **Serendipity:** Stock super-stylish and glam stuff, from designers such as Earl Jean, Liz Lange and Urban Baby.

Gym Babies

To start with, a small disclaimer, so that you don't try and take me to the High Court if things go wrong: what follows worked for me, through three healthy pregnancies, and I know many other women for whom it worked too. I'm not saying it's for you, and you know what your body can take better than I do. Get the all-clear from your midwife or doctor before you start, and ask them if you are unsure about anything. Thank you.

How Much Exercise Should I Take When I'm Pregnant?

Ahhh, a subject of such debate, confusion, conflicting advice and worry. When you are pregnant you will feel quite protective over your bump, and the idea of putting your growing baby at any risk at all seems unthinkable. To counter this, you will also feel fat and large and huge and wobbly, and you will probably want to do some exercise to try and keep things in some kind of toned order, which is absolutely fine.

It all just depends on how much and what kind of exercise your body is used to, and whether it still feels OK to do it when you have a baby taking part as well. '**If it feels bad, don't do it**' seems like sensible advice to me. Something to bear in mind is that your body will be producing a hormone called relaxin, which is not a natural laxative as its name suggests, but just loosens all your joints in preparation for the you-know-what. This means you should be more careful about how much high-impact exercise you do, even if you are used to that sort of thing.

For me, it was running. I've been running competitively since I was a little girl (why? am I *mad?*), and my poor body is quite used to being put through its paces, on the road, in the gym, along a beach or wherever. In fact, if I don't go running for a few days I get as grouchy as a pre-menstrual banshee wearing newly washed, slightly-too-tight jeans. It's just who I am and what I'm used to.

Given this starting point, I decided I would try to carry on running, lifting weights, cycling and doing everything else I usually do, until it felt wrong or I just couldn't manage any more because my bump got in the way, and it worked very well.

NB: Doctors advise against doing any exercise lying on your back after the first trimester, because the baby puts pressure on your vena cava, (the big vein carrying blood from your legs to your heart) which reduces the blood flow to the uterus, and to your brain, both of which are bad.

Here are some types of exercise you *can* do when you are pregnant:

☆ **Running:** The most vigorous and probably ill-advised type of exercise during pregnancy, but it worked for me. I ran until I was 20 weeks pregnant, at which point it started to ache a little, so I stopped. Also, I got funny looks from people as I jogged along with my paunch, and I felt embarrassed.

☆ **Cross-Training:** A perfect way to burn unnecessary calories you felt you ought to eat at the time: it's non-impact, aerobic, and you can read about beautiful, non-pregnant people while you're doing it to remind yourself why you're bothering.

☆ **Weights:** Very important, because moving your heavy body around in the later months will become hard work, and there will be lots of lifting and carrying to do after your baby is born. The stronger your muscles are the easier both will be. Your legs and arms aren't pregnant, so you can have fantastically toned limbs to make up for the fantastically un-toned tummy. Apparently doing weights is very good for reducing your risk of getting osteoporosis too, so start now and carry on forever...

☆ **Sit-ups:** I'm nervous about this bit, because I did them until I was about five months pregnant, but I would hate anyone to feel they ought to do this and do themselves or their baby an injury. If you've done your pre-pregnancy work and have strong abs before you start, then you shouldn't have too much trouble getting back into shape. Do them if you want to, but never do anything which feels bad, and ask your doctor before you start.

☆ **Cycling:** There is a point beyond which this becomes impossible because your knees bash into your huge bump. This isn't usually until the very last month or so, and until then I found cycling a fantastic way of keeping fit and having toned legs. If you can cycle outside then so much the better: fresh air is great for growing babies. Just be aware of your changing balance as you get bigger – it can get quite wobbly on there towards the end.

☆ **Swimming:** Probably the best exercise you can do, according to all the experts who know about this sort of thing. It's cardiovascular, all your muscle groups get a workout, and it relieves the weight on your tummy and back, which is wonderful. I swam dozens of lengths every day as soon as I stopped being able to run, and until two weeks after my due date. It was so boring that it nearly killed me, and now I can't go anywhere near swimming pools, but watching the attendants panic as a very overdue lady entered the pool *again* was well worth it.

☆ **Dancing:** Not only good exercise but also very relaxing and good fun. I'm a hopeless dancer, and was even more ungainly and hopeless when I was pregnant, but I found it very calming and relaxing. Not sure about tangos and vigorous dancing, but ballet is perfect. If Darcey Bussell can do it, then so can you. Some gyms offer balletcise (what a word!) classes, which sound very soothing, and aim to tone you up gracefully. Ha ha.

☆ **Walking:** Everywhere. If you really can't find the opportunity to do any of the above, then walking is a highly overlooked form of exercise, and when you're lugging a heavy baby around at the same time it becomes quite effortsome. Be warned, though: walking can become painful later on, as the baby puts pressure on your back and you start to get pains and twinges in your legs. In the final weeks walking is a great way to get things moving south, which you'll be *very* keen to do.

☆ **Pilates:** Apart from being the most fashionable form of exercise, Pilates targets the tummy and pelvic-floor muscles, which weaken during pregnancy. Many Pilates exercises are performed on your hands and knees, which is an ideal, if rather inelegant, position: it helps to take a lot of stress off your back and pelvis, and towards the end of your pregnancy can help to position your baby well when it's time for lift-off.

☆ **Aquaerobics:** I never did this, as the idea of a pool full of pregnant people was too grim for me, but those Mums I know who tried it said it was better than dry aerobics because the water made the bump less heavy.

Activities You Should Avoid

Some of the activities I was advised to avoid during pregnancy made me laugh until my stomach hurt. So there's one for starters. As well as stomach-hurting laughter, I have read that pregnant women should also avoid waterskiing, horse-riding, sky-diving (!), downhill skiing, fencing, and ice-skating. Other no-nos include doing strenuous exercise if you are suffering from vaginal bleeding, premature labour or heart disease. You don't say!

NB: In my experience, no matter how much you exercise, and how careful you are about what you eat, you will get a bit fatter during pregnancy. It's nature's way of preparing your body for the exhaustion which follows, and of cheering you up when the bulk starts to fall off at the far end. Don't try to be a weight your body doesn't want to be by doing too much exercise, and try to enjoy your new shape. Most men love the curves, and you will honestly look wonderful in your new, womanly silhouette.

TOP TIP: *You will need new sports gear: a better, more supportive bra, a longer vest or T-shirt (to avoid exposing several inches of highly stretched midriff to the hunk of muscle on the machine next to you), and a very high quality pair of gorgeous trainers to protect your legs, joints and back. This is one item of kit which you can wear after the baby comes too, so spending a little more won't feel as extravagant.*

Antenatal Classes

If you want to spend a lot of time looking at huge, panting women, then I suggest you rent a (bad) porn movie instead. Ante-natal classes teach you little more about the birth than you can find out for yourself, they are usually in the evening when you'd rather be watching telly, they take ages, and there is always the possibility of them whipping out a 'birth video', from which you will never recover. What *can* be useful about these evenings among the dungarees and bored men, is that you get to know where the maternity ward is, you might meet women who will be your friends for many years, you can try out some labour positions which you will never use, and you will discover how hard a plastic baby is.

If you are going to go then find out about classes near you from your midwife, and book early – there are usually six sessions to go to, and they can book up quickly.

You're Eating For *How* Many?

2 February. 8 p.m.
Five months pregnant with number three.

All of a sudden I'm SO fed up with feeling big. I feel that I should be eating more because the baby must be beginning to need more now, but I just seem to be expanding in all the wrong places suddenly, and I really hate it. My legs are huge and I've got that horrible big-pregnant-face thing back again. I'm trying to stick to fruit for breakfast, a light salad-y lunch with some chicken or something, and lots of veggies for dinner with some carbs, but maybe that's not enough. Yes, it is enough. It was fine last time, and the bump is definitely getting bigger so it must be OK. God, it's so hard to know if I'm getting it right. If there's anything wrong with this baby I will always blame myself, but if it all turns out fine and I've turned into an elephant I will wish I hadn't pigged out so much. Either way I'll be wrong, so I'll just try to eat sensibly. Fat chance, ha ha.

So, so, so, so many of my friends dread becoming fat during pregnancy. In fact, they're so convinced that pregnancy will turn them into a big blob of lard, that it's one of their main reasons for putting the whole thing off a little while longer. This completely baffles, and also rather annoys me, for two reasons:

Firstly, what's wrong with getting a little bigger? Maybe pregnancy is a good time to lose the boyish hips and develop a womanly curve or two. Secondly, being pregnant doesn't mean being fat. Not all pregnant women swell to the size of a salad-dodging Sumo wrestler. It all depends on how you decide to play it, and how much willpower you have. If you have no willpower at all, then now is a good time to start cultivating some.

The great news is that you *can* have a baby and still get into your normal jeans on the way back from the hospital – you just can't button them up for a few weeks. Toned thighs and abs are still a definite possibility, and unless there are medical reasons which cause excessive weight gain, it's very possible that you will go back to being roughly the shape you normally are. Like all desirable things, you just have to work at it, and in this case that means really, really, really hard.

When you are pregnant, you will get bigger. It's mainly just your stomach and breast regions which will go a little crazy, and to be honest that's hardly very surprising: there's a person growing inside you, and it's got to go *somewhere*. Unless you have some really weird internal arrangements, like no vital organs at all, then the only way is **outwards**, hence the big tummy.

And the breasts thing is fantastic! Even the flattest of flatties develop heaving bosoms worthy of a Merchant Ivory production. Any man (or woman) who has cause to be fumbling around the region will be delighted with your new arrivals. Embrace these new curves: flaunt them, feel them and enjoy every inch, because when the breast-feeding is over, so are the breasts. Gone!

Anyway, so far, 'bigger' is OK. It's a good kind of bigger. The trouble starts when you feel you have to eat enough to feed your growing baby as though it's running a marathon in there or something. It's not. It's just hanging around, swallowing, stretching, sucking its thumb occasionally, and growing a teeny bit. Hardly enough to merit a full extra meal, if you're honest.

'*But it needs to grow – I must eat more!*', you will cry, washing down another granola bar with a full-fat latte before polishing off your husband's pain au chocolat and wondering if just one more doughnut before lunch might be in order. This is absolutely fine, if you don't mind turning into a bus. It's not fine if you want to recognise yourself in a few months' time.

WARNING!!: This strong sense of having to eat tons more than usual is reinforced by absolutely everyone you know telling you to, and tirelessly offering you calorie-laden nourishment, which you would never normally have (honest). Resist! Resist! This goes doubly for your parents, and about ten-fold for any in-laws you may have acquired. Only visit these well-meaning people if you are armed with either a will of iron strong enough to decline their barrage of offerings, or a paper bag to pop any unwanted but forced-upon-you food into for future disposal. It sounds awful, but these desperate times can call for desperate measures. The alternative is just saying 'No, thank you' the whole time, which becomes very boring, and makes your mother-in-law think you hate her. Bad plan.

But I'm eating for two

No, you are *not*, or at least not in the way that it implies. 'Eating for two' makes it sound like you should be packing in *two times* the amount of food you would normally eat, or at least something approaching it. If you do that, as everyone from your second-best friend (your best friend will know better) to your favourite barista will do their damnedest to encourage, you will, as you so fear, *become enormous!*

'Eating for two' became my most hated phrase when I was pregnant (apart from 'Oh, I had twins, too.' I've never had twins, just huge bumps, apparently).

OK, so how much am I supposed to eat when I'm pregnant?

This is an impossible question to answer, but I can tell you what worked for *me*, and you can decide if you want to give it a go. Everyone is different, everyone wants different things, and I am NOT saying that this is medically or universally the best way to approach things, so please leave the lawyers out of it.

For me it was a simple question of maths. I am 1.7 metres tall and I normally weigh about 50 kgs. At twelve-weeks gestation a foetus is, depending on which book you decide to believe, about 6cm long and weighs roughly 18g. Grabbing a pocket calculator for a second, I calculate that this made my three-month-old unborn baby about 3.5% of my height, and only 0.36% of my weight.

So at this stage, going by our relative weights, it was more a case of eating for 1.0036 than for 2. Looking at a typical day's food, that's probably not much more than a few extra grains of rice, and maybe a couple of grapes.

Not two Danish pastries, a mozzarella panini and a steak tartare, then? Errrr, no.

Even at full term, when it is ready to be born, a baby is generally about 35 cms long and weighs on average 3.5kgs. That's still only 7% of my normal body weight. In food terms, I make that one extra potato and a chicken wing, at the most.

Can a baby really grow big enough that way?
Babies do whatever Mother Nature has in mind for them. Most just seem to grow as big as their genetic make-up tells them to, and there seems to be little correlation between the amount Mummy eats and the size of her baby. I've known big ladies produce tiny babies, and skinny ladies give birth to whoppers. *Que serra, serra.*

Using my very own geeky, logical approach, I managed to produce two 9 lb babies (which to you and me just means 'ridiculously big'), and one 8 lb baby. I didn't put on more than a kilo or two besides baby weight with any of my kids, and most of this was to be found in my maternity bra. I breast-fed all of them without any trouble at all, and so far they seem to be very strong and healthy children.

Now, before you padlock the larder…

Other Factors to Take Into Account
(which mean you should up the food-intake)
Your increased blood volume, higher metabolism and just general extra effort required to haul yourself around all mean you should probably increase what you eat by slightly more than I've shown above. But the general point remains the same: becoming pregnant doesn't mean you have to eat tons more. Just a little extra healthy food will do wonders.

Obviously, if you have any concerns, then go and talk to your doctor or midwife about them. At the end of the day, or rather nine months, it's *your* baby, and *your* body. If you do what feels right for both of you, you will always know that you did your best. If you don't mind putting on a bit of weight, then go for it! Being pregnant was the first time I enjoyed feeling rounder and more curvy, and it was (eventually) a very sexy feeling. But if you'd rather keep the weight gain to a minimum, then try not to eat much more than normal. As long as it's a balanced diet with all the food groups in it, you and your baby will probably both be just fine.

Body Image and Eating Problems

Here's an indisputable fact: lots of women have eating problems. Millions of us. I can hardly think of a single friend between the ages of twenty and sixty who hasn't had, or doesn't still have, some kind of hang-up about food and eating, and that's not because I hang around neurotic, anorexic, food-obsessed people. Almost everyone has food issues these days, and pregnant women are no exception.

We may like to *think*, or hope, that becoming a mother somehow changes our attitudes to life, our priorities and our self-image, but in fact it often does nothing of the sort. Just because you have a baby to think about does not automatically mean you suddenly stop caring about the size of your bum, the wobbliness of your thighs or how much carbohydrate you consume. Nor should you expect it to, or worry if it doesn't.

If you are one of the lucky, confident types who loves her body in whatever form, then I take my hat off to you. If, like me and most of my friends, you have a fairly changeable body image and have been through periods of being underweight, overweight or just-not-the-weight-you-want weight, then you will probably continue this way throughout your pregnancy. Some women get a little worse, and some women get a little better as they learn to relax about their bodies.

One thing I have discovered is that pregnancy can be the start of food problems for many women because it changes your body shape out of all recognition very quickly, you suddenly become aware of lots of parts of your body you had never paid much attention to before, and it requires you to think about what you do and don't eat the whole time. Once you've had the baby you might start to lose some of the weight gained, but this pursuit can become addictive, which is why you may have seen pictures of previously gorgeous, curvy girls suddenly looking like skeletons within a year of their baby being born. It's very sad, but it's not uncommon.

So if you are wondering why there is quite so much reference to food and body size in this book from now on, that is why. Spend 20 minutes in a playground or a toddler group and just listen to the conversations: 80% of them are about biscuits, picking at food, losing weight, trying to get fit or just feeling fat. I had a conversation with a stunningly attractive mother of four last week who told me she only started to accept and like her 'new' body when her first child was 12. It's not just me. It's motherhood.

Anorexia

If you are truly anorexic then you have done well to conceive in the first place, and you should get some medical advice about nutrition for your pregnancy. The main person who will suffer if you don't eat enough is you: I have known some unbelievably skinny women produce healthy, chubby babies, but they themselves look drained, pale, and pretty rough. Also, we don't know much about what long-term effects your being slightly undernourished can do to your growing baby. When the breastfeeding kicks in, you really do need to have extra reserves in place if you want to remain healthy, so get some help if you think you should be eating more but can't.

Bulimia

Again, if you make yourself sick occasionally, regularly or even frequently, you probably won't stop the day you become pregnant. Bulimia is so widespread these days that there are probably hundreds of pregnant women who continue to make themselves sick, and are terrified of what it's doing to their baby. I have been an on-and-off sufferer since I was about fifteen, and it was only a recent health scare which finally kicked the habit abruptly and permanently. Being pregnant didn't, and I carried on being sick every so often throughout all of my pregnancies. My babies were all absolutely fine. The worst part is the guilt and worry, and if you can get some counselling then do. Probably the worst side-effect of bulimia from a baby's point of view is that it puts your stomach under considerable stress, it can throw your electrolyte balance off-kilter, and it makes you worried.

Taking laxatives
This seems like a very bad idea to me. Laxatives reduce the amount of nutrients getting into your blood, and hence into your baby's blood. Talk to your doctor as soon as you can about this sort of problem.

There have been many studies into the effects of eating disorders in pregnancy on babies, but there is little to support the idea that having a minor eating problem can put your baby at greater risk of miscarriage or abnormalities. What does seem to be agreed upon is that issues about body image and food do not go away during pregnancy, and can even get worse afterwards unless some kind of counselling is offered. If you are worried, embarrassed or confused about any of these issues, then please, please talk to your doctor or midwife, who should be able to point you in the right direction. Hiding won't help anybody.

Pampering – Yes Please! But Is It Still Safe?
If indulging in a little luxury and pampering were out of bounds during these most trying months, then Life really would be a total bitch. Luckily, she isn't, and she has a heart after all. Either that or she just has a well-developed sense of what's important, and knows that keeping a pregnant lady looking and feeling good is near the top of the list.

So, what can and what can't you treat yourself to? Here we fall into the 'not recommended if you are pregnant' trap: manufacturers are so terrified of getting sued by irate mothers blaming every skin upset, disastrous hair colour or streaky tan-marks on a product they've used, that they slap a warning on everything from two-minute hair packs to nail buffers. Actually, not nail buffers, but that's probably only a matter of time. The only way to keep up your beauty routine and to enjoy some glamour-restoring treats during your pregnancy is by turning up the common-sense dial once again, and trusting your own instincts.

Hair Colouring
See the box of hair-care tips from Daniel Galvin on page 33.

Aromatherapy
To get all serious for a second, you should only use essential aroma-therapy oils if you know what you're doing, and **never during the first three months of your pregnancy**. Some essential oils are very dangerous if used during pregnancy, and absolutely not worth messing around with. Having said that, the correct blends of oils can restore your sense of mental well-being, happiness and balance, and an aromatherapy facial is a fantastically relaxing and effective way to care for your pregnant skin and worried brain. Book into a salon which caters for Yummy Mummies-to-be, and talk to your beauty therapist about what you need first.

Essential oils to AVOID include basil, camphor, bay, cedarwood, clary sage, clove, cinnamon, hyssop (what?), juniper, marjoram, myrrh, sage and rosemary.

Essential oils which are still OK include peppermint, for morning sickness, lemon for indigestion, lavender, geranium and rosewood for itchy stretch marks, and grapefruit and orange to combat fatigue, now that coffee's off the menu.

Massage
Essential for pregnancy survival, especially in the later months, but you need to go to a specialist who knows how to handle and pummel your changing body. There are special positions, techniques and even bizarre objects to lean yourself over to make the whole experience

safer and more comfortable. Business-savvy health spas up and down the country are cottoning on to the fact that Yummy Mummies are desperate for this sort of pampering, and there are new ones opening every month. Below is a list of some of the finest, and where to find more places near you.

TOP TIP: *Leave leaflets for some of these day and weekend spas lying around as the weeks go on, and make subtle hints about feeling very achy and knotted. If he doesn't book you a little surprise within two weeks, take yourself off with a girlfriend and have a ball.*

☆ **Nurturing Massage at Elemis Spa:** If you like a little inner peace and ancient philosophy with your pampering treat, then head straight here. Using a beanbag for the massage, camellia oil to prevent stretch marks, and specific care for stressed skin, this is sheer luxury in heavenly surroundings.

☆ **Pregnancy Massage at Space NK:** Each trimester of pregnancy is specially catered for in this aromatherapy treat.

☆ **Mother-to-be Package at Apotheke's Jurlique Day Spa and Sanctuary:** How does a float in Dead Sea salts, a body massage, a holistic pedicure and an organic facial sound?

☆ **Pitter-Patter Preparation at The Parlour:** Using the miracle-working Dermalogica products, this treatment, in fabulously opulent, boudoir-esque surroundings, will tailor to your specific needs brilliantly, and includes full body massage.

☆ Many hotels and day spas offer specific treatments for pregnancy, and babycentre.co.uk lists quite a few.

Fake Tan

Again, there isn't any evidence to say that this is dangerous in any way, but you might not turn out exactly the colour you had in mind because of your hormone situation. I had no trouble with it at all, and was glad to see a little colour in my now tired and slightly anaemic face and over my increasingly unenviable body. If you can get a professional splash of colour worked into your pampering treat, then so much the better.

Reflexology

Contrary to what you may have heard, reflexology cannot bring on a miscarriage, but most reflexologists won't treat women in the first three months of pregnancy because that's when the risk is highest naturally and they don't want hefty lawsuits. Fair enough. After this, you can have your aching feet prodded and squished as much as you like, unless you have a pre-term labour (before 37 weeks, but what are you having reflexology for if you're in pre-term labour?!), you suffer from placenta previa (low-lying placenta) or hydro amnios (too much water around the baby). Ask your midwife if you are unsure.

The benefits of reflexology include helping to relieve back pain, curing insomnia and digestive problems, and having somebody touch your feet which is my idea of Heaven at any time.

Keeping Up Appearances à la Maison

Unfortunately, it's not within most of our budgetary limits to have weekly facials and daily neck and shoulder massages. Damn. But leaving time to pamper yourself at home is just as good for day-to-day survival. This is also true of looking after your basic make-up and the way you dress: you obviously don't need the most expensive products or a stylist to help you out. Just making some time to wash and dry your hair nicely and taking some extra care over your make-up can give you a cheap but very effective morale boost to get you through the toughest 'my bum is massive in this' day.

Home Facials

I always have hundreds of face-mask sachets promising one beauty miracle or another in my bathroom, and they certainly didn't get ignored when I was pregnant. Your skin will need more pampering and care than it ever has before, as your baby starts to drain every ounce of goodness from your body, and a moisture-replacing, glow-enhancing, dead-cell-removing, mood-lifting face mask will be the cure to your greyness.

☆ **Great Exfoliators:** Clarins Doux Peeling, Dermalogica Daily Microfoliant and No. 7 Gentle Renewing No Grains Exfoliator.

☆ **Great Masks:** Botanics Vitamin Recovery Mask, The Body Shop Vitamin E Mask, and Elemis Exotic Cream Moisturising Mask for dry, dull skin. Nivea Visage Active Purifying Face Mask, Crabtree & Evelyn Deep Cleansing China Clay Mask or The Sanctuary Mint and Rosemary Mask for upset, spotty skin.

☆ **Great Moisturisers:** Olay Total Effects Time Resist Moisturiser, Dr Hauschka Rose Day Cream, Clinique Dramatically Different Moisturising Lotion, Lancome Hydra Zen Reinforced Skin De-Stressing Hydration Cream.

☆ **Great Eye Treatments:** Elemis Absolute Eye Mask, Lancome Primordiale Optimum Yeux.

☆ **Great Hair Treatments:** John Frieda Frizz-Ease Miraculous Recovery Deep Conditioning Treatment, The Body Shop Olive Glossing Conditioner.

☆ **Great Body Treats:** Elemis Frangipani Monoi Moisture Melt, Body Shop Shea Body Butter, Dove Silkening Body Lotion.

☆ **Mother-to-Be Treats:** The Sanctuary Mum To Be Body Cream, Natalia Perfect Pregnancy Kit Bodycare by Vital Touch.

---

*Debbie, mother of Luke, three,
and Helena, eleven months*

While I was still in the hospital I shaved my legs, put on a refreshing face pack and painted my finger- and toe-nails. When the health visitor called at my house the next day, she looked at me, in my Monsoon shirt, flowing skirt and full make-up, and asked if I was my sister. She couldn't believe I had just had a baby, but I felt wonderful. Fully me, and fully ready to tackle the day's chores.

Sex: How, Why And When?

Sex may not be foremost on your mind as your pregnancy really starts to take shape (as it were), but it's still there, and it needs some attention too. Pregnancy can have a huge effect on your attitude towards sex, and whatever your experience, somebody else will be feeling the same way.

Some women become nymphomaniacs, others go off sex completely for the rest of their lives, and most fall somewhere in between.

Dealing with the **WHY** first, there are two answers I have found: firstly, because you still can, and secondly, because if you don't you will worry about your lack of interest, and that your partner, becoming paralysingly frustrated, will run off with next-door's nanny while you turn into a miserable old prune. The first part is very real: when you are super-huge, sex becomes physically impossible, if not dangerous to whoever happens to be underneath you. Once the baby is born you won't be able to have sex for a good few weeks, or even months, and after that you will have to schedule it in between 'go to bed' and 'fall asleep', which can only amount to about ten seconds, on a good day.

HOW is up to you really, but any chandeliers, trapezes and highly penetrative sex toys are out for now. Sorry. Vibrators are still cool, but careful where you put them is all I'd say: easy does it... Lying on your back is uncomfortable and unwise for long periods of time now, because the baby is getting heavy and it presses down on your back and reduces your blood flow. Get a book and play around, because I'm sure as hell not going to tell you how we did it!

WHEN? Whenever you can. And can be bothered. And don't feel sick, or have terrible heartburn (although my husband swears he knows the best cure for that, if you know what I mean...), or are too tired, or want to sit in the bath squeezing colostrum out of your nipples instead. It's *your* call, because you are the pregnant one here.

Oh, and masturbation is still fine. Quick, effective, painless and risk-free.

TOP TIP: *Less of a tip than a request, really. Please, please keep having sex as much as you can while you are pregnant. It's so easy to put it on hold for a while, but getting your mojo back when you've been 'on a break' for several months is really difficult. You will need all the help you can to feel like a sexy, horny, desirable, nubile young thing once you become a Yummy Mummy as it is, and sex is one of the best ways of keeping in touch with the old you.*

The F Word: I am Definitely the Fattest Person in the World

No you're not. You are pregnant. Reminding yourself that you are *pregnant* and not fat doesn't make it any easier or less distressing at the time, alas: when you start to feel big, bloated and shapeless it's horrible, and you won't be able to see past your growing abdomen and convince yourself that it's actually not that bad. However, to most other, rational people you look lovely and womanly.

TOP SURVIVAL TIPS for this stage:

☆ **Don't spend hours looking at yourself** in front of the mirror from all angles, wondering if you are still the same shape when you try really hard to imagine the bump isn't there. It's hopeless.

☆ **It's impossible to be objective.** To your pregnant eyes, everything is bigger. And bigger is definitely not better right now.

☆ **Don't ask your partner's opinion.** It's very unfair, because he can only either lie to you or be the target of your pregnant wrath and loathing. You won't believe him anyway, because you are convinced that you are fat, so leave him out of it. Poor bloke.

☆ **Look at pictures of beautiful, sexy, curvaceous women**, and realise that larger can definitely be gorgeouser. Rachel Weisz, Jennifer Lopez, Kate Winslet, Kelly Brook and on and on. Sexy, curvy women! Love it.

If none of the above works, then this will be a difficult, depressing few months, until you become properly pregnant and have no option but to go with the flow and love your bump. In the meantime, do yourself a favour and remember: YOU ARE NOT FAT, you just have 'fat lenses' in for a while.

Testing, Testing: One, Two, Three, Four, Five, Six...

Pregnant women need to toughen up before the birth, and the best way to do this is to stick needles in them as often as possible. Or so the medical profession seems to think. By the time you've reached The End, your arms will *look* like a watering can, you'll have weed in enough small plastic vials to *fill* a watering can, and you will have had more tests than a watering can goes through before it's released onto the shelves at B&Q.

Most of this testing is just to keep an eye on your iron levels and to see if there's any protein in your urine (a sign of pre-eclampsia, aka Very Bad News). But there are other tests you will be offered, which can tell you a lot about your unborn baby, and which you will have to decide whether to have done or not.

Here are some of the main tests to expect:

☆ **Routine blood tests.** These will first determine your blood group, rhesus factor and iron levels, and then whether you have Hepatitis B, syphilis (ugh) or toxoplasmosis, and whether you are immune to German measles. If you are rhesus negative you will probably have blood tests every four weeks or so after 28 weeks.
☆ **Blood-pressure checks.** Every time you see your doctor she will check that your blood pressure isn't starting to shoot through the roof. If you are like me, the opposite problem will occur: my blood pressure gets lower throughout every pregnancy, until I can barely stand up without passing out. Hey, at least it's different.
☆ **Screening for Down's Syndrome.** This is a hard decision for some, and an obvious one for others. Only you know how you would feel about having a child with Down's, so talk it through with your partner and do whatever feels right for *both* of you. There are loads of different tests available, and different areas will offer different ones.

☆ **Glucose-tolerance test.** Some women develop a special form of diabetes during pregnancy, and this is detected by finding extra sugar in your urine. You will probably have to drink a can of Lucozade and then have a blood test shortly after. Don't do what I did, which was to drink a can of Diet Lucozade. The whole point is to get the sugar in there, Liz – duh!

☆ **Urine tests.** You'll have these throughout your pregnancy to check for signs of pre-eclampsia and to practise being humiliated. There is no simple way to get it in the bottle, so just hold it down there, hope for the best, and scrub your hands, wrists and forearms afterwards.

☆ **Amniocentesis.** By removing a sample of your amniotic fluid with a long, hollow needle, and then analysing its contents, doctors can identify hundreds of genetic disorders, including Down's Syndrome, trisomy 18, and spina bifida. It is usually offered between the fifteenth and eighteenth week of pregnancy, and you have to be very sure that you want it done: there is a 1 in 200 chance of having a miscarriage after amniocentesis, so it is a big risk to take if you don't really need it. Talk about it…

Ultrasound Scans

Oh. My. God. Amazing, amazing, amazing. Scans are one of the most incredible things you will experience during the whole of your pregnancy, on a par with feeling your baby move and looking at your cleavage. A scan makes your baby seem real for the first time, and it can be a huge shock.

If you have completely irregular periods, like me, then you might have a scan within the first few weeks of gestation, just to confirm how far gone you are. At this stage there is almost nothing to see, except for a small blob, so don't get too excited.

It's common to have another one at about twelve weeks, to check that everything is hunky-dory, and to terrify you a little. By this stage your baby is about six centimetres long, and you may clearly be able to see the beginnings of little limbs, and a definite head bit. This is a good chance to get the first 'baby photo', which you can stick on your drinks cabinet to remind you why you're not going to have that gin and tonic, or hide in your wallet and peek at on the way home.

The BIG SCAN usually happens at twenty weeks, and you should prepare yourself well. This time you will see a proper-looking human baby sucking its thumb, kicking its legs, waving at you (yes, really waving at you), scratching its head, turning somersaults and all sorts. Most people cry, some can't speak for hours, and others get hysterical.

Tips to make the experience better:

☆ **Never go to a scan alone:** This is one of the most important moments of your life, and sharing it with a four-year-old copy of *Hello* is not a good idea. You will need a cuddle when you come out, so take someone special.

☆ **Drink lots of water:** It makes the image better, because a full bladder pushes the baby closer to the ultrasound thingy…

☆ **Wear some beautiful knickers:** They will be seen.

☆ **Check your bikini line:** They make you pull your knickers down very low, and it will just make the nurse's day if there are no wayward hairs sticking out. Eeek.

☆ **Bring some cash:** Trying to pay for a baby photo with a credit card won't work, and you only get one chance to buy one.

☆ **Tell the scan-lady (or man) if you want to see the screen better:** They are usually very kind, and will turn the monitor round for you to see everything. Otherwise you end up with a cricked neck as well as a belly covered in jelly.

☆ **Ask if you can't identify anything:** The image from an ultrasound is very dark and confusing, and unless you are used to looking at such things, it may look like nothing but black and grey blobs. Don't lie there saying, 'Oh yes! I can see her tiny fingers', when really you could be looking at her earlobe for all you know. Ask, and ye shall learn.

Try not to think about having a scan as a way of finding all sorts of things wrong with your baby. A lot of people get really worked up about scans, but they are usually just a great chance to see your baby for the first time, and to make the pregnancy feel more real. Very, very real, in fact. Yikes!

Come Fly With Me (while you still can)

If this is your first pregnancy, then please trust me on this one: travelling will never be as easy or enjoyable as it is now, so GO ON HOLIDAY and enjoy yourselves while the going's good. If you don't, and you duck out because you can't be bothered, feel too tired, or don't look nice in a bikini any more, you will regret it forever, and really annoy me because I'd *love* to go, thanks very much.

If possible, fly away somewhere beautiful, because this will be the most tricky form of transport once the baby arrives, and you can get somewhere much more exotic on a plane. Flying short distances is perfectly safe for your baby and cabin pressure, dry air and ugly seat-covers won't harm it. Do tell your doctor before you go though, because everyone has different medical circumstances...

TOP SURVIVAL TIPS for pregnant travellers:

☆ **Fly before you are 28 weeks pregnant.** After this, some insurance companies get a bit panicky, and either refuse to insure you at all, or require a letter from your doctor confirming your due date.

☆ **Carry your travel medical insurance with you at all times.**

☆ **Take your medical notes with you.**

☆ **Drink lots more water than usual** to combat swollen feet and ankles, and to stave off dehydration.

☆ **Go to the loo every time you see one.**

☆ **Walk about even more than usual** on a flight, to prevent varicose veins, backache, thrombosis and so on.

☆ **Learn how to say 'pregnant'** in the language of the country you're going to. 'Stop staring at my big stomach' is also handy.

☆ **Don't go scuba diving**, or use saunas or hot jacuzzis.

☆ **Go to the British Insurance Brokers Association** if you are having trouble getting travel insurance.

Health Matters

Yes it does, and here are some.

As well as what you eat, drink, do and think, there are yet more things which could affect your pregnancy, and which you should be aware of. Because we'd *hate* any pregnant ladies to be having too much fun, wouldn't we...

Gardening

Assuming you can still bend down and reach some soil and filth, then wearing gloves and washing your hands thoroughly afterwards is essential. Earth contains parasites which can cause toxoplasmosis, which in turn can cause brain damage to the foetus, or even a miscarriage. If you let these get under your nails and into your mouth, you could be in real trouble.

Pets

If you still have a pet, then try to get rid of it as soon as possible. Ok, obviously don't *really* do that, but you might like to spend a few minutes honestly trying to think how manageable this will be soon: a baby is quite enough for most new mums to handle, without also having to feed the goldfish, clean out the hamster or take the Labrador for long walks. In the meantime, being near animals is not a good idea when you are pregnant, because they carry all sorts of bugs and nasties, which are potentially very harmful to a Yummy Foetus, for example toxoplasmosis, chlamydia, listeria, E. coli and salmonella. It's also not a good idea to visit a zoo, a farm or a vet. The worst domestic offender is the cat litter tray, and if you *must* clean it out then dress like a bee-keeper and wash your entire body thoroughly with TCP afterwards.

Medication

If you are on any, your doctor should have gone through whether you can carry on taking it while you are expecting. If you have to take some medicine at some point, make sure it's OK to.

A small problem: Almost everything carries a 'do not take this if you are, or think you might be pregnant' warning in case somebody drinks an entire bottle of Night Nurse and sues the pharmaceutical company when her baby has three heads. This makes it impossible to know whether something *really is* potentially harmful, or if there's virtually no risk at all unless you are armed with common sense. If you truly believe that taking one Nurofen for the headache you've had for two days will do more harm to your baby than the stress your headache is causing you, then you must carry on suffering.

Definite no-nos: aspirin (it thins the blood), ibuprofen, decongestants containing ephedrine.

Safe medicines: paracetamol (hooray!), antacids containing magnesium or aluminium, and most other over-the-counter medicines, but ask first!

External Factors

These include working in a smoky atmosphere, being very trigger-happy with the bleach, living under the M4, painting all your walls in leaded paint, and other such nasty things. Try to avoid inhaling, ingesting or spending a lot of time hanging around any nasty chemical or biological substances, which could pass into your blood, and then into your baby.

PART FOUR

Nearing the End

The third trimester (aka 'the last lap') can feel disproportionately long. It's a bit like standing in the Co-op behind an old lady who wants to buy a half-bottle of Vodka with an out-of-date cheque book, when all you need is a pint of milk and this month's *InStyle*, and you've parked outside illegally.

With only a couple of months left, the time for burying your head in the sand is well and truly over, and things are hotting up on all fronts. If you looked at yourself in the mirror at 24 weeks, and swore you wouldn't/couldn't get any bigger, this last stage will come as quite a shock. You are about to get very, very big indeed, and it's time to start getting organised for take-off. It's an uncomfortable, exciting, frustrating and nervous stage, and the only way to survive it is to keep busy.

More **Physical Changes** (nearly there though...)

Never wishing you to become bored, or too comfortable, your body saves a few surprises for the last month or two. Cheers, love.

Is There a Loo Around Here?

In the last month your baby presses down on your bladder quite hard, so you will need the loo constantly. Added to this is the fact that you feel you need to drink lots to keep hydrated and avoid getting piles, so it's not uncommon to have to wee more than once an hour. And when you have to go, you have to go *NOW*.

Backache

A big stomach means a sore back. Mostly this is your lower back, as the baby weighs down so heavily there, and maintaining a good posture is critical now. Backache can be very bad during the night towards the end, and upping the number of Johnny Depps between your legs to two, or even three, can help.

I Can't Get Comfortable

Nope. And you won't until Junior is out. Lying on your back for long periods is, as you now know, not a good idea. Lying on your stomach became impossible months ago, standing hurts your back, and sitting down squashes the baby into your rib cage so you can't breathe or eat anything. The best positions for me were perching on a high stool, and lying on my side with pillows in position. It is a tough time, but you're nearly there now…

Twinges and Cramps

These can be really painful and also terribly embarrassing: there is no subtle or ladylike way of relieving cramp in your groin when you are in the middle of Selfridges. Leg cramps and twinges in your back, abdomen and groin ligaments happen a lot now, but unless they are painful and prolonged they are probably just caused by your baby getting big and heavy. Moving around as much as you can helps, as does gentle stretching every few hours.

Haemorrhoids

Don't panic: I never got any. Promise. If you do, drink more water and up your fibre and fresh fruit intake to keep things, errr, moving more easily.

Stretch Marks

Just when you thought you'd made it they can pop up like a bad zit before a party. Keep going on the oils every night, and pray for a lucky miss.

Burping and Farting

This is so much fun, because you can fart as much as you like, and blame it on the baby. Seriously, it's really common to get somewhat gassy towards the end, so if you have to be in an enclosed space with somebody for a long time, then sit near the window or be prepared for some funny looks. It was around this stage that my two-year-old learned to say "Whodunnafart?" It was *always* Mummy.

Braxton Hicks contractions

These have been going on since the middle of your pregnancy, but you may start to notice them a lot towards the end. Your body is just doing lots of dummy runs for what a proper contraction should be like, so it makes your uterus tighten for 30-60 seconds every so often. Your abdomen may feel harder, and it may hurt a little, or you may hardly notice it at all. If I sound a bit vague, it's because I have to: every woman has her own experience of Braxton Hicks contractions and there are no hard and fast rules. Oh, except these: if you have any vaginal bleeding or leak water, and if, before your 37th week, the tightenings are accompanied by lower back pain, come at more than three per hour or seem to be very regular, call your midwife. You may be in premature labour. Them's the rules, girls.

What To Buy Now

Baby Clobber

Considering how tiny they are, babies need a head-spinning amount of clobber. If you are ever accused of owning too much 'stuff', then point your longest manicured digit at the youngest consumer in your family and plead innocence: next to your baby, you look positively frugal.

I say babies *need a* lot of clobber, but it's probably more a case of 'are expected to have' a lot these days. When your grandmother was a baby, she probably made do with some swaddling clothes and an old rag doll, and was much better off for it. But these are 'these days', and Yummy Mummies can choose from a baffling array of equipment, toys and aids to make their babies happier, comfier and more stimulated, and their own lives much easier.

Here are some essentials:

1. Car seat

The only legally required bit of kit. Newborns' car seats need to be rear-facing because babies' necks aren't yet strong enough to withstand any force. Some come as part of a three-in-one system, which means you can lift the car seat straight onto your pram chassis and off you go. Don't scrimp on a car seat: get a good new one.

2. Pram

Probably your biggest investment, and worth every penny. The best advice I can give is push them around the shop and see how they handle. Things to look out for include:

☆ **Swivel wheels or fixed?** I'm a fixed girl – give me swivel wheels and I'm like a drunk ice-skater.

☆ **Suspension.** Will it withstand bumping up and down kerbs and over potholes? Will your baby get whiplash between your front door and the end of the road?

☆ **Space.** Does it have enough underneath for piling all your shopping into? Remember that your shopping list will quadruple the minute you become a Mum: nappies, wipes, baby-food jars, nipple cream, gin…you need a lot of room under there, and that's before you have piled in the baby's changing bag, some toys, your handbag and last week's Sunday supplements, just in case you get a moment to yourself.

☆ **Handle height.** Will it break Very Tall Daddy's back when he pushes it?

☆ **Folding and dismantling.** If you are likely to do a lot of travelling, then getting a pram which comes apart easily, or better still just folds away in one piece, is essential. We have wasted hours at airports removing the top half from the chassis and putting it back together again.

☆ **Size.** Does it fit in the back of your car? You'll feel *so* stupid (and cross) if it doesn't.

☆ **Lining.** Does it come out and can it be washed?

☆ **Can your baby sit up properly, as well as lie down?** New babies should lie down all the time, because of the weak neck problem, but after a few months they will love sitting up a bit and looking at the world whizzing by. Then, when it's time for a nap, you can just lie them flat again.

☆ **Can your baby face forwards or backwards?** This, for me, is one of the most important factors. All my babies have faced me (i.e. backwards) when I pushed them in the pram, because that way they could see me, I could talk to them and point things out, and I could also see whether they were being strangled by some loose strap or other more easily. I am also convinced that all the talking, smiling and singing you can do with your baby facing you can dramatically improve how fast they learn things. And if they've just been sick out of the corner of their mouth you will notice before anyone can tut-tut you.

☆ **Can it have a buggy board attached to it?** This ride-on platform will be indispensable once you have another baby (which you might, despite it seeming like a ridiculous notion right now).

And, finally, if it ticks all of these boxes, ask yourself one last question:

☆ **Is it stylish enough for me?** Your baby's pram will become like a fifth limb to you, so if it doesn't make you proud, don't get it. Get one *you* like – the baby doesn't care.

3. Buggy

A pram *and* a buggy? Isn't this a little unnecessary? Not at all: prams are big, heavy and cumbersome; buggies are small, light, fold-down-in-a-flash-able, portable and absolutely essential. For day trips, quick hops to the shops, and travelling abroad, a good buggy is the piece of gear you'll need. NB: babies can only go in a buggy once they can sit up properly. Otherwise they just slide down into a heap at the bottom and you'll be picked up by Social Services. Not glam at all.

4. Raincover and sunshade

Ooooh, don't get me started on these. I *hate* raincovers. They are ridiculously expensive, they never fit on properly, they rip, they snap, they stick out so far that you'll clear supermarket shelves as you go down the aisles, and, most annoyingly, they are essential. I think it's called being caught between a rock and a hard place – wet baby or infuriating rain cover?

NB: there are loads of different models available, so make sure you get one which fits your pram or buggy, and don't take the shop assistant's word for it. Get her to fit it right there in the shop, and watch *her* struggle to get the damned thing on. If you're not sure, find a different model. Good luck.

I have no such murderous thoughts about sunshades, but I would complain that they are very drab. Where are the beautiful, stylish sunshades out there? If you can get one where the sunshade is detachable from the bit which screws on to the top the pram, then do: it'll save a lot of time screwing and unscrewing.

5. Moses basket

I was sure we didn't need one of these, partly because the name is as unappealing as the object itself, and partly because I didn't see what was wrong with letting my baby sleep in the top half of the pram for a while. Or a large cardboard box – it's not as though the baby will notice. Having bought the least hideous one I could find, I was very glad I did: much more comfortable (and socially acceptable) for the baby, and it was even quite cute. However, I would never leave my baby in a Moses basket in a stand: a disaster waiting to happen, surely? The floor is the best place, preferably right next to your bed to start off with, so that you can just finish a feed, turn over and pop your baby back in again.

6. Cot and travel cot

Not much to say here, except that the top bar should be high enough to stop a nine-month-old baby from nose-diving onto the floor. Choosing a cot bed is quite cunning, because you will be able to squeeze a good few years out of it. Just using a travel cot is a bad idea, because they are less sturdy, they often have fabric sides which rustle if your baby wriggles against them, and they look fairly hideous. Get a nice wooden one, and sit back and admire. We swore we didn't really need a travel cot (did we think we needed *anything*, in fact?) but it has come in useful on hundreds of holidays and weekends with friends.

7. Mattresses, sheets, blankets

For some weird reason we are happy to spend a fortune looking after our own backs and necks, but make do with a horrible synthetic-foam mattress with a plastic cover for our babies. Considering how much time they spend on it, this is pretty mean, not to mention unhealthy. Get a supportive, breathable mattress made from natural fibres if possible (The Natural Mat Company is a great place to start looking) for your baby's cot, and find sheets which actually fit. There seem to be a million different cot shapes and sizes, and buying a 'standard' sheet size never worked for me. Or maybe I'm just hopeless at making a mini bed.

NB: **Don't put your baby under a duvet for at least six months.** They wriggle around all over the place, and will end up kicking the duvet over their head and suffocating. Stick to blankets or a baby sleeping bag, and if it's cold then put an extra layer of clothing on the baby, rather than in the cot.

8. Baby gym

Excellent, excellent investment. No sweat or Lycra involved here, just some bright, shiny objects which dangle above your baby's head as she lies on a mat. There are loads of different types, but my favourites were the soft ones which fold up – you can take them away with you and ensure a happy, occupied baby while you're on holiday or visiting relatives.

9. Bouncy chair

Bouncy chairs allow for more stretching and bouncing than car seats, which babies like. Until your baby can sit up unaided, a bouncy chair is the only way you will be able to go to the loo, wash your hair, or do anything else which requires two hands.

10. Non-slip rubber bath mat

Cheap, not very pretty, but very useful – it makes bath-time less like trying to catch an eel in a Jacuzzi.

11. Changing mat

Always far too flouncy and unattractive, but as they're going to have a fair amount of poo and other nasties wiped on them, I don't suppose it really matters. The most important thing is that it's long enough – you don't want your baby to have outgrown it within four months, and have her bottom resting on the carpet.

12. Cupboard and drawers

Junior fashionistas have a ridiculous amount of clothing considering how little there is to actually clothe. The wardrobe I started out with was woefully too small, and I upgraded within three months to something much bigger. Twenty babygros, ten snow-suits (because everybody will give you one), hundreds of socks and unworn baby shoes, and all the clothes your baby is yet to grow into have to go *somewhere*, and anything smaller than a full-sized armoire with five drawers is too small.

13. High chair

Not for at least six months, if not more, but at some stage within the first year you will need something better than a bouncy chair for feeding your growing baby. A high chair should be the opposite of your desired body shape: think sturdy, chunky and practical. Those tall ones with long, skinny legs terrify me – my babies would topple those over in three seconds during a particularly lively feeding session. Ours converts into a table and chair, which will be very useful just as soon as we can stop producing yet more babies who need it as a high chair. My daughter is still waiting for a desk…

14. Muslin squares

When my first college friend joined me in Yummy Mummyhood, I remember giving her a box of beautifully wrapped muslin squares – they were the most useful baby things I ever bought myself, and I knew that everybody else would plump for impractical bonnets and My Baby's First Photo Album schmaltz instead. Her face displayed a look I can only describe as something between disappointment and disgust. I bet she regrets it now. I became so used to having a muslin square over my left shoulder to catch any post-feed spills that I frequently walked around with one even though my baby was somewhere else. They are also indispensable for lying your baby down on if you need an emergency change somewhere less than spotless, as a very thin layer in hot summer months instead of a blanket, or as a makeshift sunshade if you've left yours at home as I always seemed to.

15. Bibs

Loads and loads and loads. Soft ones which do up at the back are best, unless you want to smear egg into your baby's hair as you remove it. Done that many times.

16. Changing bag

This will go with you everywhere from now on, and should be able to fit a nappy, wipes, a bottle of milk, a food jar, a spoon, one change of baby clothes, small toys, a travel changing mat and some lipstick. It doesn't need to be designer, but something pretty which you will be proud to carry everywhere with you will do.

17. A baby sling

This is not in case you *do* break one of his arms while getting him dressed, but to carry him around in if you don't fancy heaving the pram over any rough terrain, or when you could do with sharing some body heat. Front carriers (aka papooses or slings) are very useful for times when a wheeled vehicle is unnecessary or inappropriate. Make sure the part near your baby's mouth is removable and washable – it will get disgustingly pasted with slobber and bits of sick.

That covers the essential items you should get for your new baby. It's a huge list, and it costs a large fortune, but, unless you subscribe to the 'swaddling clothes and an old rag doll' approach to childcare, then you should find them all very useful or even essential. Best send your bank manager some flowers, smartish.

Things You Will Feel You Should Buy, but Don't Need and Won't Use

☆ **Baby bath.** See **Bathing Your Baby** in Part Six.

☆ **Cot bumpers.** Totally unnecessary, very flouncy and possibly dangerous due to the loose ties.

☆ **Pillow.** Babies need to lie flat, because their necks just aren't up to any crooking. Apart from the fact that they'll just end up underneath the pillow anyway. No pillow.

☆ **Changing station.** The floor will do. Safer, cheaper and takes up much less room, which will now be at a premium.

☆ **Baby rucksack thing.** Unless you live in the Highlands, you will spend a lot of money (upwards of £60 for a good one) on a large unfoldable object which lives in the attic. Borrow this from a friend for the three occasions you'll ever need one.

☆ **Playpen.** Huge, ugly and never used. If you must lock your baby in a cage, then a travel cot would be as good.

☆ **Nappy disposal system.** Why would you want to keep nappies full of poo inside your house for more than two minutes? Throw them in the wheelie bin immediately!

The Ultimate Luxury Baby Gear – Because Looking Good Doesn't Stop with You

☆ **Storksak Classic Shoulder Bag:** Finished with a chic leather trim, with a wipe-clean interior and pockets for hot or cold bottles.

☆ **Posh Baby Changing Bag:** As used by Ms Paltrow and Ms Cox-Arquette, has metal feet so everything doesn't get soaked from the bottom up, and is the most sturdy I've seen. The Reversible Day Bag/Tote is slightly cheaper, machine-washable, with straps long enough to stretch right across the pram handle, which I could have done with at times.

☆ **Petit Planet:** Made of soft nappa leather and pony skin, these luxurious bags have been designed to cater for every emergency in true Yummy style. Mobile phone pouch, make-up compartment, washable changing mat and much more.

☆ **Dior Baby Bottles:** Oh go on – it's quite funny!

☆ **Bill Amberg Sheepskin Snuggler:** This supremely cosy snuggle-bag is fully machine-washable and mouth-wateringly stylish. It is also great for lining prams on cold winter walks.

And some cheaper alternatives...

I am always happy to buy second-hand baby clothes and toys, but somehow when it came to the basics of pram, cot, high-chair and so on, I had to have them new, clean and unexposed to another baby's snot and spit. Just a personal thing, which probably involves some irrational motherly pride too. You can get some fantastic second-hand bargains at car-boot sales and by looking on good old eBay, and never be too proud to accept a hand-me-down from a friend or relative. I've just inherited a friend's buggy, as our old one finally caved in after seven years of hard wear, and, while it's not the loveliest piece of baby equipment I've ever owned, it's free, and it'll do the next six months perfectly.

If none of this sounds appealing, and new is really what you're after, try these for value and no loss of style:

High Street Clobber

Mothercare has come a long way since the days of shapeless dungarees and flowery blankets. They stock all the necessary basics at reasonable prices, and just occasionally you can spot a really stylish piece.

Other stores to take a look at, while you are actually shopping for yourself and not your baby, include Boots, Argos and John Lewis, and if you can set an entire Sunday aside, then never forget Ikea. Flat-pack equals better value, remember?

Online

This is the best place to start to get an idea of the styles you like. If you can bear to buy without touching and smelling first, it's also the easiest way of baby-furnishing your house. Search under 'baby equipment' and you'll have enough choice to satisfy even *your* high standards.

TOP TIP: *I have heard miserable tales of cots and prams arriving late, with bolts and screws missing, leaving the baby to sleep in a drawer for a few weeks and Mummy unable to go out until the extra parts arrived. Order online items with plenty of time to spare, and be ready to get your Ikea 'how does this fit together' head screwed on.*

For You

☆ **Yummy Mummy clobber.** There is a complete list in Part Seven, but for now you might want to sort out some earplugs and a blindfold, if you are intending to get any rest in the hospital at all, and maybe the new Mummy-friendly handbag should make an appearance before you go into labour – because it's fun, and because you will need it the moment you step out for the first time. Your new make-up and beauty routine will be helped if you get loaded up with beautiful products now: trawling around the heavenly 'pamper-me' counters at John Lewis will be a lot less fun in a few weeks' time.

☆ **Baby announcement cards and thank-you cards.** Obviously you can't be 100% certain which flavour you will end up with (even seemingly enormous penises have turned out to be nothing more than enormous umbilical cords or fingers, though what exactly they are doing down there is anyone's guess), so hold off the 'It's a Boy!' stationery for now. Much better to go for something neutral and classy, which can apply to either sex.

You will hopefully get lots of presents in the next few weeks, and there's nothing like a prompt, beautiful thank-you card to set your Yummy Mumminess off on the right track. Smythson has the most coveted ones, but if you're after something more afford-able it's worth a rummage around your nearest 'lifestyle' shop, which is bound to have something gorgeous and unusual, and WH Smith can also come up trumps.

☆ **A lovely bedside table.** If you don't have one already, then get something which has enough room for several baby bottles, wipes, all your creams and lotions, acres of maternity bras, and a loud alarm clock.

☆ **An equally lovely bedside radio.** I'm quite sure that I've spent more hours in bed with John Humphreys than my husband, but when you're a heavily pregnant insomniac, or a breastfeeding Yummy Mummy in the wee hours of the night, you'll take any company you can get. And you might learn a thing or two while you're at it. A nasty black affair, which doesn't tune properly and makes your bedside table look like an Argos catalogue, will not cheer you up every time you hit the On button. A sleek Roberts 'Classic' Radio, made of ash wood with a pink leather trim, on the other hand, is much more like it.

Audio books are worth a try too. Reading with your eyes closed? Now there's a great idea!

Due Dates: Due for a Re-think

New Year's Day 1998. 12 days overdue.

I can't believe it's 1998 and I'm still pregnant. After an alcohol-free Christmas, I though I'd at least be ready for a booze-up at New Year, but one glass was all I was allowed again. I'm very frustrated, almost angry, and I feel annoyed with the baby and with myself for not planning for things to get so overdue. I thought she was coming out weeks ago, and got all excited, but now I just feel stupid for being so naïve. I've been having Braxton Hicks contractions for weeks, but they just annoy me now, because they never seem to get anywhere. They just hurt and make me tired. They're going to induce me on the 3rd, which will be such a disappointment after all this waiting. I want to know how my body does it on its own, not through intervention. This is such a confusing, surreal time.

(Clearly terrified of being induced, sensible Emily was born naturally on 3 January at 3.30 a.m. Clever girl.)

'So, When is Your Baby Due?'

That's an annoying question you'll be asked over and over again, and you will duly give the only answer you know, which is the date given to you by your doctor right at the beginning of your long journey to the delivery room. This date is your EDD, or Estimated Date of Delivery, and the only word we care about here is the first one:

ESTIMATED

Not actual, likely, probable, desirable or chosen. Just ESTIMATED. Now, to be fair, they can't be sure: complications can arise, every woman's body is different, and you might even be telling a tiny fib about when you *really* think you conceived, for personal reasons. (Naughty girl.)

But 'estimated' by what means? By calculating the average length of gestation in women today? No. By dividing your last credit-card bill by the number of times you went to the cinema last month and adding it to Sarah Beeney's date of birth (because she is a groovy Yummy Mummy and we should all aspire to be more like that)? No, but it might as well be.

In the UK, here's how your due date is calculated:

Last Known Menstrual Period + 7 days – 3 months = EDD

And why? Because in about 1850, well before Mummies had even thought about becoming Yummy, some German science dude called Dr Naegele decided that the average length of human gestation was 266 days from conception. There. That's it. No allowance for variations caused by age, race, stress, nutrition, how many times you've been pregnant before or the fact that half of us ovulate completely irregularly. That was his theory, and that's how we still do it today. Well, thank God for advances in modern medicine!

The mad thing, given how unbelievably important this date is to you, is that there are about ten different ways of calculating it, different countries use different methods, and all of them give you a different date! The only thing you can be almost certain of is that **your baby will NOT be born on its due date**!

Psychologically, it's better to think it will be late. Practically, it's better to get ready early. Emotionally, it's a minefield whichever way you look at it, but at least the tips below should make it a little less traumatic.

TOP TIPS for Surviving the Big Wait:
- ☆ **Ignore your due date**, and pretend it's actually two weeks after the date you're given.
- ☆ **Book yourself loads of treats** for the two weeks before your due date.
- ☆ **Book yourself loads *more* treats** for the two weeks afterwards. Your baby is bound to come out if there's a full-body massage and dinner for two somewhere special lined up for the next day.
- ☆ **Tell everyone it's due two weeks *after* your official due date**, so they don't ring you every five minutes the second you're overdue to ask if there's any news yet. Like you wouldn't tell them. Grrrrrr.
- ☆ **Stock up your freezer** with all your favourite food. You won't be going shopping for a while, and your partner will forget that you wanted low-calorie everything.
- ☆ **Stock up your cupboards.** I filled mine with herbal teas, decaf everything and enough non-perishables to last several decades. This applies to your bathroom products as well, and to any household cleaning products you will need so much of now, especially washing powder!
- ☆ **Take your phone off the hook** when you pass your due date, or re-record your answering-machine message to something like: 'Yeah, so I'm just hanging out this week, not doing much really. Bit of reading, that sort of thing, so can't come to the phone. Oh, and did I mention? *The baby HASN'T COME OUT YET SO LEAVE ME ALONE!*'

And While We're At It – Some More Questionable Facts
I can't wait to be an Old Wife, so that I can sit around in a croch-eted shawl and concoct some Tales. Old Wives' ones, to be more

precise. When you are pregnant, lots of well meaning people will tell you lots of complete nonsense about your unborn baby, which you will listen to intently, nodding your head, and half-wondering whether they are right. They are not.

Even the most up-to-date ultrasound scans can get things wrong, so the chances of Mrs Mopplethrop from Number 25 knowing instinctively that you are expecting a boy with dark hair and a talent for spin bowling are very slim indeed.

Here are some of the most common and totally groundless Old Wives' Tales you are likely to come across:

☆ **The shape and height of your bump can indicate your baby's sex.** Many people belive that 'all out front and low' is a boy and 'all over the place and high' is a girl, but this is totally unsubstantiated and for every woman for whom this turned out to be true (like me) you will find one for whom it didn't.
☆ **Heartburn means your baby will have lots of hair.** I had terrible heartburn for all of mine, and they all had tons of hair, but I know just as many friends who also suffered and then produced baldies.
☆ **If your face gets very full and rosy, you are having a girl.** Nope.
☆ **The foetal heart-rate can indicate the sex.** This is the most convincing one for me, but there still hasn't been conclusive evidence that it's true. The thinking is that faster is a girl and slower is a boy, but there will be so much variation anyway, depending on how relaxed you are, what you had for lunch and whether your trousers are too tight, that it's hard to say what makes a heart-rate faster or slower at any given time. Sorry to be such a killjoy.

There are many more, but all are equally scientifically unproven, and they should be treated as a bit of fun.

Last Chance To...

However high-achieving, Yummy and utterly brilliant at multi-tasking you are, there are certain things that will become either extremely difficult or just impossible after your baby is born. This is something you will become completely used to after about two years, but to begin with you can feel as though you've been sent to a boot camp, with all of life's luxuries locked away.

I'm not even talking about *big* luxuries, like going skiing for two weeks or buying a season ticket for the Royal Ballet. Not being able to do *these* things can hardly be considered hardship, on anyone's scale. No, the real problem when you have a new baby is that everything becomes more difficult, and if you don't indulge yourself in the last few weeks, you will regret it very soon. Even if you don't feel like doing any of the things suggested below, please drag yourself off the sofa and try one of them, because this might be the last chance you get to:

☆ **Read a newspaper.** Not just *buy* a newspaper and then recycle it four days later, but actually read some of it.
☆ **Read a Sunday newspaper.** Obviously not all of it (does anybody do that?), but at least a fair chunk of it.
☆ **Go to the loo when you need to, and on your own.** From now on you will only be able to go when it suits your baby, and you will rarely, if ever, be able to go without a baby in a bouncy chair for company.
☆ **Go to the cinema** every day! GO! GO! Peace, popcorn and pure escapism. I spent the last two months of my final pregnancy virtually *living* in the Cambridge Arts Cinema, watching films I didn't even want to watch, just because I *could*. It ended in a huge row, because I *was determined* to call our baby Igby, as an homage to my favourite film of the year, but my other, more rational half told me I was prenatally insane and our baby would have the piss ripped out of him forever. (I hate it when he's right.)
☆ **Be spontaneous.** It's a little hard to *plan* to be spontaneous, but see how often you can suddenly change your plans and do something you enjoy on a whim.
☆ **Wash your hair** when you want to, and in an unhurried, un-stressed, un-covered-in-water-and-bubbles sort of way.
☆ **Have a lie-in.** It's hard to sleep in these final weeks, but force yourself to stay in bed, spread those Sunday supplements around

the place and try to hold that feeling as long as you can. Three or four years would be good if you can manage it...

☆ **Go everywhere that kids can't go.** Eat in über-stylish restaurants, walk through the glassware section of Habitat and try to go to all the upstairs places you'll have a nightmare getting to in the future (prams and buggies mean the hassle of lifts and automatic doors forever).

☆ **Have sex in the morning.** Or evening, for that matter, but sex in the morning is a true luxury of the child-free and the over-forties whose kids have left home. Or the brave and uninhibited who don't mind their toddler walking in to find Daddy's bottom bobbing up and down on top of Mummy. Too many questions there...

☆ **Be reckless.** You will be so reck-*full* once you become a mother, watching where every hot cup of tea, small plastic bag or box of drawing pins is put, that now is a good time to throw caution to the wind and live on the edge a bit. Is that a razor I see lying on the side of the bath? Rock and roll!

☆ **See your friends.** I didn't do enough of this before I had kids, because I didn't believe how much being a mother would affect our relationships. You can obviously still spend time with your childless friends, but it will never be quite the same again, and you will always feel a small rift there, as you wipe milk off your baby's chin and she looks at you as though you were a stranger. If you can, throw a small party and sneak some of the alcohol into a secret hiding place for you to enjoy when you are finally allowed to drink it again. Such fiendish cunning.

☆ **Shop very, very slowly.** Maybe even spend an afternoon window-shopping if you're really serious about it. Take your time, try lots of shoes on, ponder a little, stop for a coffee, go back again and have another think about those earrings, and then decide to come back again tomorrow and see if they still take your fancy. Because you can.

Baby Showers

This originally American tradition has been adopted so well over here that we are practically ready to claim we thought of it first, as we do with most other fun things. I think the objection most English people have to baby showers is the unashamed 'give me lots of presents' aspect of the celebration. If there were more scope for our customary 'Oh, you shouldn't have, really. Please do stay for a cup of tea, but only if you want to or feel free to go straight back to decalcifying the kettle or whatever it was you were doing before I so rudely interrupted you. Sorry the cakes are a little flat', then I think baby showers would catch on even more.

It's a shame, though, because the idea of a girly party to celebrate your exciting future is a lovely one, and I think every Yummy Mummy-to-be should organise (or get her friends to organise) something special. If you don't want to call it a baby shower, then why not a 'Last Chance To' party, or, less depressingly, a 'Here we go!' party?

Tips for a Perfect Baby Shower

☆ **Have it at least six weeks before your due date.** Just in case…

☆ **Send out the most gorgeous invitations you can afford** – this is supposed to be the most stylish, indulgent treat you will have for a long time, so don't spoil it with some smudged computer printouts. Your local 'gorgeous things' shop should have some fun ones, or you could just spend a few hours making your own funky ones – it'll take your mind off the heartburn, anyway.

☆ **Don't have the party at your house.** There will be lots of house-dressing before and clearing up afterwards to do, and you are not in the best state to be hanging balloons from the top of a tall ladder. Ask your best friends if they would like to have it chez them, and really enjoy the treat.

☆ **See if you can get somebody to come and give you all a pedicure** or a head massage. Although you are the one having the baby, this party is for all of you, and the more you can spoil your friends the better.

☆ **Make sure there is plenty for everyone else to drink** – and don't forget to have a glass yourself. You deserve it more than anyone, and the baby will appreciate the relaxed vibes.

☆ **Get everybody to write in a special book**, for you to look back on when you are breastfeeding in the middle of the night and need to remember something fun you once did.

☆ **Have some strict policies about baby and birth talk in place** – this is NOT the moment to try on your Yummy Mummy hat. That will come in a few weeks' time…

☆ **This is a good opportunity to force all your friends to sign some kind of fidelity agreement**, whereby they promise to call you at least once a month forever, and not disappear into the 'Friends I Used To Have' wilderness. This is where the lashings of champagne come in handy – the drunker they are, the better the promises you can squeeze out of them!

☆ **Keep all your receipts from any presents you receive.** My first baby was so massive that she went straight into the second size of baby clothes, rendering all the newborn stuff only good enough for her big teddy bear which I felt guilty about. He was very well dressed, though.

☆ **If you don't want to have it at home, and you fancy spoiling yourself (and a few friends) rotten** then book a Girls Night-In Weekend at the Berkeley Hotel in London. If someone offered me this as a baby shower now, I would consider getting pregnant again – food, drink, candles, girly DVDs, Bliss beauty treats, access to the Spa and all its treatments (at extra cost but who cares – you won't be able to do it again for a very long time!), an in-room mini manicure and room-service at the touch of a button: this is a huge treat, and one you'll never forget.

What's in a Name?

If you don't know the sex of your baby yet, choosing a name will be impossible until after the birth, but it's a good plan to have at least a top five or ten that you both like. We spent hours reading the Baby Names book, and laughing condescendingly at some of the weirder ones. (I've kept it in case we really run out of things to talk about one day…best to be prepared.)

It's quite fun 'What are they like'-ing at celebrities and would-be celebrities who call their children odd names. I mean who *name* their children odd names, not *call* them odd names. I *call* mine any name, word or sound which comes to mind most of the time, but almost never their actual *name*, and I have this to say to the finger-pointers:

At least they chose something they *liked*.

It may be a bit unusual, but if you both love it, go for it. Obviously there are a couple of things to bear in mind, which the fuzzy-brained pregnant lady might overlook until it's too late. Take note:

☆ You will have to shout this name in very public places. Can you *really* see yourself yelling 'Chastity, put the Bran Flakes box down, please' in the middle of Asda?

☆ Just because every man in your family has carried the name Bartholomew, does *not* mean the tradition can't stop right here.

☆ Whatever you go for, your child will probably hate it. My daughter hates the name Emily (Why? What's wrong with 'Emily'?) and I would change my name immediately if it didn't mean filling in loads of forms and stuff.

All the other stuff about nicknames – such as avoiding first letters which spell out something rude (Toby William Arthur Thompson), names that create unfortunate combinations with your surname (William Williamson, Hugh Jarse), current trends (Angelina, Sienna or Manolo), embarrassing rhymes, impossible spellings and trying to piss your parents off by going for something you know they will hate – obviously still applies.

Nobody Else Likes the Name

So? Nobody else has to like it. It can be very difficult if it's your own parents who dislike the name you have chosen for your baby. I remember being met with raised eyebrows on all three occasions when we announced our newborn's name, and it hurt every time. Parents should at least *pretend* to like the name you have chosen for your beloved, but if they don't manage a fake 'Oh, how *lovely*!' just remember that you like it, and you have made the right decision to go with what you want.

We Can't Agree on a Name
Oh boy. This isn't like agreeing on the colour of your bathroom towels. This calls for some Big Time agreement, and as there is no correct way of sorting the dilemma out, I can only offer one answer: **Go with whatever *you* want**, and he'll have to get used to it. Why? Exactly *who* carried this baby and gave birth to it again? That's right. Remember: you win all domestic disputes forever. Prada it is, then.

Hospital Bag (got lipstick? good to go then)
If, like me, you always pack industrial quantities of clothing and toiletries when you go away, but you only end up using about 10% of it, then this section is for you. You will read lists longer than the credits of a Jerry Bruckheimer movie, of 'essential items' to pack in your hospital bag, but the fact is that you *need* very little on the big day.

What You Must Pack
For You
☆ **Lip salve/Lip balm:** Going through labour is as sweat-making as running two marathons and doing eight rounds with Muhammad Ali, so you can get very dehydrated and your lips will dry out. Every mother I know has this as their number-one recommendation, so I'd take the advice if I were you. Burt's Bees 100% Shea Butter is great, as is Vaseline.
☆ **Make-up bag:** Just some foundation, concealer and some colour which does cheeks, lips and eyes in one (if you think you'll need any help with the rosy glow after all that effort) can really perk you up. My skin was quite blotchy and spotty after the huge physical strain, and I wanted to go straight to the bathroom and slap some foundation on as soon I could walk. You could be

wandering around for hours before the actual birth, and you might be in for a few days afterwards, so making yourself look a little prettier at these times could be the pick-me-up you need. Also, there really are some lovely doctors around, and it's nice to make an effort to look good. For their sakes, obviously.

☆ **A mirror:** To check you've blended properly, NOT for taking a look Down Under.

☆ **Wash bag:** You will probably have a shower or a bath at some point, so bring your cleanser, moisturiser, mini shampoo and conditioner to get all that sweat off, and a toothbrush to freshen up. Luxurious body moisturiser is an absolute must and a product like No 4 Aloe Vera Face Gel can save you from any hot, dry, nasty skin situations.

☆ **Food:** Hospital food is hospital food, and if you like things just a little more special then bring it with you. I craved fresh fruit after the birth, and needed lots of chocolate beforehand. Dextrose tablets are a good idea if you need some extra energy, and if you like herbal teas then pop some teabags in too – it's strong English Breakfast otherwise.

☆ **Beautiful going-home outfit:** Hold the pre-baby jeans for now, but pop in something you *love* wearing, which is clean, sexy and makes you feel beautiful, to make the trip back to the real world more glam. You can throw away all your stretched trousers now!

☆ **Disposable knickers:** These are so horrible, they actually made me laugh, which made looking at my saggy bottom all wrapped in some meshy, blood-stained granny-pants a whole lot more enjoyable. Not your finest hour, but not your finest underwear either. Keep the La Perla ones for next month, and compensate with some drop-dead gorgeous maternity bras instead.

☆ **Sanitary towels.** Not super-lightweight 'Look I can go swimming in these and still look inviting' ones. You need maternity ones, which are like mattresses, and you need hundreds of them.

☆ **Breast pads.** If you're not wearing them already.

☆ **Feeding bra:** Ditto.

☆ **Bottle of water with a sports cap.** Drinking out of an NHS cup while lying down is impossible, and you will get terribly thirsty.

For your baby:

☆ **Baby car-seat:** Duh!

☆ **Your favourite baby outfit**, which you will treasure forever as the first thing your baby ever wore. *Not* a plain babygro – this needs to be the loveliest outfit you (or whoever buys it for you) can find. It could influence your child's sense of style from now on, so make an effort.

☆ **Newborn nappies:** Bring at least ten, in case you're in for a day or two, and because you will probably waste a few by putting them on upside down or dropping them in the bowl of water. Bring a few bigger ones too, in case yours – like mine – has a huge bum at birth, and doesn't fit newborn ones. Bless her lovely bum.

☆ **Hat:** Not just because they need it, but because newborn babies look much more 'newborn' in a teeny hat. And their heads *do* need protection from the elements, summer or winter.

☆ **Blanket:** Soft, luxurious and beautiful. This blanket will go everywhere with your baby, and be associated with her forever, so if it's whatever Mothercare had left in the sale, you will feel very un-stylish and mean. Cashmere is ideal, as it's *so* soft and thin, which means you can fold it over and over to get as many layers as you need. BUT this blanket will get very dirty and mucky, and it will need frequent washing. If you're not prepared to do it by hand, then either buy five of them and throw them away as they disintegrate, or stick to a material which is more washing-machine-proof.

☆ **Packet of dummies:** If you are going to use them, start as soon as possible after the birth, so your baby's mouth gets used to the shape and feeling. If you are not planning to, then plan to change your mind when you haven't had more than three minutes' sleep in 48 hours.

What You Could Also Pack

☆ **Slippers and cosy socks**.

☆ **Massage oil:** If having your back rubbed eases the pain, then having oil as well makes it just a bit more enjoyable, and you could almost imagine that you're in a health spa. (A really crap one, with bright strip-lighting, no music and a beauty therapist with huge, clumsy hands, but it's worth a shot.)

☆ **Cooling foot spray:** You can't reach your own feet, I know, but your birthing partner could spritz some on for you, and feel useful for a minute. The Body Shop's Peppermint one worked for me.

☆ **Hair bands:** In all the struggling, forehead-wiping and position-changing you might lose a few, so bring spares.

☆ **Something to read:** For *after* the birth, not before. This is the time you most need to escape into a world of beauty and fantasy, so bring a glossy or two to relieve the hospital grimness. And this book, of course.

☆ **Antacid:** When I was giving birth for the first time, what I wanted more than anything was something to relieve the agonising heartburn. (NO, that's a lie. I wanted to die, or I wanted the baby to come out NOW!) Heartburn was the final straw when everything else was hurting so much, so don't get caught out like me. I always pop some into my 'birth survival presents' for my friends. They think I'm weird, but always thank me afterwards. Pleasure, babe.

☆ **Camera: and charge the batteries!** This only applies to the lucky first-borns, because after that you will forget to take any pictures of your children, ever. Taking newborn photos is only for the thick of skin: you won't believe how horrible you looked or how unsightly your baby actually was in the hours after the birth. Fun to pull out for the wedding one day, though… It might be an idea to agree on what is and what isn't to be photographed before you start. If you decide you don't want a camera shoved between your legs, that's your call entirely.

☆ **Radio and favourite music:** You seldom have time to get round to DJ-ing, but if your labour is *very* long, listening to the radio can be a life-saver. It drowns out the noises from the next delivery room too…

☆ **Dressing gown:** Why slouch around the hospital corridors and TV rooms in a faded 1970s hospital number when you could proudly wrap-up in a stylish robe? Just in case of any leakage (you will bleed for a long time after the birth), avoid your best silk or other high-maintenance materials.

☆ **Notebook and pen:** You never know – you might want to record some of the events while you still remember any of them. *If* you remember any of them.

☆ **Extra batteries for the TENS machine:** Running out half way would be too awful to bear, but *he* would get the blame of course.

What You Absolutely Will Not Use

☆ **A stopwatch** to time the contractions. By the time you are in hospital, you don't care about timing anything. You just want to survive, get it over with, and keep *some* dignity intact.

☆ **Photos of people you love.** You will hate everyone in sight for the duration of your labour, and after that you will be too consumed with staring at your new baby to care about anyone else. Keep the extra room for more body moisturiser or a bar of chocolate instead.

For Delicious Daddies

He may have to spend a lot more time in the hospital than he anticipated, so it's a good idea to bring:

☆ **Man food**, in case he gets the munchies when all the shops are closed, and your dry crackers are not substantial enough.

☆ **A change of clothes**, or at *least* some clean underwear. A baby has the right to enter the world with *one* parent wearing clean undies, surely?

☆ **Arnica:** for the bruises. I bit my husband's finger so hard that I drew blood, and he also suffered minor bruising to the upper arms and chest. Oh the poor, poor, poor man. My heart bleeds.

☆ **Something for him to do.** There's only so much being-fussed-over you can take, and he will need some chill-out time before the next round starts.

I realise this a very long list, but labour can last for a very long time, and it's unpleasant enough as it is without having dry lips, bad skin, greasy hair and a hideous bra. Have your bag packed well before your final month, just in case, and make sure your partner knows where it is. You will have other things on your mind when you have to leave for the hospital, and if he leaves it behind, or brings his gym bag by mistake, there will be Hell to pay. Still, you'll have good grounds for divorce if you ever need them.

Pedicures
(and other essential preparations for handsome doctors...)
I know people who would scoff at such silliness, but luckily you are not one of them. You are, or are going to be, a Yummy Mummy, which means you appreciate the vital importance for yourself, and for the pleasure of others, of looking good whenever possible.

When you are in labour you will be seen by quite a large number of medical professionals, from nurses and midwives to paediatricians and surgeons (hopefully not surgeons, but you never know). With so many people meeting you for the first time, it is deeply unfair that you will be looking your absolute worst ever: you will be sweaty, blotchy, irritable, half-naked, bleeding, possibly vomiting, and quite probably doing a few other unmentionable things at the same time.

Under such miserable, unflattering conditions, attention to detail is crucial to maintain a basic level of glamour and polish, so bear this in mind and make sure you put some time aside to take care of the following:

☆ **Have a pedicure.** All sensible women do this a couple of weeks before they are due, because by this stage you cannot *see* your feet, let alone reach them any more. When you are in an ugly grey maternity ward, looking down to see some buffed, painted toes can be the boost you need to get you through to the next feed. While you're there, you should definitely get a **manicure** too. It's one other part of your body that can still look fantastic.

☆ **Get your legs waxed.** A good form of training for some of the pain which is to come, having smooth legs is essential for boosting your glam-factor in the delivery room, and you won't have any time to do it afterwards.

☆ **Sort your hair out.** If it could do with a little tidy up, or if your roots could do with a touch-up to see you through the next six weeks, then doing it now will not only fill another day of waiting, but it'll make you look lovely, and you won't need to go to the salon with a pram, changing bag and bored baby in tow. A simple wash and blow-dry is all you need to look instantly wonderful. How do you think all the A-listers do it?

☆ **Tidy up your wash bag**, and fill it with only the loveliest, cleanest, newest products. Clogged-up mascara and leaky moisturiser bottles are out of the question when you've just given birth – everything has to be as nice as possible. If you need a new wash bag, now is the time to get one.

☆ **Go to the dentist.** Not very glamorous, I agree, but the point is that it's FREE and it will be for a year after your baby is born. I don't think you can get the full Hollywood Smile on the NHS, but a check-up and any minor bits of maintenance should be done now if you want to save a bob or two.

The Nesting Instinct
(pass me the hammer drill – I'm going to have a baby!)

I'd love to know what the nesting instinct is all about. I mean, I know it's all about making your home look gorgeous and tidy before your baby comes, but what about in evolutionary terms? How does the nesting instinct further the survival of the human race? When Countess Caveman of Bleak Outdoors approached the birth of Tarquin Caveboy the First, did she start frantically sweeping out her cave, organising the yak skins into neat piles according to their thickness and colour, and putting up (stone) shelves, on which to display her *du jour* stick and bone collection? Of course she did, but the question is, *WHY?*

Your own urge to de-clutter, organise and majorly redesign your nest can kick in at any time, but there is a very definite increase in this energetic lunacy in the last month or so. Just when you should be taking it easier, in other words. It can feel like taking a huge hit of caffeine and adrenaline, mixed with euphoria, panic and obsessive-compulsion. If you get the nesting bug badly, you should be given a wide berth and free access to all tools and cleaning equipment. This is an instinct, remember, and trying to fight it will lead to terrible frustration and interior-design withdrawal symptoms.

When I was eight months pregnant, my husband came home to find me making holes in the bathroom tiles with the hammer drill pressed firmly into my abdomen for extra force. I'm not sure he agreed that putting up some giant mirrors was *very* important, but he was wise enough to let me carry on – a pregnant, nesting lady with a hammer drill is *not* to be messed with!

Zoe, mother of Daniel, ten months

About six weeks before I was due, I went into nesting mode: no cupboard was too high, no bed too low. I cleaned and de-cluttered and threw away old junk we never used any more. It was fantastic. I didn't get tired at all – in fact I think it invigorated me, and it felt great to be getting on with so many therapeutic, organising jobs.

This is a really enjoyable phase, so get out your back copies of *Elle Deco* and start painting. A couple of **TOP TIPS** to bear in mind are:

☆ **Don't start any job which could take more than a few days.** The baby could come at any time now, and having drill-bits and tins of emulsion lying around will not help at all.

☆ **Try to be objective**, if possible. Your ability to judge anything objectively is completely shot through in the later stages, and unless you have *always* wanted to cover the kitchen cupboards in black gloss, it might be worth holding off for six months or so.

☆ ***Try* to listen** to your un-hormonally-challenged partner and friends if they give you nesting advice. I know *they* can't see how important it is to alphabetise your condiments, but they just might have a point.

☆ **Don't climb high ladders.** Your balance is all funny, and you are also more prone to fainting. I got very dizzy up there while I was painting clouds on the nursery ceiling, and I nearly fell off several times. It does look lovely, though...

☆ **Inhaling strong chemical vapours** and other toxic, noxious substances is a very bad idea so open lots of windows.

☆ **Don't throw away lots of clothes you think you'll never wear again.** It's that 'clouded judgement' thing again, and you will regret giving all your skinny, dark denim to Oxfam when it screams into fashion once more next season. Be patient.

PART FIVE

The Birth

Let's Bring It On: Getting Labour Started

13 June 2004. Ten days overdue.

This is driving me nuts. I'm well overdue again, and I am having false labour contractions every single day, at least once. It hurts like mad, and I'm getting exhausted by all the pain and nerves. Every time it comes on I wonder if this is it: should I rush home and call H, am I going to have a baby in the playground, have I had a show? All the sex seems to be doing nothing, and time is going by sooooo slowly.

If you cannot stand the wait any longer, there are some supposed ways to get things going, but you should definitely ask your midwife or doctor first. If you're only 35 weeks gone, she might suggest you hang in there a while longer... Here are some things which are *believed* to get labour started:

Sex

Straight in there (so to speak) at number one is good old shagging. Sperm contains prostaglandin, which can soften the neck of your womb, and sex can also trigger the release of oxytocin, which causes contractions to start.

BUT: in my experience, all sex does is to trigger false labour (see below) and make your groin ligaments ache. It may keep your partner smiling night after night, but after every session I had four or five hours of painful, tiring contractions which eventually petered out, leaving me miserable and exhausted. The other problem with using sex as a method of labour-induction is that it becomes almost as un-spontaneous and agenda-driven as the sex which got you pregnant to start with. 'Oh, I suppose we'd better give it another go' is hardly the come-on he'd like. Hang on – why do we care what *he* likes at this point? He's having sex every night! He should be very grateful.

Curry
Great fun, but totally ineffective. This rumour was started by the proprietor of a chain of Indian restaurants in Manchester in 1974 when McDonald's first arrived in the UK. No, that's rubbish. I have no idea where this one came from, but I and many of my friends ate chicken madras and lamb vindaloo every night for weeks without any sign of labour. Delicious but useless.

Raspberry Leaf Tea
This brew, available from most health-food stores, tastes disgusting, but contains a uterine tonic which helps to prepare the uterine muscles for labour. You shouldn't drink it until you are seven months pregnant, but one or two cups a day after that is *supposed* to make labour faster and easier. I drank it religiously every evening, and had three long, painful labours. *So* not fair.

Tweaking Your Nipples
Ooo-er. Didn't work for me, but I did feel some tightening of my bump for a while afterwards. And it was kind of fun.

Falling Downstairs
No.

Castor Oil

No. *Very bad idea.* Midwives used to use this in the Very Ill-informed Ages, but it's highly discouraged now. I was so desperate that I did buy a bottle, but after staring at it for a few hours I decided that if I'd waited nine months, I could wait another week.

Am I in Labour *Now?*

Here's a conversation I had recently with the first of my college friends to finally, FINALLY, decide to have a baby. With her being six months down the road to Yummy Mummyhood, we were discussing the actual birth part (something I try hard not to do, because I am always far too honest and graphic), and she had 'just a couple' of questions to put to me. She seemed to think, quite reasonably, that I would have some answers. I think I disappointed:

Friend: I'm really starting to worry about going into labour, Liz. I mean, how do you know when it's started properly?
Me: Ummm, I don't know really. You just sort of realise you probably are, after a while.
Friend: After a while of what? After your waters break and stuff?
Me: Ummmm, well, I don't really know, because my waters never broke.
Friend: They never broke? But how can you be in labour if your waters don't break?
Me: I'm not sure, really, but that's how it went for me. I was in practice labour for three weeks, but then the contractions seemed a bit stronger one day, and hurt a lot more, so I figured I was probably in real labour.
Friend: Oh. Practice labour? So how did you know when to go into hospital, then? I don't really get it.

At this point I had to tell my poor, confused friend that I didn't go into hospital when my real contractions started, but decided to go and see *The Talented Mr Ripley* instead to take my mind off the pain. This was not the right answer either.

I should explain. Labour is very weird, and totally unpredictable. How and when it decides to start, and how it proceeds until the glorious end, is up to your baby and your body, with your baby definitely having the upper hand. **Every labour and birth is different**: no woman can choose how it will happen, however many books she reads or expensive consultants she asks. What you do know is that it will happen in the one way you didn't expect or plan it to.

False Labour

If this is Nature's idea of a joke, then I'm not impressed. It is completely un-funny, and it will have you confused, nervous and tired out well before you need to be. Basically, false labour falls somewhere between Braxton Hicks contractions and real labour, but it's hard to be more precise than that. In the last weeks of all my pregnancies I had very strong contractions every ten minutes, and this would go on for hours before dying away gradually and stopping until the next day. I started to dread the next practice session because it really hurt and it made me very tired. Little did I know that this was *nothing* on what was to come... It also made me not believe when things started to get going for real, because I was so used to being teased and then ultimately disappointed.

Real Labour

Not a political slogan, but the stage at which your baby lets you know it has stopped arsing about with false labour and is thinking about coming out soonish. Things which suggest you might be in Real Labour are:

☆ **A show.** Yippee! A show! Steady on – this kind of show involves less popcorn and more blood-tinged mucus than the ones you are used to. Mmmmm. If you see a little plug of pinkish or brownish jelly stuff in your knickers, then things are starting to happen. BUT not necessarily soon: it can be several days before the baby actually comes, so keep calm.

☆ **The lightening.** Apart from being a great title for M. Night Shyamalan's next thriller, this is also something which sometimes can happen in early labour. Your bump can suddenly feel much lower down, you can breathe more easily and you can eat more than two mouthfuls before feeling full. This is because the baby's head has dropped into position (or has 'engaged') in your pelvis. BUT: with subsequent pregnancies it can come back out again, so if this isn't your first pregnancy, don't get over-excited when the baby's head engages. It might disengage again.

☆ **Your waters break.** I virtually camped out in Marks & Spencer's for a week, hoping for my year's free supply of whatever it is they are rumoured to promise you if your waters break while you're in there. Apart from spending a lot of money on fruit salads and fresh croissants, I achieved little else. My waters never broke of their own accord, and I was always left disappointed. If they do break, you will think you've weed yourself, but it's much less dramatic than the 'water was gushing all over the dairy products aisle' scenario you might have read about.

☆ **Contractions.** You are only in *real* labour when your contractions are regular, and becoming more frequent. **You will know when you are having real contractions**. There is nothing more to say on the matter, except that if you *don't* know, then you are very, very lucky, and should keep it quiet from all your Mummy friends who suffered fifteen hours of agony. Like me. At some point you will notice that they are regular-ish and getting stronger, and you might think about starting to time them. This is harder to do than you would imagine: because you are so relieved that the pain has disappeared, you forget to make a note of the time, and end up wildly estimating the intervals, which leads to all manner of confusion and panic.

☆ **Speaking of which...**

Panic: How to Avoid the 'No Petrol, No Hospital Bag, No Idea' Disasters

Most books will advise you to do a practice run: time yourselves from the starting position of screaming in the kitchen, through to grabbing the ready-packed bag, jumping in the car, sitting in traffic for twenty minutes, having a row, and finally arriving at the wrong entrance to the hospital.

In reality, there is little point in doing this, because your baby will almost certainly decide to come in the middle of the night, when you can't think straight, forget half of what you meant to bring, and there is no traffic at all, making your journey time considerably shorter. (And your speeding fines greater.)

There are some things you might think of doing, though, which can make those last crazy moments at home a little smoother:

☆ **Pack your hospital bag well before you are due.**
☆ **Check that the car has petrol in it every day.**
☆ **Talk through the logistics with your partner.** What if he's at work? Does he know where your hospital bag is? Will he remember to bring the baby car-seat? Does he know that when you tell him you hate him, you don't really mean it?
☆ **Make a contingency plan for getting to the hospital.** Have a friend or two on standby who could take you there. Preferably someone with a nice car and very thick skin to take all your curses and insults.

The Birth Plan: Prepare to Improvise

Robert Burns sure showed what a bright spark he was when he penned those famous words: 'The best-laid plans o' mice and pregnant women gang aft aglay'. That's Scottish for 'screw the birth plan – it's coming out however it chooses to'.

Making a birth plan is a good, er, plan, but *not* if you are intending to stick to it. The best reason for talking it all through with your midwife and partner is so that you are both aware of all the options and situations which might present themselves, and can ask any questions you may have. 'How can you make all the pain go away and get the baby out quickly?' for example.

But, however well you plan it, whatever your preferred choice of pain relief, position, music or bed linen (unless you are very rich, you will get whatever the NHS can find, which is usually off-white), it will almost certainly never go as you planned.

The best piece of survival advice I can give you, which should see you through your labour in better mental shape, is as follows:

Don't expect anything to go as planned, and be prepared to change your plan many times.

If you can approach going into labour with that in mind, it should make things much easier when the spanners start being thrown into the works.

Here's how my three labours went not-at-all according to plan:

My First Labour
The Plan: Nice and quick; no drugs; baby not too big.
The Reality: 36-hour labour; pethidine, epidural, gas and air; 9 lb 1oz baby (that's fucking huge, by the way). Excellent midwives – all 7 of them.

Labour Number Two
The Plan: Nice and quick; epidural immediately; baby not too big.
The Reality: 17 hours; no drugs (no one available to give me an epidural); 8 lb baby. Merciless midwife.

Labour Number Three
The Plan: Short labour; epidural immediately; smaller baby; nice midwife.
The Reality: 9-hour labour (including trip with whole family to see *Pippi Longstocking* at the Arts Cinema, with me grimacing and 'ouch!'ing every 20 minutes or so); no drugs; 9 lb baby (how about some variety, guys?); angelic midwife.

And so you can see that the best laid plans really *do* gang almost always totally aglay. Well done, Mr Burns.

Kate Winslet, actress

I had two completely different experiences of childbirth: my daughter was born by emergency c-section after a lengthy labour, and my son was born (three years later) vaginally. So, to anyone out there who maybe doesn't realise that it is indeed possible to have a vaginal birth after a c-section, I am very proud to be able to tell you – it is!

Midwives

21 June. Charlie one week old.

I wrote a letter to my midwife today to thank her for being such a star during Charlie's birth. I know I am terribly rude and nasty to the staff when I'm in labour, and I dimly remember telling her she was a liar, because I didn't believe the baby was really coming. I even told H to tell her to go away, because I thought she was making it all up. I'm sure she's used to it, but I feel very ashamed and guilty.

I always find this such an grim word. Midwife. It makes them sound like insensitive, unattractive, matronly gorgons, who cackle and whip you to make the experience worse. Thankfully, most midwives I have come across were rather attractive ladies with a good sense of humour, who love helping gorgeous babies into the world and women to have the best experience possible under the somewhat trying circumstances.

When you are in labour she (or he, but it's mostly she) is there to oversee your labour until the end: she will make sure everything is going OK, comfort you, help you, advise you about which pain relief you can have, keep you informed about the progress, and get a doctor if one is needed.

She is not there to take verbal or physical abuse. I know that seems unnecessary to point out, but believe me, when you are having your insides ripped out by 4 kg of baby and another 3 kg or so of placenta, you will behave in ways you wouldn't believe possible. I have sworn at midwives, shouted at them, and I have heard many stories of people even hitting them during extra-painful moments. Unfortunately, being in extreme pain is not a reasonable defence. If you can, try to remember how hard she is working for you, and that she is honestly doing the best she can to get your baby out quickly and safely.

However, there *are* a few nightmare midwives around, and if you are unlucky enough to get one of these aforementioned insensitive, unattractive, matronly gorgons who encourages you not to have any drugs, or tells you that you are looking a little puffy in the face, then you are probably allowed to have a sharp word.

Choosing a Birth Method

This doesn't mean choosing between 'easy' or 'difficult', but trying to decide how and where you want to deliver your baby. Very often you don't end up having a choice, because complications arise, like you forgot to order the birthing pool, and you end up giving birth on the back seat of your best friend's car.

1. At Home

Personally, I wouldn't advise anybody to *plan* to give birth at home. You may end up *having* to do it there, but there will be a LOT of blood around the place, and if you are worried about any of it ending up on the white sofa or all over the parquet floor, then don't even consider it. The following points are worth bearing in mind when you're sketching out your birth tactics:

- ☆ **You will bleed and sweat** through about twenty towels, and dealing with all that laundry will be the last thing you have energy for with a new baby to look after.
- ☆ **The phone will ring**, and somebody will have to hear you screaming like a strangled cat.

☆ **If you suddenly need medical assistance immediately**, both you and your baby will be at considerable risk if you can't get to the hospital very quickly.

I do know people who have had home births and who rave about it, but the potential risks involved are worth very careful consideration.

2. Water Births

Many women love the calming, soothing aspect of birthing pools, but be warned:

☆ **The water is lukewarm at best**, and you will be in it for a long time, so you will resemble a shivering sun-dried tomato giving birth.

☆ **You will probably shit yourself**, and will have to sit in the water with bits of shit, mucus, wee, blood and many other foul things floating about.

☆ **You can't have an epidural**, pethidine, or use a TENS machine in the water.

☆ **Your partner might feel that he should come in too**, and he doesn't want to swim in your poo either.

☆ **There's all the hassle of getting dry and dressed** once the baby is out, and you will get even colder.

3. Active Birth

Moving about as much as possible during labour can really relieve some of the pain, and keep the baby moving in the right direction. Babies have an annoying habit of forgetting what it is they're supposed to be doing (coming out!), and this can cause labour to slow down for a while. Walking about and keeping active helps to keep their mind focused on the task, and keeps your mind off everything else. If you need an epidural or more examinations, you might not be able to stay as active as you like. Make sure your midwife explains everything to you at the time, and that she knows you want to keep moving if possible.

The Truth Hurts (I probably shouldn't tell you this, but...)

I come from the 'well-informed is well-prepared' school of life, and it's my duty to prepare you for what it's like to have a baby. This won't take long, but it might scare you.

Childbirth, it seems to me, is like Mother Nature sticking two fingers up at us and saying: 'Look, ladies, I've given you curves, intelligence, sensitivity, great beauty, sensuality and multiple orgasms, but I'm really knackered now, and I can't be bothered to figure out a smart way for you to have a baby. I know it's a bit crap, but I've decided the baby should grow inside you for nine months, until it's unfeasibly large, and then it should come out through your vagina. Will it hurt? Oh shit yeah, but like I said, I'm really tired, so you'll just have to live with it.'

Well, cheers for that. **Giving birth does indeed hurt.** If you can imagine sticking both your hands up your derrière and very slowly stretching the tight little hole until you can fit a giant marrow through it, over a period of about ten hours, while simultaneously disembowelling yourself with a red-hot poker and experiencing faint-inducing painful stomach cramps, then you are on the right tracks, except that it's about 5000 times worse. Still, you're a strong girl: you can handle it!

Some facts about the pain of childbirth:

☆ **If you haven't been through it, you can never imagine how painful it is.** This is Nature's way of making sure we don't die out within a generation.
☆ **Once you have been through it, nothing will ever seem sore, uncomfortable or unbearable again.** You are now as hard as nails.
☆ **When it's over, the pain goes away almost immediately** and you'll be ready to do it all again a week later.
☆ **You will believe you are about to die**, because you can't withstand the pain any longer.
☆ **Even the most unpleasant form of pain relief will seem desirable.**
☆ **You will always have the upper hand in any domestic rows.**
☆ **At the end of it, you have your baby.** Your very own, tiny, perfect, beautiful, wonderful, unbelievable, irreplaceable baby, and there

is no pain on earth that wouldn't be worth enduring to have that. It is worth it a million times over.

Now that you know all of this, you will dread the birth even more than you did five minutes ago, but hopefully you will *survive* the whole episode much better. It probably won't be half as bad as all this, and you will be pleasantly surprised. I wish you all the luck in the world.

A Happy Bit of News

The above reflects *my* three experiences of giving birth. For me, it hurts. BUT, there are women for whom it doesn't hurt. I haven't met one yet, but I have read about them, and I thought it only right to point this out, and to remind you that you *might* also enjoy labour and the moment of birth. It is a truly fantastic event, and you should never assume it will be awful and agonising. Some women give birth without batting a eyelid, and go back to looking for shabby chic mirrors on eBay within hours. Hats off to them, and try to think more along these lines if you can. Then when it starts to really hurt you can swear at me, and take the drugs instead.

Free Drugs! Free Drugs! Take Them All...

There are no prizes for enduring a painful birth. Nobody will care, there will be no parties, day spas or free babysitting for the woman who refuses all pain relief, because she thinks it makes her more of a Mother than anyone else. It doesn't. Perhaps in days gone by there was some kind of admiration heaped on stoical mothers who would go through it alone, but these days nobody has any hang-ups about spoiling yourself and trying to make your life as enjoyable as possible.

With this in mind, I have the following **TOP TIP: Take the drugs**! There is absolutely no point in refusing them if they are offered, and the minute you get some relief from the agony you will be very glad you did. If you really have a problem with admitting that you can't take the pain, then you can always lie. Who's going to know, anyway? Drugs used in labour are a little less exciting than the recreational ones you may be familiar with (naughty you), so here is a very brief explanation of the *à la carte* menu chez le delivery room:

1. Epidural
I'll spare you the details – oh, all right, then: they stick a hollow, curved needle between the vertebrae in your spine, and then into the space outside the coverings which surround your spinal cord. Then they inject anaesthetic in there, and the entire lower part of your abdomen goes numb. See? It's terrifying and I shouldn't have told you. I can only do the joy of epidurals some justice by saying that having one is like experiencing all your best, longest, most intense orgasms in one go. Really. The feeling of relief, ecstasy, relaxation, joy, and every other wonderful, satisfying sensation comes the second the heavenly anaesthetic gets into your bloodstream, and it lasts for as long as they keep you topped up with the stuff.

BUT there are some disadvantages to be aware of. For example:

☆ You will probably have to stay in bed, which can slow things down.
☆ If you are nearing the end they might advise you not to have one in case the labour slows down again.
☆ You have to have the baby's heartbeat monitored constantly, which some people find uncomfortable.
☆ You can't feel when to push at the end, which can be very frustrating.
☆ There's a greater chance of having to use forceps or suction to get your baby out.

Even taking all of these into account, they hardly outweigh experiencing all the orgasms you've ever had in one go, do they?

2. Mobile Epidural
This newish technique leaves some sensation in your legs, allowing you to keep walking around and still get complete pain relief.

Genius. It's best for early stages of labour, but many hospitals don't have them yet, so check.

3. Gas and Air (Entonox)
For lots of my friends, this worked a treat and it was all they needed to stave off the pain. For me, it was always an unpleasant waste of time: it made me feel sick and woozy, it didn't seem to have any effect on the pain, and it dried my mouth out. It's quite fun offering some to your birthing partner, though, and watching him or her get high.

4. Pethidine
If you've never taken hallucinogenic drugs, and fancy having a go for free, then pethidine is your answer. Very similar to morphine, pethidine is an analgesic, which also helps you to relax. A lot. I have been told that I had a bath and listened to the whole of the shipping forecast and the evening news while I was on the stuff, but can't remember any of it.

Some disadvantages:

☆ It can make you very sleepy and even sick.
☆ It crosses into the placenta, so your baby might be very sleepy too for a few days after being born. And this is a *bad* thing?
☆ It can slow labour down.

5. TENS
Rather like the gas and air, I didn't find this effective at all at relieving any pain, unless you count taking my mind off it as pain relief. Which it is, in a way. A TENS machine (Transcutaneous Electrical Nerve Stimulation, if you must know) gives off little pulses of electricity, stimulating your body to produce endorphins, which block the pain in that area. Theoretically. Actually, it just tingles a lot, but you can have some fun twiddling the dials and seeing how much electrical pulse you can withstand before it starts to hurt. It's best to start using this very early on (when you are still at home and starting to get nervous about the pain), because it takes about an

hour for your body to get into gear and kick the lazy endorphins out there. Look after your TENS machine, because you'll have a big fine to pay if you don't take it back to wherever you hired it from in working order.

You can hire TENS machines from Boots, and from many places advertised on the Web. Ask your midwife or doctor where they would recommend locally.

The Moment of Birth

The actual moment that your baby enters the world, and becomes a 'baby' as opposed to a bump, is never as you might have read, or hoped. Babies rarely fly across delivery rooms, or emerge looking beautiful and pink. The actual moment feels like someone has knocked all the wind right out of you, and you can feel completely empty, light and almost unable to speak.

Some women describe it as feeling like you've just done the biggest poo of your life, which has been building up for weeks. (In many cases you have also done this, but it's best not to think about that too much.) The relief is so intense that I just laughed for a minute or two every time. If you end up having a caesarean, the moment of birth will be a little less dramatic, but the knowledge that your baby is in the world and the labour is over will be fantastic enough.

☆ **Don't worry if all you want to do is lie there in a daze** instead of seeing and holding your baby immediately. This is very common. It doesn't mean you feel no love for your baby, and after a couple of minutes of recovery you will be ready to meet your new friend.
☆ **New babies are usually blue when they come out,** until the oxygen gets into their lungs and blood. Don't panic!
☆ **If you don't hear any crying immediately, this is not necessarily anything to worry about.** I don't remember any of mine bringing the house down after they were born – I think they were too tired after all that effort, and they seemed very calm and peaceful to me.

☆ **You might not even realise the baby is out.** If you are as confused as I always am at the very end, giving birth to a flamingo will be no more surprising than anything else. I had to ask several times if everything was over, and what flavour I had got.

After the Birth

Just when you thought it was all over, here's a whole lot more stuff that happens to you just after you've given birth:

☆ **You deliver the placenta.** I always forget about this bit, being somewhat preoccupied with having stitches, gazing at my baby and so on. It's quite painful, but nothing like delivering the baby was. Some people like to have a good look at this surprisingly large, bloody bag, which kept your baby nourished for the last nine months. Others like to take them home and plant trees over them. I like to deliver them as quickly as possible and move straight on to something more beautiful, like my baby.

☆ **Somebody will cut the umbilical cord.** This can't always be your partner if things get complicated, or if he's popped out to check the football results. If either of you are unsure then don't force anything. Some guys get squeamish and some new Mummies decide they've had enough indignity for one lifetime.

☆ **You may need stitches** following an episiotomy or a tear. This can be quite painful, but it's mostly just annoying, because you feel so glad to get the birth over with, and now somebody is still poking you about and hurting you.

☆ **You may shake a lot** due to the adrenaline your body releases after the birth.

☆ **You might be sick again** for the same reason.

☆ **You will hold your baby.** And your life will change forever. Aaaaaaah.

That's It: Over to You Now

3 January. In the hospital.

What is happening? I am lying in a huge hospital bed, bleeding slowly but constantly, with a wrist band and an ugly nightie on, and lying two feet away from me is my baby, sleeping in her plastic cot thing. She is much bigger than I expected, and she has red, blotchy skin with lots of scratches on her face. Her black hair is matted to her scalp, and she has huge, dark blue eyes, a lovely button nose and huge cheeks. Her hands are flaky, and her fingernails are really long and sharp. She lies there, covered in a white sheet and blanket, breathing fast and sighing occasionally. She is beautiful, and perfect, but I don't really know who she is. Does she know me? Can she recognise me? Will she like me? I don't know how to make a baby love me – I am who I am, and I just hope we will love each other. I want to stare at her all the time, and smell her and kiss her. Please love me back. I will do everything I can to make you happy, to make your life happy and how you want it to be. I will always be here for you. I can't wait to know you, but I have to go to sleep again right now!

When the deed is finally done, **YOU BECOME, IN AN INSTANT, A MOTHER!!** Not a Yummy Mummy just yet, but an actual, factual mother! Massive congratulations, hugs all round, well done you, and all of that. That was the easy part over, and now you just have to be there, do what's required, love your baby every day for the rest of your life, and be utterly Yummy.

Should be a piece of cake, really.

Just in case it isn't, there are another 248 pages with some helpful notes on how to survive the start of the most exhilarating ride of your life, without falling off too many times, and without losing your beauty, style, flair or mind. Really, I am too kind.

PART SIX

A Yummy Mummy is Born

In the Beginning, a baby is born. In the Beginning, there is a new mother, hopefully a man or some other life-partner, and at least one new baby. This is the beginning of the rest of your lives, the end of your lives as you knew them, and the absolute beginning of your baby's life.

The first few weeks of motherhood are too bewildering to explain, and to go into detail wouldn't make a lot of sense yet. The Beginning is a period of colossal adjustment on your part, as well as physical endurance and emotional turmoil.

The Beginning is the hardest bit. If anyone ever tells you it just gets harder from now on, then remember this:

IT DOES NOT GET ANY HARDER

This is as hard as it ever gets, so struggle through and congratulate yourself when you come out and enter The Rest, which should be after six months or so.

I get quite annoyed when experienced Yummy Mummies of three or four children look at first-time mothers and smugly remember how 'easy it was when I only had one'. Of course it's easier to only have one baby when you're used to having four, but when you're used to having none, just the one is nearly bloody impossible! No mother should *ever* tell you it's easy with one. **The jump from zero to one is the biggest change you will ever experience.** Once you've mastered that, it makes almost no difference how many you squeeze out – you've done the hardest part.

The following pages contain some things you may encounter in the first few months of Yummy Mummyhood. Some are fantastic, others are awful – but they are all perfectly normal.

24

Thank God the makers of this cool, slick, gripping drama didn't set it in a maternity ward. The first 24 hours of being a mother are not cool, not slick, and more baffling than gripping. And Kiefer Sutherland wouldn't look sexy in a green hospital gown. Come to think of it, he would – all that thin cotton over taut muscle… Sorry. Back to you.

A better celluloid comparison would be *Memento*: your body cunningly erases all memories of a Yummy Mummy's first 24 hours, and you spend the next year or so gradually remembering bits, and piecing the whole trippy experience back together. To save you from covering your lovely body with tattoos bearing such glamorous memory-joggers as 'uterine contractions', 'night sweats', and 'vaginal discharge', here is a list of things you might notice in your first 24 hours:

☆ **Breastfeeding hurts like hell.** This gets worse with every feed for about a week, until your nipples crack and bleed enough to get hardened to their new requirements. I used to shake uncontrollably and cry at the start of every feed because the pain was so intense.

☆ **When you breastfeed, your uterus contracts** so hard that you might as well be in labour again – my toes curled until my feet cramped up. The upside is that every contraction makes your stomach smaller. Which makes the pain almost bearable.

☆ **You will bleed and bleed and bleed.** You might be lucky enough not to, but most women spend the first day or two just soaking through those gigantic sanitary pads, and most of the bedding as well, at a furious rate.

☆ **You will feel very faint.** I remember stoically heading off to the hospital toilet, determined that I didn't need any support, and collapsing about ten paces down the corridor. Humiliating? Yup.

☆ Just in case you hadn't lost enough fluid for one lifetime, **you will probably also sweat like a disco diva on the dancefloor**. Feeling rivers of cold sweat pouring down my face, back, legs and neck is a memory I would be quite happy to erase permanently. This is where a face cloth and some moisturiser come in very handy – and shampoo. This excessive sweating can last for a few weeks, so please don't worry that you may have hit the menopause within 24 hours of giving birth as a clever preventative against ever having another one. You're just having very unpleasant, post-natal night sweats.

☆ **You might forget that you have a baby.** This may sound very unlikely but when you have just given birth, you haven't slept or eaten properly for three days, and you are in yet another strange, badly decorated, uncomfortable room, you will be so spaced out and exhausted that remembering you also have a baby to tend to can slip your mind. Luckily there are nurses on hand to remind you, and it doesn't mean you are already a useless mother.

☆ **People will keep pestering you.** Midwives, paediatricians, visitors, your baby, more midwives – the list of people who want a piece of you is very long, and if you want a break then say so. You need to rest and to take some time to get your head around what has just happened to your life.

☆ **You might feel on top of the world**, euphoric, strong, indestructible and completely content. This is very common, and it's caused by the rush of Happy Hormones you produce after such an ordeal. Be very, very wary of this feeling of euphoria: it's lovely, but it almost never lasts more than a few days, and the landing can be very hard.

☆ **Or you might feel frightened.** Panic can set in very early, especially if you spend a night alone with your new baby in a ward. I called my husband about five times just to hear something familiar, and for some reassurance that everything was going to be OK, and normality would be restored one day. It also ensured that I wasn't the only one having a broken night. Hee hee.

Despite all of these warnings, there is little you can do to prepare for that first 'Mummy' day. It will be the strangest day of your life, you will almost certainly forget most of it, and it will never go as you expected it to.

We Are Family

Yes you are now, and it's something which will take a lot of getting used to. Being a couple, even a married couple or a pair of 'committed' co-habiting people, might *feel* like being a small family already, but it's nothing like it. Offspring are what really make a family, and the second you have one you shift from Groovy Couple to Proper Family.

Don't expect to feel at home with this concept immediately. It took me about five years to get used to saying 'my husband' after I got married, and I still find it odd that I am somebody's Mummy. That we now have to look for 'family' holidays and 'family' cars and 'family-friendly' restaurants still feels fairly weird to me, so give yourself at least two years to feel comfortable with being a family rather than a couple. It's a great feeling, but it might not come in the first 24 hours.

Instinct? Schminstinct!

What if I don't know what to do with my baby when it's born? What if I'm not as maternal as other mums? What if I fail this basic test? Will the baby know? Will everyone else know?

Worrying about your levels of maternal instinct is absolutely normal, if you are someone who has had very little contact with babies and children, has a healthy level of self-awareness, or if you just like freaking yourself out a lot. To make you feel better, here are some common myths:

☆ You will feel an overwhelming love for your baby the moment you hear, see or hold her.
☆ You will instinctively know how to hold her, and what to say to her.
☆ Breastfeeding will be as natural to you as exfoliating.
☆ Your life will feel complete and perfect.
☆ You will feel a strong maternal instinct, and just *know* how to do it all.

And now to de-mythstify: all of the above *might* happen to you. You might take to motherhood like a wannabe to the limelight, and if you do you are a lucky lady with more maternal instinct than me and all of my Yummy Mummy friends put together. Most of us were terrified during the latter stages of our pregnancies that we wouldn't cope with a new baby the way a more 'natural' mother would, and that we would feel inadequate, humiliated and a complete failure. And, sure enough, most of us didn't feel an overwhelming, instinctive understanding of how to be a mother, or what to do in any of the gazillion new situations our new baby threw at us.

Eva, mother of Chloe, two

The pressure to feel maternal, and know immediately how to be a mother, was almost unbearable. I had no idea at all how I would cope with anything, but the amazing thing is that I have coped, and I have amazed myself. I could have saved myself a lot of wrinkles if I'd just waited a few weeks to see how it all turned out.

It was the same for me: **I had absolutely no idea what to do with a baby** until mine was a good few days (oh, all right, *months*) old, and even *then* I wasn't really sure I was doing anything right. Come to think of it, I'm still not sure that I'm doing anything right, and I'm eight years down the road. If you are worrying about all of this instinct stuff, then all I can say is:

Welcome to the club

It's called being a parent, and it rarely gets any simpler or any clearer. It just becomes normal and you manage most of the time. Somehow. So stop worrying.

When I was handed my first baby, about three minutes after she was born, it was the first time I had ever *seen*, let alone held, a new baby. I was terrified, still in shock after the birth, and hopelessly unsure of how to hold her. But there she was: tiny (and she was a huge baby), velvet-soft, warm, tightly wrapped in a pink blanket, snuffling a little, her head covered in soggy, matted hair, opening and closing the most fragile-looking fingers I had ever seen and, mostly, staring intently and calmly at me with huge, dark blue eyes. At *me*, her mother. Ohmygod, this was *it*: cue Maternal Instinct. *Hello? Help me out a little here: tell me how to react, what to feel, what to do.*

And then it came: no fanfare, no razzmatazz, red carpet or launch party: just a slow realisation that I *loved* the way this baby was looking at me, that I had never smelled anything as good as her forehead, and that I was never, ever, ever going to let her go.

[Break for huge crying session. Dammit, I promised I wouldn't cry!]

Just as I was starting to sink into a fluffy pink haze of smug, maternal competence, she did something which made me almost drop her into the plastic sick bowl beside my bed:

She moved.

This may not seem very remarkable to you, but believe me, when you first feel your baby move and wriggle and stretch, you suddenly realise that this is not just a doll, or a gadget you can play with for while and then put back in its box, but a real, live, breathing, living PERSON who needs you, and it's a whopper of a realisation.

After that initial shock, motherhood has all been a case of dealing with each situation as it arises, and trying to do what seems like the right thing at that time. If *that's* what constitutes a 'maternal instinct' then maybe I have one after all, but it's not something that I can remember *feeling*, or being aware of.

Top Survival Tips

☆ **Stop worrying about it.** Everything is new, confusing and scary right now, so give yourself a month, and see how you are doing then.

☆ **Try not to look at too many other Yummy Mummies** who seem to be doing everything very easily and naturally. They are probably just better at acting cool than you are.

☆ **Think of it as like taking a masters' degree, in something you have no training in.** If you have very low expectations of what you should be *programmed* to do, you can only amaze yourself when it turns out you do know something.

☆ **Treat everything you manage to do well as a huge success**, and not as something you were *expected* to be able to do. Managed to change a nappy without consulting the book? Reward yourself with an extra ten minutes in the bath tonight. Got through a whole day without panicking once? The remote control is all yours. Just because you're a woman doesn't mean you already know everything a woman needs to know. Did you know how to wax your bikini line the first time you did it? No, so why should you know how to put a babygro on a new baby? There's no difference, so don't believe there is. (I realise there is a difference, but come with me, please.)

☆ **Remember that love takes time:** love at first sight doesn't apply to babies any more than it does to any well-dressed, smooth-talking, drinks-buying piece of male flesh you meet in a bar after work. You and your baby may have been together for nine months, but you are actually no more than two complete strangers, thrown together. To feel that you should instinctively know this stranger's wants, likes, sleeping requirements and bowel habits is ridiculous, and to think this way is to pave the way to a big disappointment.

☆ **Try to spend as much time getting to know your baby as possible.** Sometimes it just takes a little small talk to break the ice, and before you know it you'll be best friends.

☆ **If you really feel no love or bond with your baby after a few days, talk to your health visitor** as soon as you can. It's normal not to have a clue how to manage being a mum, but it's not normal to actively *dislike* your baby, except for a short while after yet another grizzly sleepless night, but this should melt away the moment she smiles at you.

Even after many years of practice, most of my Yummy Mummy friends admit they are still fairly clueless about how to be a parent, and we have all worked out our own, widely differing ways of doing it. There is only one thing we all agree on, and it should cheer you up: **You can only do your best**, and no matter how wonderful, instinctive, lousy or erratic your mothering skills turn out to be, you will get a lot wrong, and get a lot right, and your child will both love you and hate you anyway. Amen.

The Brain Drain:
Some Useful Advice and a Long Rant!

Giving birth seems to be all about gaining and losing things:

☆ You gain a child; you lose your figure.
☆ You gain the ability to do eighteen things at once; you lose your sense of humour.
☆ You gain a million new jobs to do every day; you lose any time to do these in.

And so on. It's all a bit of give and take (and take and take and take, on your baby's part). Happily, **one thing you do NOT lose is your BRAIN**. It may be a bit fuzzy and confused for a few months, but it's still there in all its weird-looking glory, and it still works.

The only reason I mention this otherwise obvious fact is that since getting to know enough mothers to clean out every Baby Gap in the country, I have been amazed at the number of intelligent, able, sensible women who give birth and then promptly lose all ability to make any rational judgements when it comes to looking after their children. At some point during the birth, probably the moment when they first held their squashed, helpless bundle of joy, these women abandoned all trust in their own instincts, and ceased being able to make any parenting decisions of their own without worrying themselves silly.

The sad truth is that I did it, most of your friends will do it, and you will probably do it too. I'm sure many eminent sociologists, psychiatrists and pedicurists have clever theories about why this is: the breakdown of the extended family, today's information overload, the evil, wasteful Coffee Culture, *Heat* magazine, mobile phones and 24-hour shopping probably all have a hand in it, and some of this may even be true. My personal theory, having observed and experienced this Brain Drain myself, is that it's **fear**. Fear of getting it wrong, fear of screwing up, fear of being blamed for, or of blaming ourselves for anything which might go wrong with our children. While previous generations seem to have been quite happy to ignore the emotional needs of their offspring (OK, OK, not all of them, but you know what I mean), **we are a generation of parents completely paralysed by fear of making any mistakes at all**, lest we end up with screwed-up kids, and the therapists' bills which will go with them. And the only guaranteed result of all of this worry is very screwed-up kids. All of the Yummy Mummy friends I have asked agree that they feel under considerable social pressure to 'do it right'. Everyone from newspaper columnists to next-door's cleaner seems to feel free to advise and judge mothers, and it's a very strong lady indeed who can stand up to such pressure and scrutiny and do things her way.

And so we wind ourselves up into a frenzy of self-doubt and worry, and do whatever anyone else tells us to do. Literally anyone. I have even taken (and followed) advice on whether my three-month-old baby was ready to eat bread yet from a woman sitting next to me in a restaurant. Why? What made me so convinced that *she* knew what my baby needed better than I did? This made me so annoyed with myself that I vowed to start believing in myself more, and have never looked back, except to check whether anyone is tut-tutting at the way I'm looking after my kids, of course.

NB: Getting advice is still really important: the more tips, suggestions and experiences you can listen to the better, because one of them might just solve the latest baby dilemma you're having. But you've still got your own brain, and you know what's best for your baby and for you. Below is a mildly patronising but hopefully also helpful list of quite obvious things to remember when you become a Yummy Mummy, because very occasionally a thick, maternal fog can descend on your brain, which will severely cloud your otherwise perfectly good judgement.

☆ **Trust your *own* instincts.** Even I can be wrong.
☆ **What works for someone else might not work for *you*,** or for *your* child.
☆ **Be prepared to change your mind.** If it doesn't work, try something else.
☆ **Don't do anything which feels wrong to *you*.**
☆ **If you really think your brain came out with the placenta, then throw your hands in the air** and do whatever people tell you to, until your kids leave home.

Weight a Minute!

Oh! This is so mean and cruel, but it's true for almost every woman who breastfeeds her baby, and for many who don't. Just when you thought you could finally start getting back to the 'Old You' shape, your body digs its heels in and decides to hold on to any fat it can get. The result is that far from shedding pounds like a wallet in

Harvey Nichols, you may well put *on* some weight, regardless of how careful you are about eating (or not) and exercising.

There are several **SURVIVAL TIPS** I can offer:

☆ **Prepare yourself mentally**, and don't fight it when it happens.

☆ **Remember that your body is making sure there are enough fat stores to feed your baby** if a sudden crisis occurs (if Tesco runs out of *everything* for a week, for example). It can do this even if you are not breast-feeding, so beware.

☆ **Stick to a healthy diet**, because your baby needs it.

☆ **Most of the extra weight is on your boobs**, which is a good thing.

☆ **Don't look at your smallest-size pre-pregnancy clothes just yet.** You may well be much smaller than you were before you gave birth, but perhaps the figure-hugging hipsters can wait another few months.

☆ **Look at pictures of yourself when you were pregnant:** who's feeling fat now?

☆ **Set yourself a target for** when you want to be back to your pre-pregnant weight again, which should be at least two months after you stop breast-feeding.

So Can I Start To Diet *Now?*

Hold the wheat-free, gluten-free, fat-free, sugar-free, carb-free wonder-snack! The day after you give birth is **not** the day to start a full-blown weight-loss programme. You may think you're free to do what you like now but there are three people to consider when working out what to eat when you've had a baby:

☆ **Yourself,** who is recovering from a massive physical and mental ordeal.

☆ **Your baby,** who might be relying on you for all her nutritional supplies.

☆ **Your partner,** who has to live with you. If you're on a diet, you will be grouchy. End of story.

So, with these three characters in mind, when can a Yummy Mummy start to get her figure back?

If You Are Breastfeeding

Since you are making all the breast milk, you need to have enough energy to do so. But, as in pregnancy itself, the number of extra calories used up by your baby is a TEENY amount compared with what you normally eat, and cramming in two extra jacket potatoes with grated cheese at lunch will eventually turn you into one.

Don't feel you need to keep eating as much as you did in the last months of pregnancy to make enough breast milk. Remember, if you eat normally your body will make just the right amount of milk to feed your baby, and quite possibly too much (hence the breast pads). A breastfed baby can use up to 500 calories a day, a lot of which can come from the lard on your bum and thighs you are trying so hard to shift, if you watch what you eat. It's one of the best things about breastfeeding – your baby does all the work for you.

Remember that **your body will hold on to some stored fat** while you are breastfeeding. Some say it's about 10% of your new weight, and this feels right to me. Trying to shift this last little bit is almost impossible until you stop, but there is so much other work to be done in the fitness and toning departments that it's not a huge disaster. Annoying, yes. A reason not to breastfeed? Well, what do you think?

So, assuming that your body has changed during pregnancy to a shape and tone you don't like as much as you did before, and assuming that you want to lose some flab and trim things up a bit, here are some top tips for post-baby shedding:

☆ **Don't lose weight quickly.** This can release toxins, normally stored in your body fat, into your bloodstream, and thence into your milk. Considering how much more body fat you have now than you used to, that's an awful lot of toxins!

☆ **Do lose weight, if you want to.** Not losing it quickly doesn't mean not losing it at all. If you set yourself a realistic target (which you probably won't, but at least go for a *semi*-realistic one) at which point you want to have a flatter stomach again, this will spur you on. There's an irritating saying among many Mums which says: 'Nine months to put it on, nine months to get it off.' This is quite untrue unless you have put on five stone. If you've been careful during your pregnancy, and if you have any willpower at all, then three or four months is a perfectly reasonable timescale for getting most of your figure back, with some careful eating and exercising.

☆ **Try to wait for six weeks** before you really cut down: limiting your food intake a lot in the early weeks *can* reduce your milk supply, and who wants a Zone, Atkins or Macrobiotic baby anyway? Starting to shed some bulk by eating lots of fruit and veg, cutting down on sugar, fat and salt, and drinking gallons of water is a sensible start, and it'll massively boost your self-esteem. Crash-dieting and detoxing is totally ill-advised – you won't have the energy anyway.

☆ **Do take exercise.** Exercise releases happy hormones called endorphins. These are definitely passed into breast milk, because every time I breastfed after a workout my baby would be perky for about two hours afterwards. Whether this is a good thing or not, I don't know, and maybe they will all turn into adrenaline junkies. But if you don't start to tone up while you're still breastfeeding, you'll never bother, and losing weight without exercising leads to skinny but still wobbly bodies. Yuk! Work out a good exercise routine, and get some realistic personal goals stuck to the fridge. Monday: bum; Tuesday: legs; Wednesday: tummy; Thursday: arms; Friday: look like Laura Bailey is not the kind of thing at all.

☆ **Do whatever your body seems OK with.** Some women lose post-baby weight like I lose pairs of gloves; others struggle with it for years. Some are back in the gym after three days, others need to wait a few months. Your pre-pregnancy fitness and weight will have a big say in the matter, as will your determination, but if you are not managing to keep on top of things because you are trying too hard to lose weight, then stop being a wally and re-prioritise.

☆ **Be patient**. I hate this one, because I always want everything to fall back into place immediately. It will take a few months, but just look at Sara Cox, Sarah Jessica Parker, Thandie Newton, Zoe Ball, Cate Blanchett and so on. Were they ever even *pregnant*? It won't take long, but it might be a tad longer than you hope. Patience and hard work – oh, it's a Yummy Mummy's life for me!

☆ **Tell your partner to compliment you**. Don't suggest, or hint and hope. Tell him outright that you are trying to lose weight, and that this is his Big Chance to make up for the fact that he read a newspaper for half of the labour. Daily offerings of praise, compliments and encouragement, however insincere, are a minimum, and not offering you any cookie-dough ice-cream or eating his right in front of you, are but small additions. If he is unwilling to co-operate, point out that he has some vested interest in your figure-regaining pursuits: the sooner you love your body again, the sooner he might get a load of it again. It's bribery, but it works.

If You Are Not Breastfeeding

I guess you have a fairly free rein if there's no breast-milk quality control to worry about, but starving yourself is still a stupid idea. Even if you are cutting down your calorie intake, keep your energy levels up with low-fat, slow-release foods. Fruit is a brilliant way of keeping the blood sugars up, and don't forget your carbs. They are not

the Devil's work as you may have heard, and are only evil if you eat *all* the pies. One pie is fine. Also, because your baby isn't helping to eat up all the extra stored fat, you will have to work a bit harder at burning it yourself.

The Name's Bonding, Baby Bonding

Everyone seems to have some kind of hang-up about bonding with their baby, and the person who started this obsession has a lot of Yummy Mummy stress to answer for. There's never as much pressure on new Daddies to 'bond' with their newborns: as long as he *likes* his baby, and the baby doesn't scream non-stop when Daddy is in the room, he is considered to have bonded properly. We women, on the other hand, feel expected to establish a 'special bond' with our offspring before the dust from the birth has settled; to feel a unique, powerful love from the moment our tired eyes meet. Failure to do so guarantees our children will take drugs before they are old enough to pay a full fare on the train, and spend their teenage years in a Brat Camp in Arizona.

To think this way is not very helpful, because baby bonding can mean many things, from simply feeling comfortable with your baby (when holding your baby stops feeling like gripping a Fabergé egg with some chopsticks, you know you're getting somewhere), to getting to know each other and learning to communicate with each other (soon you *will* know what each cry, gurgle, grimace and wriggle means), to finally starting to really *like* each other's company.

In the same way that bonding two bits of a smashed vase back together requires two parts (and some glue), so Baby Bonding is a two-way process: if you adore your baby but she thinks you are a cold-blooded She-Devil, things are not going very well. That said, it's almost impossible that your baby will do anything other than worship the ground you walk on – who could resist the lady who thrusts her ample bosom in their face every couple of hours and lets them drink sweet, warm milk from it? Actually, I could, because that sounds quite gross to me, but then I'm not a new baby, am I?

Stressing about Baby Bonding will almost certainly make the process fail. The best way I've found to bond with a baby is to spend as much time as you can doing absolutely nothing with her. Just holding her, staring at her, smelling her, feeling her, listening to every sound and watching every reaction. If you let her do the same – touch your face, smell your skin, watch you smile, laugh, grimace and so on – she will think you are a bit weird but at least she'll get to know what she's got to work with.

Rock Bottom: Part One

What goes up must come down. Winnie the Pooh knew that, and so should you. In your case, you're not as likely to land with your bum in a gorse bush as you are to spend several days in bed crying, because – well, that's just it. Because *what*?

The elation and euphoria you might experience to counteract the hell of giving birth is almost guaranteed to be followed by an equally intense period of gloom and sadness. This is usually referred to as the Baby Blues, but it's more like the Baby Black, Black, Black. It shouldn't last much longer than a few days, and if it does you should probably talk to your doctor, or a very good friend.

My personal theory of why we hit Rock Bottom so soon after our adorable baby has arrived concerns the coming together of several factors as well as hormones:

☆ **You are now too tired.** Anyone can live without sleep for three or four days. We all do it when we are students, when we first start dating somebody hot, and when we come back from a weekend in Rome to discover that some dickhead has deleted all the work we did before we left, and we have to write it all over again. (You know who you are.) But after four crazy days and five sleepless nights, we've had it, and can't even cope with making a cup of tea, let alone looking after a hungry, needy baby 24 hours a day.

☆ **The novelty has worn off.** This is a whole lot less callous than it sounds. The first days with your new baby are so exciting that you really are doing little more than playing with the best new toy in the world. It's like all your Christmases rolled into one sleepsuit. But once you've pressed all the buttons, worked out how to programme it and have shown it to all your friends, it does become less exciting for a while.

☆ **You want to press pause.** This was the biggie for me, every time. After four days of relentless baby-care, everyone craves a little break. Not a long-weekend kind of a break, but a little tiny pause, just to pop out for a coffee or to catch up on some correspondence. And somewhere around day four, it suddenly hits you: YOU CANNOT PRESS PAUSE. Not today, not tomorrow, not for the whole of the next year, and not for the four, five or six years after that. Your baby will be right there, every day, every night, every weekend and every holiday, and you cannot have a proper break. Even if you get somebody to babysit for a while, and get a *physical* break, some part of your brain stays with your baby all the time. When you realise the enormity of what you have undertaken, having a minor breakdown seems like a mild reaction to me.

☆ **You miss your old life.** A change *is* as good as a break, but when the change is as vast and permanent as this one it may seem like more of a nuclear bomb than an energising break. It's often after a week or so that you reach your 'not going out for a drink, to the cinema, for dinner with friends, to a club, to an art gallery, to anything in fact' threshold, and start to miss that old life terribly.

If you hit rock bottom after a few days, then there are several things you can do to cheer yourself up:

☆ **Don't feel bad about feeling bad.** Everyone does, and it just shows how conscientiously you are treating motherhood. Well done.

☆ **Let it out.** Denying that you need to cry and that you find everything overwhelming will not help you at all in the long run. People will be more supportive and sympathetic in these early days than at any other time, so get all the attention and help you can.

☆ **Talk to your partner, family and friends.** This sounds obvious, but loads of Yummy Mummies battle on, scared to show how hard they are finding it. Nobody will think any less of you, and the support you'll get will help enormously.

☆ **See if you can get a few hours in the Real World.** I still remember my first walk into town and back, without each of my babies: I skipped half the way there, felt all the 'new baby' weight lifting off my shoulders, and was very happy to get back to feeding again, having had a short break.

☆ **Go to bed even earlier for a few nights.** Sleep deprivation is the biggest downer, so arm yourself with an extra hour or two of kip.

☆ **Make an extra effort to spoil yourself.** Even if it's only a hot bath and a glass of wine, make time to enjoy it. *This is very, very important!*

☆ **Try to remember that it's only for six months or so.** This may seem like forever, but it will go a lot faster if you set yourself targets, and...

☆ **Arrange something to look forward to in the coming weeks.** It doesn't have to be a huge thing: just a day trip somewhere nice, lunch with a friend or a pampering massage can be the mental boost you need right now.

Being the capable, proud woman you are, you may shun half of these suggestions and take the 'I'm OK, I can manage just fine, thank you' route. Every Yummy Mummy I know regrets doing this in retrospect, and wishes she had been much more sensible and opted for the 'take it easy and look after yourself' method instead. Do what feels right, but I can't recommend going easy on yourself for the first few months highly enough.

Rock Bottom: Part Two

Your bottom will not resemble any solid geological specimen right after you've had a baby. If you have a wobbly bottom, then fret not your pretty, postnatal face. All newborn babies have Yummy Mummies with wobbly bottoms, and this is only so that they don't feel too bad about theirs.

You may have heard about things Going South after having a baby, and this is true of several parts of your body, including your bottom.

The bad news: your breasts will always be nearer the ground, unless you go for a boob job.

The good news: your bum can get right back up where it should be within a few months. It all depends on how much butt-firming action you go for. (See **Sexy Mama: Getting That Body Back in Order** in Part Seven.)

Dummies

You may not like the idea but dummies (pacifiers, binkies, dinkies, or whatever silly name you decide to use) can be incredibly useful. Very ugly, but very useful.

To avoid total dependence and withdrawal symptoms later, here are some handy rules which have worked well for us. In our family dummies were only used for:

☆ getting our baby to go to sleep.
☆ soothing our baby if she was so upset about something that she wouldn't stop crying after all the usual distractions.

If you always take the dummy away as soon as these needs are met, then your baby learns very quickly when she can and can't have one, and there shouldn't be too much of a fight over it.

Some babies don't want to have a dummy, no matter how hard you try, so don't force it! Two of mine did, and the middle one didn't, but that's middle children for you. Sigh.

Baby Basics

Looking after a baby is like the ultimate *Krypton Factor* challenge: babies don't come with any instructions, they don't offer you much in the way of assistance or handy hints, and you can't start all over again so there's little scope for screwing everything up.

If you already know how to look after a new baby, then you are either in a hyper-talented class of your own, or you are just very dishonest. Assuming that, as I was, you are unsure about any of the basic daily requirements of a delicate, demanding baby, then this section aims to shed a little light on some of these basics. If it all seems very obvious and patronising, then I simply say 'Just you wait…'

Bathing a Baby

Terrifying. Absolutely terrifying for the first few attempts, until you realise where you are going wrong. Imagine you're a new baby: you've been in a warm, protected environment for nine months, and suddenly here you are in the cold, bright, confusing, noisy outside world. Now imagine you have all your clothing removed and are being dipped into lukewarm water by a pair of clumsy hands which are clearly petrified of letting you go in case you drown, and don't know how to hold you comfortably in such a slippery, hard baby bath. A recipe for a very unpleasant washing experience for both parties, I think you'll agree.

The solution: **have a bath together**. We used our new, sparkly baby bath twice before abandoning it in favour of a *lavage-à-deux*, and it was the best move ever. Screaming, slipping, splashing and panicking were replaced by calming, soothing, heavenly bath-times. If you get in with your baby (in your bath, not your baby's one!), you can hold her much better, she feels safe in your arms, you can kiss and cuddle her, feel her naked skin against yours and have the most amazing bonding sessions. Babies will gaze intently into your eyes when they're in the bath with you, and I cannot recommend it highly enough.

You may have heard that you should do an 'elbow test', where you stick your elbow in the bath water, and it should feel neither hot nor cold. You will probably do this for a few days, so determined are you to do the 'right thing', until you realise that it's really very silly, and just swishing your hand and forearms around a bit will tell you whether it's OK or not. Babies should go in bathwater which is only a *little* warmer than their body temperature, which to you will feel a bit like 'Ooooh, I'm not going in *there* for long.' It's also best to leave any bubble baths or other products out for the first few months, to keep baby's skin clean and free of irritants and chemicals. If you must, then go for something organic (see list later on).

☆ **Washing hair:** Assuming that your baby has hair (and many don't for about a year), you really don't need to 'wash' it for a very long time. Shampoo is unnecessary, and a rub down with clean bathwater is fine.

☆ **Non-slip bath mat:** You won't really need this if you're in the bath with your baby, but as soon as she can sit up (after five months or so) and you pop her in on her own while you lean nervously over the side, you will.

☆ **Bath toys:** A plastic cup for pouring water is all you'll need for a while – they love watching and listening to water being poured beside or directly onto them. After that, anything goes, but our big hits have been a colander and an empty bubble-bath bottle. Cheap chic, I like to call it, but if the latest Disney bath entertainment centre is more your thing, then who am I to argue?

☆ **After the bath:** This is Golden Time. This is the time when your baby is most relaxed, sleepy, cuddly and attentive, and it is the best time for ignoring all the toys and distractions, and just talking, reading or singing to him. It's also the ideal time to try some baby massage, as his body is warm and his skin appreciates the massage oil better. When your baby is screaming his head off after a bath, you will wonder what on earth I'm talking about, but for every time they do that there will be a time, if you play your cards right and keep things quiet, dark and gentle, when you get this Golden Time.

☆ **Towels:** Soft, soft, soft. And warm – stick the baby's towel on a warm radiator in the bathroom, and preferably the sleepsuit and nappy as well. Babies get very cold when they get out of the bath, so having everything warmed and ready makes the crying peter out sooner.

☆ **Skincare:** If it looks perfectly fine to you, then it's always best to leave a baby's skin well alone. It will come into contact with chemicals and products in good time, and the longer it can stay *au naturel* the better. If it seems dry, or if there's any eczema, then applying baby lotion or E45 cream is a good idea. The best dry-skin solution I ever found was aqueous cream: it smells horrible, looks unappealing and goes on like putty, but it cures dry skin within 48 hours, and that goes for your own dry bits too.

Baby Massage

Why didn't anyone know about this when we were babies, eh? How lovely it must be to be lifted out of a warm bath, wrapped in a soft, warm towel by your adoring Mummy, and then given a gentle, soothing massage complete with soft lighting and aroma-therapy oils.

It's generally accepted now that massaging your baby can have enormous benefits, both to her and to the way you bond with her. I loved getting to know my baby's body: feeling all her bumps and curves, her soft, squishy limbs, and her smooth, strong back. Most baby massage is little more than stroking to begin with, but it's a fantastic way to learn about your child's body, her reactions to your touch, for you to gain confidence in handling her, and for her to gain confidence that you know what you're doing.

TOP TIPS for baby massage:
☆ **Do it after a bath when your baby is warm and relaxed**, and in a darkened, warm room where your baby is comfortable. Not the kitchen table, in other words, but in front of the telly with the volume very low is fine if there's something unmissable on – it's not ideal, but they like the flickering lights.
☆ **Don't do it within half an hour of a feed**, or it'll be baby vomit instead.

☆ **Make sure your hands are warm.** You wouldn't like your masseuse to put her freezing cold hands on your warm stomach, would you?

☆ **Make as much eye contact as possible**, and smile, talk or sing gently all the time. Unless you sing very badly. Some babies hate being naked, and if yours does then only expose the parts you need to get at. Then have a long chat with her about it – this sort of prudish behaviour won't do at all when she gets to secondary school, so best to stamp it out now.

☆ **Don't apply much pressure at all.** Think stroking rather than pummelling.

☆ **Massage the face, head and back of the neck** (gently!) as well.

☆ **Stomachs should be massaged in a clockwise direction**. (I still haven't worked out how clockwise for *me* can also be clockwise for the *baby*, but it seems to work that way. If you do it the wrong way, your baby can get digestive problems, so do a double-check of your watch to make sure.)

☆ **Don't massage *on* the spine** – put your fingers on either side of it. Some babies love having the dimples at the base of their back massaged.

☆ **If your baby doesn't like it, stop!** Obviously.

Yummy Baby Products You Could Indulge In:

☆ **Little Me Baby Organics, available from Boots.** They do everything from body wash and soaps to heavenly scented lotions for happy days and calm nights, and a lovely massage oil.

☆ **Crabtree & Evelyn Baby range.** Pudy Cat Comfort Cream, Liza Lamb Shampoo and Babywash – you get the idea. They look sweet, and are all very gentle on your baby's soft skin.

☆ **Avant SPF 15 Out and About Cream.**

☆ **Burt's Bees.** This famous, Earth-friendly range now does natural products for babies too. If you can't decide what to get, then try the Baby Bees Starter Kit – contains a small sample of everything your baby could ever need to keep her body smooth and cared for.

☆ **Neal's Yard Baby Massage Oil.** The beautiful blue bottles are available for babies too – just try not to steal it for yourself.

Bedtime Miracles and Disasters

3.30 a.m. 10 February. Six weeks after birth.

Breastfeeding again. I am so, so, so tired. I am tired, and I don't want to be feeding this baby. I have to sleep. Why won't she just sleep? My eyes are so dry they hurt when I blink, and my head is too heavy to hold up, so it's just flopping down to my chest, which is hurting my neck. I have to sleep. I keep dropping off halfway through the feed – maybe I'll fall over on top of her and smother her. Oh God, I have to stay awake. Hurry up and finish. And I'm so angry and jealous and hateful of Harry, just lying there, heavily and deeply asleep, breathing slowly in and out, just resting. I want to rest too. I'll be up again at seven for the next feed, while he just lies there and then goes off to work. I need a break. This was such a bad idea. Oh FUCK, I'm so tired. I hate this, I hate this, I hate this. I want to sleep for a week. And now she's finished at last. Now I just have to put her back in her Moses basket and HOPE that she goes to sleep. If not, I don't think I've got it in me to pick her up again.

4.10 a.m.

I can't put her down. She is so beautiful. I'm just holding her head in the palm of my hand and her hair is all fuzzy and smooth. I can't stop staring at her, even though I'm so tired I can't think. And she smells delicious – I love putting my nose just by her mouth and letting her breathe on me. It's so sweet and clean. I love her. I love her. Her tiny nose, her open, perfect lips, her huge closed, moon-shaped eyes. And her skin! It's the smoothest thing I've ever felt. I kiss her and kiss her all over her beautiful face. She is so tiny and helpless and dependent on me. I will love her forever and look after her and make her so happy. Lovely little Emily. Oh I'm so tired. I have to put her down in her Moses basket or tomorrow will be Hell, but I don't want to. I want to hold her all night. She is breathtaking. I love you, my beautiful, wonderful, perfect baby. I love you.

Sleep! Ahhh, sleep. Once upon a time, sleeping was something you did just to separate one day from the next, or possibly because you had drunk too much wine and couldn't stay awake any longer. Once you've had a baby, sleep becomes your most valued commodity in the entire world, even outdoing a full-body aromatherapy massage or the chance of some good sex. Really. Nothing makes us more grouchy than chronic fatigue – it makes our skin dull and dry, we get bags under our eyes, and we tend to eat more and put on weight, which is always cause for a hellish mood.

Babies are lovely. They are funny and beautiful and fascinating. But after 14 hours of funny, beautiful and fascinating, you may start to find your baby exhausting, annoying, and just far too *awake*. I always felt terribly guilty wishing my baby would go to sleep at the end of the day so that I could have some time to myself, but there's actually nothing bad about feeling that way at all. Everyone loses their appeal a little bit after such a long, unbroken period of cuteness, and you need a break to recharge and find your baby lovely again.

If, like me, you find you cannot cope any longer because you are so tired, the only answer is to get a good night's sleep, and the only way you can do *that* is to get your baby to have a good night's sleep. But how? Bedtime can be terribly fraught, because you are exhausted, your baby is exhausted, you have lost your sense of humour, and there is a comfy sofa and a good book waiting in the living room. Under such conditions it is almost impossible to remain patient and calm while gently soothing your stubborn, bright-eyed child off to sleep.

Sarah, mother of Jack, eight months

Jack takes ages to settle down. One time I took him for a drive in the car. I drove him around the block about ten times, and it was two junctions of the A14 which finally did the trick. He settled quite well when I moved him into his cot but I am not doing that every night. What a nightmare.

I have also had some horrible evenings trying to get one baby or another off to sleep for what seemed like hours, trying technique after cunning technique, and longing for silence. I've tried controlled crying (which really upset me and it didn't work for any of my kids), gentle singing, leaving a light on, total darkness, with a dummy, without a dummy, getting cross, with a teddy bear, tucked under a blanket, left uncovered, facing the window, facing the wall – you name it, I've tried it.

Mostly, nights like this end in tears for you, and a huge sense of failure, hatred and gloom. When this happens, try not to get too upset, and start afresh tomorrow. All babies eventually get so tired that they crash out, but it is a miserable experience, and the following will hopefully help you:

Routine, Routine, Routine

According to 'Liz's Theory of Baby Sleep', babies are little more than small animals who can learn really quickly. So are dogs (except some dogs are big). Now, if Pavlov managed to teach his dogs that the sound of a bell ringing meant it was time for food, (or was it fish and lights? Well, whichever) then I think babies can learn that it's time for sleep when they are given a certain signal, or sequence of signals. It's just training through repetition, and it's really boring and unexciting, but I have found that it works brilliantly.

Here's the plan: From the very first day you take your baby home, establish a bedtime routine, and stick to it like bikini wax. It may be boring and repetitive and it may even mean you have to miss the first ten minutes of *Property Ladder*, but it works and it really is worth it.

Now, I don't know about you, but I find it very difficult to go to sleep straight after I've been out with friends, playing tennis, watching a film or if I'm lying in a bright, cheery, noisy room, and I think we can only assume that babies and children are the same. They need to calm down, chill out and have a bit a peace and quiet. About an hour before you want your baby to go to sleep, start to calm the playing down, read some books, sing a few gentle songs and so on. Prepare the last feed of the day, get everything ready for bed (remove all the junk which is lying at the bottom of the cot, find some sleepwear, a clean nappy, a blanket and whatever cuddly toy is the current hot favourite), and dim all the lights. In the summer time, we shut all the curtains ridiculously early, just to make the house darker and calmer, but it also keeps the nosy woman opposite curious, which is fun. It's also a good idea to talk in a deeper, quieter voice and to be more cuddly and close. Just do anything which calms them down and this will get their brains ready to start shutting down for a few hours' kip.

'Bath before bed' is gospel in our house, and again, it's a fantastic way to get babies drowsy, warm and relaxed before they go to sleep. It doesn't even have to be a very long bath, just so long as it's a bath, and it's always followed by stories, the last milk feed of the day and then sleep. It's just a pattern which they learn, and which works for us, and for most of our friends.

Try not to miss story-time out. Even the shortest picture book is better than nothing – the calm period after their bath is the best time to get them to enjoy looking at the pictures and listening to your voice.

In theory, after all that they just lie down and go to sleep, and, amazingly, about 70% of the time, they do. The other 30% is just awful, fraught and miserable, and can be caused by anything from teething, to colic, a cold, nightmares, earache, trapped wind, wet nappy, too much sleep during the day, too much excitement in the afternoon, and so on and on and on. Not forgetting stubbornness, which is a big player here.

Don't despair if your baby really won't go to sleep. Keep calm, and try again in ten minutes or so, after some more stories or a quiet cuddle. Repeat the whole thing again tomorrow, and it may just work then.

What if I can't stick to this every night?

Oh no. You're not going to be one of those bad, neglectful, uncommitted types, who occasionally throws caution to the wind and *ignores* the Bedtime Routine for a night, are you?

Well, I hope you are, because a mother who sacrifices every

opportunity for a bit of fun – having friends round for a drink, going for a cheeky after-dinner ice-cream in the park, hanging in there for that last sausage which has just been thrown on the barbeque – in favour of religiously performing bedtime rituals is a very misguided person indeed, and has completely lost sight of what life is about. I know several Yummy Mummies like this, ruled by their babies' demands and requirements, who are unable to make exceptions for anything. And then they complain that they can't ever do anything or go anywhere. What difference is the odd night of frivolity *really* going to make? You go and have a bit of fun, but prepare yourself for a couple of difficult nights to come, as your baby cottons on to the fact that there is life after he goes to bed and decides he wants some of the action too. The cheeky little so-and-so.

What time should I put my baby to sleep?

Seriously? I get asked this all the time by my pregnant friends, and I have no idea what to say, let alone which face to pull to cover the 'waddaya *mean*?' look in my eyes. How should *I* know? Are you a morning person (you'd better start practising if not!)? Would you rather put your baby to bed early and have an evening with your partner, or keep your baby up later and pray for a lie-in? Your baby will have her own ideas about what suits anyway, but when you decide it's bedtime is up to you and your partner, not a book.

My rule has always been 'If it's after 7.30 p.m., I don't want to know any more, so good night!' In order to free up this DVD-watching opportunity, I keep my baby out and active as much as possible during the day, try not to let her sleep for more than an hour or two at the most, and then get everything calmed down at about 6 p.m. for the 7.30 'lights out'. It means we are up horribly early, but I don't mind because I'd rather have the child-free evenings to feel like an adult again. You just do what fits your own life best.

How many blankets is too many blankets?

Well, I guess this depends on how cold it is in the baby's room, no? There is no 'correct' answer to this oft-asked question, but I have always relied on the following to decide how many layers to tuck my baby under: too cold is always better than too hot. A baby who is too cold will cry until you sort him out. A baby who is overheated can die. I'd go for cold toes, personally. If he's in a body and a thick sleepsuit he will need fewer blankets than if he's in a thin, skimpy number. A good general rule of thumb is that babies need one more layer than you do. That's about it, so use your clever head, and figure out what's required every night.

Front or back?

Oh my God – will you stop worrying so much?! Look, the advice on whether to put babies down on their fronts, backs, sides, heads or whatever changes all the time: it even changed between my first and last babies, so I couldn't win. Whatever the current fashion as you read this, it will almost certainly ignore this overriding fact:

All babies have their own favourite sleeping position, and you can't argue with it.

Currently, I am dealing with a two-year-old who will only sleep on his front with a huge bear tucked under one arm. Previously I have had one daughter who slept flat-out on her back with her arms sticking out to the sides, her legs sticking straight up in the air and all her blankets kicked off. In between, we struggled with the middle child, who changed her mind every two weeks, and we never knew what she wanted. Still don't, come to think of it.

See what works best for your own baby, and just pop in to check on him every half-hour or so, if that makes you feel any more relaxed.

My baby won't sleep.

This is not right, after a month or so. If you have a six-week-old baby who is still waking every three hours for a feed or for some comfort, he is abusing your kind nature and needs to be taught some new rules. Like, 'It's night-time, so go back to sleep for another three hours, please, or Mummy will collapse.'

It's easier said than done, but there are some things which can help:

☆ **Establish a clear night and day.** As above, day is for daylight, noise, activity, and lots of change. Night is for dark, quiet and peace.

☆ **Keep your baby awake for longer periods of time in the day.** They can go for a good two hours of awake time in one go after a couple of months before zonking out yet again.

☆ **Start to have fewer, longer naps.** Not you, your baby. Within about two months you should be able to get it down to two long sleeps a day (of, say, an hour or an hour and a half, depending on how tired your baby is that day) rather than six 20-minute kips.

☆ **Try to make the feeds bigger and spaced further apart.** Babies rarely get a decent feed if they are suckling every two hours. Be really vigilant, wait until your boobs are about to explode and your baby is really ready for some food, and then deliver a proper, long, filling feed. This should keep him going longer, until the next good feed. Snacking is a devilish habit, which is easy to give in to, as all women know!

Isabelle, mother of Tom, two, and Daisy, nine months

I remember evenings of constant crying, with my husband carrying Tom around in a sling while trying to watch the World Cup, and me trying to think of toys and noises which would make Tom happy. In the end, we read about 'overstimulation', and as soon as we went for a darkened-room-and-soft-voices approach, things got markedly better.

I can't keep my baby awake!

This may sound a little strange to you if yours is an insomniac, but it's a common problem in the first few months to have a baby who just wants to sleeps all day long, and then wakes every three hours throughout the night. This is the worst habit to get into, and if you can't get your baby to learn the difference between day (this is when you're awake, honey, OK?) and night (I don't want to see you for the next six hours) then you will suffer terribly from lack of sleep. Even more than normal, I mean.

To break this hellish cycle you need to try and keep your baby awake during the day as much as possible, but this can be really hard. Taking a baby out for a walk puts them to sleep almost immediately, as does a trip in the car, a feed, listening to music and watching Mummy do stomach crunches.

The only thing which worked for mine was frequent changes of activities. Doing any one thing for longer than ten minutes made the eyelids start drooping (the baby's, not mine – mine were permanently drooping for six months), and it was only the constant moving from place to place, stimulus to stimulus and activity to activity that worked. If all else failed, pretending to change her nappy *again* usually kept her awake for another ten minutes, and walking around the garden looking at all the flowers was a hit. Until the bright light made her fall asleep again. Dammit!

All Change Please!

Poo. Great word, horrid thing. If poo is an unfortunate by-product of being alive, then wiping poo off a baby's bottom is an unfortunate by-product of being a Yummy Mummy. That said, I find it very irritating that most depictions of motherhood seem to centre around piles and piles of poo-filled nappies. It's all nappies, poo, stinks, and general foulness. Why?

Obviously there is a whole lot of bum-wiping and poo disposal to be done in a day with a baby – in fact, much more than would be expected from a creature so small and cute. But it's not *that* bad. Changing nappies is not in the same *league* as removing pubic hairs from hotel-room plugholes, or sharing a bed with a man who has drunk ten pints of strong lager and smells like a urinal, yet we do this quite regularly without fuss. (Actually, I make a *huge* fuss about it, and refuse to sleep with him for the next two weeks – a great opportunity for some rest.)

In the first few weeks baby poo goes through a series of truly bizarre changes: it starts out as a tarry black gloop called meconium, and then becomes yellow with little white bits in it as your milk content changes. This is all perfectly normal, if a little surprising, and you shouldn't expect to see anything resembling real poo until they start having solid food. If you are breastfeeding, your baby's poo will smell fairly inoffensive (another bonus of breastfeeding), but as soon as you introduce a bottle, something meaner is produced, which really does smell quite bad.

TOP TIP: *Bottle-fed babies are often more dehydrated than breast-fed ones, and they can become constipated. If you think your baby's poo is too dry, and seems hard to, um, expel, try to give him some cooled, boiled water as well as milk feeds to loosen things up a bit.*

Back to the poo removal. With practice, changing a baby's nappy will become as automatic and easy to you as applying fake tan: after the first few nervous attempts, poring over the instructions and hoping for the best, you will soon be able to do it in double-quick time, without a hitch, while holding a phone to one ear and catching up on the latest non-baby news from old work colleagues. Poo? What poo?

Until you reach this point, however, changing a nappy will test your agility to the limit. It's all legs, folds, poo, wipes, mess, smell, more legs, some arms – oh God! – nappy sacks, spilled water, baby lotion and a crying baby.

Help is here. Before you change a baby's nappy, get the following ready:

☆ **Changing mat.**
☆ **Cotton wool balls:** I found the smaller ones were better, and they go further.
☆ **Fresh, warm water in a bowl** (or margarine tub, in my case), unless you are using…
☆ **Wipes:** Always buy them when they are on buy-one-get-one-free,

but try to stick to cotton wool balls dipped in warm water for as long as you can bear it. It's cheaper and gentler, and this goes for wiping baby's face as well. The fewer chemicals the better. Poor baby's bum.

☆ **Kitchen roll:** Economy stuff is fine – you'll get through kilometres of it.

☆ **A clean nappy:** Open and ready for immediate use.

☆ **A nappy sack:** Or any other small plastic bag to put the offending item in. (I assume you realise I mean the nappy and not your baby.)

☆ **Something to distract your baby**, and keep stray hands occupied.

☆ **A cordless phone:** It will ring the minute you take the nappy off, and dashing out to fetch a handset is ill-advised, unless you want to return to a scene from *The Messiest Babies in the World Ever!* which is probably in production somewhere.

Even with all this in place, there's plenty of scope for disaster, but it does, honestly, get much, much easier. Here's what will go wrong:

☆ Your baby will wee *the second* you remove her nappy, so get that kitchen roll ready to catch it. If it's a boy, be extra vigilant – they have terrific range, but appalling aim. I've had wee in my eye, down my front, and all over the wall. This explains why urinals smell so awful, I guess.

☆ Your baby will bend her knees and put her heels in the poo before smearing it all over the changing mat. This is where the long mat comes in handy – try to keep her feet out of the messy part by holding tightly to her ankles and lifting them above her head. Yes, they are that bendy.

☆ You will knock the water over, and all the baby's clothes will be soaked, so she'll need a complete change. Give yourself plenty of room, and keep the clean, dry stuff well clear of the changing area.

☆ You will take your eye off your subject for a nanosecond and you'll be covered in poo. Don't. Keep focused on the danger zone, and all will be well.

☆ You will put the dirty nappy somewhere near your baby's feet, and, as you reach for a wipe, she will get her feet caught up in the nappy and...yes, well, anyway, it's not pretty, so try to put the dirty ones well clear of wriggly appendages.

This is by no means an exhaustive list, and eight years down the line (which means I must have changed – shit! – somewhere in the region of 10,000 nappies. Shit, indeed) I am still occasionally caught out by some new complication.

Lots of books I have read strongly recommend getting a 'changing station' to perform the odious task, but I've never had one, and I have never found it a problem. I've always just put the changing mat on the floor and kept all the bits I need in a cupboard next to it. What these books often neglect to mention is that within a few months your baby will be able to turn over and crawl off the mat. Fine if it's on the floor; lethal if it's three feet off the ground.

Another thing to bear in mind is that lots of babies find having their nappy taken off very unnerving, and they get quite upset. If you talk to them the whole time, sing songs and look them in the eye as much as possible (hard, when I've just told you never to take your eyes off the critical parts, but you know what I mean), then you can make the whole process more relaxing for both of you. It can even be a nice time for a chat and a giggle, especially when blowing raspberries on a bare tummy is involved.

Disposable Or Real?
(See also **The Eco Baby** in Part Ten).
For me it was disposable all the way. I had very good intentions of doing the real nappy thing for about 24 hours, at which point I realised that I was just kidding myself. The fact that it was the middle of January and my entire house would have been full of drying muslin squares didn't help much. In my defence, the services offered today for laundering nappies and delivering clean ones to your doorstep were much scarcer when I had my first baby, I went back to work within a couple of months and I travel a lot, making disposables essential. But if I am totally honest, I'm not sure anything would have made me change my mind: there is so much else to do, and

you are so exhausted to start off with that anything which makes your life easier is worth doing, even if it's only for while.

If you are a committed eco-warrior then all of this will severely piss you off, and I do apologise and acknowledge that you are right. But for everyone else, don't beat yourself up about using disposables, try to do your bit for the environment in other ways, and do whatever feels right for you and your circumstances.

Breastfeeding – How Hard Can It Be?

VERY.

To begin: breastfeeding kicks arse in terms of healthy, practical and effective ways to feed your baby. If you can breastfeed, then no reason you could ever think of is good enough to prevent you from doing so. *Yes, but it's really gross* and *I really don't want to have droopy breasts afterwards* are rubbish excuses. What's a droopy breast or two when there's setting your baby up for a healthy life at stake? And anyway, they'll be droopier than they were before you were pregnant whether you breastfeed or not.

Here's why you should *try* to breastfeed:

☆ **It's the healthiest option:** Breast milk contains *exactly* the right ingredients your new baby needs, and these ingredients change as her requirements change. Everything from antibodies to the correct amount of certain vitamins come through in your milk, and you don't even need to know what you're doing – it just happens! Magic.

☆ **It shrinks your uterus** down quickly after the birth. This is a good thing, because your tummy will get smaller.

☆ **There is no better way of bonding,** literally, with your baby. When your baby looks up at you as he drinks from your breast, it is a look of trust, love and need that you can never imagine, and which cements something between you forever. It's also handy to remember this moment when your three-year-old breaks the DVD player or your fifteen-year-old announces she is pregnant. They were perfect once.

☆ **It's quick and easy:** No preparation or cleaning required here: it's sterile, warm and ready whenever and wherever your baby needs it. For any Yummy Mummy who intends to travel with a baby, breastfeeding is almost essential.

☆ **Men can't do it:** Not the most positive reason, I'll admit, but anything we can do to make ourselves feel a little more special and needed, the better. You might not be bringing in the cash, but you sure can feed a baby.

☆ **It's free.**

☆ **It can help you lose a few inches of lard quite quickly.**

To Continue: Breastfeeding can be very difficult and distressing. With so much pressure on all mothers to breastfeed, it is very upsetting if breastfeeding is either extremely difficult, or impossible. There are many reasons why you might not be able to breastfeed. These include:

☆ **Medical complications** during or after the birth involving separation from your baby, or taking medication which makes breast milk unsuitable.

☆ **Physical incompatibility:** Some women have very oddly-shaped boobs and nipples, which makes it very hard for the baby to get a grip. Not your fault, just a shame.

☆ **Your physical and mental state:** If you are too tired, not eating properly, or suffering from bad postnatal depression, your milk supply can dry up. This can happen amazingly quickly, and it happened to me several times for a short while. Things can get going again with enough rest and nourishment, but sometimes when the tap is switched off, that's it.

Breastfeeding is another of those 'it's so natural that you should instinctively know how to do it' things that turns out to be very tricky and not instinctive at all. Some babies just can't get the hang of it either, which doesn't help the situation: there you are, tit out, ready to go, and your little sproglet just cranes her neck in the vague direction of your heaving bosom, but fails miserably to get any milk down her throat. The worst thing is that you know the more annoyed and upset you become, the less likely she is to succeed. The only way to master breastfeeding is to stay as calm and relaxed as possible, and not to let your baby know you are screaming with frustration and pain inside. This is unbelievably difficult, but then you are unbelievably amazing, so you will manage. If you really can't get anywhere at all, and you are becoming agitated and upset, then tell your health visitor as soon as you can.

Hannah, mother of Rachel, four, and Ben, two

I was very surprised at how hard it was to do something so natural. My midwife said 'give it three weeks' and she was right. My nipples bled, and it was agonising, but suddenly I passed a point and it didn't hurt any more, and it became wonderful, easy, cosy and special. I would recommend it to anyone; don't give up trying!

Eva, mother of Billy, eleven months

I'm not sure if I will ever get over not being able to feed Billy myself. It was something I knew I wanted to do, and when it didn't work, because I had terrible mastitis and he also couldn't get the hang of it, I felt I had failed the first, huge hurdle of being a mum. If I have another baby I will try again, but I am prepared for it not to work. There's nothing you can do if you can't breastfeed, but that doesn't make the disappointment any less hard to bear.

If you can manage it, breastfeeding is the business. It takes ages, it means you can't leave them for more than a few hours for many, many months, and it may feel a bit weird and even gross for a while (not helped by *Little Britain* sketches at all), but no words can describe how beautiful it is to feed your own child from your own body, and to see how much they love you for it. *Bitty?* Yes please.

Here are some breastfeeding terms and tips you'll need:

☆ **Colostrum.** For the first few days you don't actually produce any 'milk' as we know it, but a thick, sticky liquid called colostrum. Apparently this is the wonder stuff for your baby, so go with it.

☆ **When the milk 'comes in'.** This usually happens on day four (or Black Day Four as I like to call it), and it coincides with quite a big hormonal change for you. You will probably feel more tearful, moody and 'down' at this stage, and the sudden abundance of milk can be very unsettling. It will all seem normal very soon.

☆ **Let-down reflex.** Nothing to do with male impotence or getting no birthday cards (again). The let-down reflex is an astonishing, automatic reaction to your brain announcing 'Cabin crew, breasts to automatic and cross check: feeding commencing in 30 seconds.' At this command, hoards of chemical messengers charge towards your helpless boobs in a mad frenzy reminiscent of a crowd of Yummy Mummies at the Liberty sale, and tell them to become rock hard, to make their nipples tingle and hurt, and ultimately to start expelling milk at high pressure. Groovy. If there's no mouth ready to receive this lactic eruption then it's a wet shirt for you. (Unless you've been clever enough to wear breast pads and to have several spares to hand.) Let-down reflexes usually only happen when you want them to (i.e. when you settle down for a feed), but be prepared for the occasional false alarm, such as hearing another baby cry, buying nappies or flicking through *OK!* magazine and glimpsing the latest celebrity baby. Fatal.

   Sometimes let-down reflexes don't happen. This can be frustrating, and if this happens, try to relax and think of something else while keeping your baby at your breast, and it might just come when you're not looking.

☆ **Latching on.** This just means getting your baby's mouth properly around your nipple in order to make a seal, allowing her to drink the milk. This is the most important thing to master, because without it your baby's mouth will come off the whole time, she will be permanently hungry, milk will go everywhere and you will both get very upset. In the maternity wards, scary paediatric nurses will come around and show you how to get your baby to latch on, but it's always an unpleasant experience. The temptation to tell her to 'just sod off and leave me alone' can be overbearing, but try to resist and remember that she is only doing her job, and trying to help you.

Study all the positions suggested in baby manuals to get your baby into for latching on but don't treat them as gospel. With a bit of experimenting you will find what works for you and your baby.

Squeezing a drop of your breast milk onto your baby's lips so that she knows what she's missing can help to make her turn her head towards you and get the right idea. Stroking her cheek on your breast side will also make her head turn that way. If all else fails, just get that nipple to her mouth somehow, and hope for the best.

☆ **Foremilk and hindmilk:** Basically, the first bit that comes out is thin and watery, and satisfies your baby's thirst. After a few minutes this turns into hindmilk, which is thicker, and has more sugar and other goodies in it. Your baby needs enough of both, or she will become either dehydrated or lacking in energy. If, for example, your baby always has a good start but drops off after two minutes, then she's only filling up on water and will be starving later on.

☆ **Feedback loop:** Not when your baby turns around and feeds you, but a very clever and also very annoying system, whereby the more you feed, the more milk you make, and vice versa. What this means to you is that if you let your baby snack on tiny feeds very often, and don't let him finish a proper big feed, your body will go into overdrive and make pints and pints of the stuff, which will be thinner and less nutritious than it should be because your body hasn't had the time, or energy, to make good-quality super-food in between all this feeding. The consequence is that your baby gets hungry every couple of hours, so you feed him more often, and you make lots more watery milk. See? Try, if possible, to avoid this feedback nightmare by having fewer, bigger feeds.

☆ **A little note about nipples:** All the sucking, pulling, wetting and drying can cause trouble in the nipple department. Everything from a bit sore, to dry, cracked and even bleeding is possible, but the good news is that most of this is curable. Cracked nipples often means your baby is not latching on properly, so try changing her position when she feeds. Other causes are that your baby has thrush in her mouth (not uncommon, so don't worry) or that you have eczema. The best cure for sore nipples is breast milk, oddly enough, but if things get very bad then try some nipple cream. Buying this is more embarrassing than buying condoms by a factor of a hundred, but buy it you must if your nipples are badly cracked. And preferably before then. You can also use vitamin E oil if you can't summon up the courage.

The hardest part: try to keep very calm and relaxed. I've breastfed in tears, exasperated at the difficulty of doing what should be so natural. And I've got cross, and annoyed with myself and my baby too. In other words, I've done everything they tell you not to do. It's very hard not to get upset when feeding isn't going well, but babies are sensitive little creatures, and when they sense you have become tense, they offer consolation by tensing up too. Chill, breathe, don't worry and keep trying.

Common Concerns
I'm not making enough milk!
Yes you are. We are *all* convinced at some point, or several points, that we are not making enough milk for our baby, that she will starve to death any second now, and that it's all our fault because we've started cutting the carbs already or we stayed up late to finish a novel. All is well. Somehow (don't even think of asking me how, because I still haven't got a clue) your body makes just enough milk at just the right temperature and with just the right ingredients to

keep your baby healthy and fed. Lucky really, because if we had to do it we'd mess it all up and get in a flap.

Every baby is different, and if yours suddenly seems to need feeding more often, then feed her more often, providing you are sure she is actually getting the milk down properly and not just having a little play with you. (They do this.) If it is starting to wear you down, if you don't think you are producing enough milk, or if you think something is not working for either of you, then just ask your health visitor, who might suggest topping up with a bottle every so often.

Where to Feed

Most childcare books will tell you to find a quiet, comfortable place, where you can have a relaxed, uninterrupted feed. In reality, you will sit wherever you can when the time strikes: in a café, at a bus stop, on a park bench, or, occasionally, in a quiet, comfortable place. This is especially true for subsequent babies, who are lucky to get fed at all, frankly, what with all the chaos caused by Baby (now Toddler) Number One. It is a good plan to have 'a place' at home where you do day feeds, and for me this had to be within reach of the television and remote controls, a phone and a huge glass of water.

Some Yummy Mummies can even feed *on the go*, which impresses me beyond measure, but I'm not convinced it's such a good experience for the baby, and I've never tried it. I'm always happy to be proved wrong, though.

Feeding in Public

You must, must do this. Feeding in public has become much more acceptable since my first baby was born, back in the Dark Ages of 1998 (that it was ever *unacceptable* still brings me out in a rage), but lots of us still feel shy about it. We mustn't. The more we give in to prudish, antediluvian ideas that doing what Nature intended is somehow gross and unsightly, the longer the pompous, shallow-minded, uneducated, ego-centric philistines who spread these ideas will continue to win. If your baby is hungry, then get 'em out and feed the poor wee thing. If a sexually frustrated man finds it awkward then it's no concern of yours. **Be bold, be proud and show them who's boss** – even if, deep down, you are horribly embarrassed and would far rather cut your left arm off. It's the principle of the thing.

Don't sit down without:

☆ A huge glass of water – it's very thirsty work.
☆ An extra pillow, to support your arm: a baby's head gets very heavy after fifteen minutes or more.
☆ Cordless and mobile phones – perfect 'catch-up' time, and your mum will always phone the minute you start feeding.
☆ The TV remote control/a radio.
☆ A magazine full of beautiful people to aspire to, or a book which can be read in ten-minute chunks. This one is ideal of course.
☆ A cloth for spillages.
☆ Something to eat – it's also hungry work.
☆ Something to put your feet up on. Beating the varicose veins while you breastfeed means you are multi-tasking already. What a pro.

Eating the Right Stuff

You are what you eat, and so is your breast milk. If your baby seems to be unhappy to drink what you are producing, then take a look at your diet and see if it could be something you are consuming which is causing the trouble. Here are some good starters:

What to cut out

☆ **Caffeine**: It's worth trying this one out – drink a couple of coffees before a feed, and see if your baby gets a bit edgy. It's a neat demonstration that what you consume goes straight into your breast milk. Or you could just believe me and be done with it.
☆ **Alcohol**: After nine months of abstinence you would have to be *mad* to continue refusing all alcoholic indulgence now. Of *course* the odd tipple is fine, but getting thoroughly wasted will make your milk taste odd, and your baby very drowsy too. It can come in handy if you want some extra sleep in the morning (you'll need it after a night out), but it's not something I would recommend. And a baby hangover can't be very nice either.

☆ **Colic-inducers**: Some of my friends have noticed that their babies get worse colic after Mummy has been eating broccoli, garlic, onions, cabbage, apples and Brussel sprouts. The cabbage soup diet may well shift the baby flab, but my guess is it causes some dreadful colic too. Mine didn't like apples, but since I love them I decided to live with the colicky baby and enjoy the crunch.

☆ **Spicy foods**: I never found this to be a problem and I continued to eat curries, chillies, you name it. But I have heard reports of babies who don't like what spicy food does to Mummy's milk, so if there's resistance I'm afraid you may have to go bland for a while.

What to add:

☆ **Iron**: Eating extra iron, or taking supplements (if your doctor gives the all-clear), can be very helpful when you're breastfeeding, because your own supplies may be depleted, making you very tired, and tired ladies not only look bad, but also find it more difficult to produce good breast milk.

☆ Apart from iron, all the usual **'quality, not quantity'** advice applies to breastfeeding, and if you stick to the good old 'plenty of fresh fruit and veggies, low-fat dairy produce, whole grains, protein, calcium and iron' you will be able to feed your baby perfectly well.

☆ **Water:** If you haven't got the message yet, let me say it again: breastfeeding makes you very thirsty and tired. Water rehydrates you and makes you feel perkier.

The Crying Baby Checklist

Your baby will cry sometimes. Even if you are the best Yummy Mummy in the world there will be crying, because it's a very important part of being a baby and learning to use those tiny yet incredibly powerful lungs and vocal cords. If your baby never, ever cries then, rather than awarding yourself an Elemis Spa weekend, you should definitely go and see a doctor about it.

The noise of a small baby crying is one of those mad, biologically linked stimuli, which, to anyone who hasn't had a baby, is simply irritating and socially unacceptable, but to anyone who has, is stomach-knottingly upsetting and impossible to ignore. Before I had a baby I don't think I'd ever really noticed babies crying much. Now, and I suspect forevermore, I'm like the kid from *The Sixth Sense*, except that instead of seeing dead people I hear crying children. Mildly less shocking, but equally distracting and gut-wrenching.

Why? Why do they cry? We spend all day looking after them, tending to their every want and need, and yet still we get the high-pitched noise? Why? Couldn't they just, oh, I don't know, point or something? No, coz it's all bi-o-logy, innit. Crying is a remarkably effective weapon, given the relative uselessness of newborn human babies. Don't get me wrong, I drool over a sweet-smelling, soft-skinned, teeny-weeny-fingered new baby as much as the next Yummy Mummy, but compared with the rest of the animal king-dom, our offspring are woefully unable to do anything for them-selves for a very long time. They can't even sit up until they are about five months old, and most still require regular help and guid-ance until they're well into their thirties.

The result of this 'needing lots of help' combined with the 'not being able to tell you *what* they need' is a highly effective alert mechanism, which we call **crying**. The first time you hear your baby cry can affect you so strongly you can feel like you've been plugged into the mains. Suddenly, your entire body is attuned to this sound, as you search desperately for a way of making your baby happy. Your baby will only cry because it wants something and you are not sorting it out. Until you do, your clever baby will carry on crying, while you try desperately to rule out every possible cause for this upset.

The good news is that most crying is very easy to sort out, because your baby is simply either:

☆ hungry
☆ sitting in a wet or dirty nappy, or
☆ tired.

Or all three, in which case you should probably get some help for the morning, because life's getting on top of you. Once you've ruled out any of these (if, say, she's been asleep for two hours, and you've just fed and changed her), then the next hit-list is as follows:

☆ She needs winding after all that food/milk. Always, *always* spend five minutes with your baby over your shoulder, patting her back while you jog gently up and down. Trapped wind hurts like mad, and the burps a baby can produce are very impressive.
☆ She is too hot/too cold.
☆ She is teething.
☆ She is thirsty.
☆ Something is uncomfortable (check clothing and positioning carefully: you've probably dropped a baby fork down the side of her bouncy chair or something).
☆ She is frustrated (this happens quite early on, and can be because she wants to reach something, express herself, crawl, or many other things).
☆ She is ill or in pain.

Another very common cause of crying, which is often never thought of, is that your baby is BORED. I remember discovering this for the first time and feeling rather stupid that it hadn't occurred to me before. I don't like sitting in the same position, looking at the same thing, doing the same thing or even being in the same room for long periods of time, so why should my baby? Babies are just mini versions of adults, and they suffer from boredom too. Sometimes a change of scene or activity is all that's required to make a really fractious, bad-tempered baby happy again. It's usually good for *your* mental wellbeing too, so take a cue from Junior, and go and do something else.

And my favourite **top tip** for cheering an unhappy baby up?

Putting a CD on and dancing! Just make sure you're not being overlooked by the whole street.

Is That a Cry, or a Moan?

To say that 'babies cry' is far too simple, because there are as many different types of crying as there are things a baby is trying to tell you. As well as your bog-standard, Economy Class crying, babies also moan, whimper, scream, screech (quite different from screaming), howl, sob, bawl, and so on. The amazing thing is that you will almost certainly become so familiar with all of these different noises that you'll immediately know whether your baby is hungry, angry or simply has his finger trapped in the shopping-trolley seatbelt-fastener. After a few months, you will recognise whether your baby's protestations require immediate first-aid, or whether a soft toy will provide enough distraction and entertainment for the three minutes it takes you to unload the last bits of shopping before it's back to feeding time again.

I can't stop my baby crying.

Some babies cry a lot more than others. A baby who cries and cries and cries is not only a cause for concern, but can also become so unbearable and draining that you can start to hate your baby and never want to see or hear him again. **Don't panic if you feel unable to deal with it any more.** You **must** get help from a health professional if you are worried about your baby's health or wellbeing, and equally so if you feel you are not coping. Prolonged crying *could* mean there is something peculiar going on, so go and get things checked out if you are worried at all.

Once any health problems are ruled out, and it just turns out that you have a very moany, colicky baby, it's time to start finding ways of getting through this difficult period, which could last for many months. Friends and family are the first port of call here: tell them about your troubles and frustration, and see if somebody could look after your baby for a few hours a couple of times a week, to give you a break from each other. This constant crying can be one of the most trying things about a new baby, and simply soldiering away on your own will help nobody.

The Curse of Colic

Colic is a complete pain in the neck. Actually, it's a pain in your baby's tummy, but for you it's a complete pain in the neck and the ears: it makes your baby scream for hours on end, and you both feel rotten. It can start at about three weeks, and lasts more than three months in many cases. Basically, your baby just cries and cries, especially in the evening, and it's as painful for you to hear your baby in such distress as it is for the colicky cherub.

Nobody is exactly sure what causes colic, but it always looks to me like trapped wind, or some digestive problem, because all the stomach clenching and screeching often stops soon after a good burp or something more fruitful at the other end. If I ate more acidic foods the colic seemed to get worse, and I've also heard that drinking cow's milk can be a cause (that's you drinking the cow's milk, not your baby – I hope you got that already...)

Colic-busters

There really aren't any absolute solutions to colic, but trying anything at all is worth it when things are very bad.

☆ **Gripe Water:** I tried this once, but it just went everywhere, and there was no improvement. I did feel virtuous for trying though. Available from Boots, and other good chemists.

☆ **Water off a teaspoon:** This did work for our babies. We would get a teaspoonful of cooled boiled water, and try, using all four of our combined arms, and all 20 of our digits, to get one spoonful down the screaming hatch. After much terrifying coughing and spluttering, said baby was usually content within five minutes or so, after a huge burp.

☆ Another way we got our colicky babies to calm down was by **lying them across our lap on their tummy and rubbing their back**, occasionally quite strongly, while trying to keep a dummy in with one finger. If there was a telly on in the background this worked a treat as well, especially if it was something high-octane and fast. The ten o'clock news was hopeless.

☆ **Carry your baby face down on your forearm**, with your hand firmly between their legs and their cheek resting by your inner elbow (if you can imagine that) and rock and swing them to and fro that way. Either it really does sort the colic out, or they are just so frightened by the ground zooming by at a weird angle that it shuts them up completely. It works well, so never mind why.

☆ **Try putting your baby in a warm bath.** This can calm her down enough to make her forget her woes and loosen the trapped wind – and we all know where it's going from there. Oh it's only a tiny baby fart, chill out.

Most importantly, **don't feel that you are to blame for the crying**, and that you are somehow failing by not being able to cheer her up. If you've tried everything in the lists above, and probably some other things I haven't thought of, then you really are trying your hardest, and you should feel good about that. Don't give up: one day the sun will rise and your baby, miraculously and without any warning, will suddenly decide she doesn't need to cry any more. Nobody will ever be sure why, but it will happen, and your life will move on to pastures quieter.

Baby Clothes: Dolce & Gabbana or H&M?

Every Yummy Mummy wants a Yummy Baby. This is only natural, since your baby is basically an extension of you for quite a long time, and there's no point making yourself look lovely only to push around a grubby pram with a badly dressed baby in it. And anyway, choosing clothes for a new baby cheers most girls up, and there's less pressure to get it right: their bums always look big in everything.

BUT buying baby clothes is not just a case of 'see a really cute outfit and buy it'. There are some crucial things to know, which I only discovered after making every mistake in the (at that point, sadly unwritten) book. With such fantastic babywear available these days, our offspring can be better dressed than we are, and it's very easy to get carried away. The following should help you out, and save you a small fortune on unused garments:

☆ **Babies grow.** Not that surprising, really, but the rate at which they outgrow clothes never ceased to shock me. Some gorgeous garments were literally worn only once (or even never, if they managed to lie hidden at the bottom of a drawer for a week or two). The solution is always to buy clothes which are slightly too big and to resist buying too much. It may all look dead cute but if it's never worn it's a waste.

☆ **Babies crawl.** Not such an issue for little boys, but crawling is very hard on the knees, and new tights will be worn through quickly. Dresses tend to ride up badly and just get in the way, so trousers are probably best for this stage.

☆ **Babies throw up.** All the time, and usually within three minutes of getting dressed. Even the teeniest little posset will ruin the front of a baby's top, and if, like me, you always forget to put a bib on your baby, then it's best to get clothes for the upper body which don't mind being wiped a lot. I still think there's a market for rubber baby clothes. **NOTE**: you will become very familiar with possets. These mouthful-sized portions of baby sick (mmm!) usually contain little more than fresh milk, but can occasionally be very nasty indeed. It's just a tiny bit which follows through after a baby burp, and doesn't count as being sick – but try telling that to the stained shoulder of your favourite shirt. Muslin cloth – quick!

☆ **Poppers.** All baby clothes must have poppers at the crotch. When my parents gave us some stunning hand-made dungarees from Peru, with no poppers, I swore I wouldn't mind removing them completely every time I had to change a nappy. What actually happened was that I ended up swearing a lot more, and wishing I'd never seen the impractical things. No poppers, no buy.

☆ **Fastenings.** Again, I never thought about the practical side until I had wrestled several babies into complicated but pretty garments. Babies wriggle and squirm when you try to dress them, and they only need to be a little older than newborn before they can put up quite a fight. Carefully inserting rows of tiny buttons into buttonholes the size of a pumpkin seed is a complete nightmare, even if they do look sweet. Velcro may seem brilliant, but it's far too easy for determined fingers to pull open again, and ties are a complete no-no for me: too scary to think of the strangulation potential there. Zips are great on coats and for everything else it's poppers all the way. Whoever invented them is a genius, and should have a statue in Trafalgar Square.

With all of this knowledge under your belt you are now ready to stock up your baby's wardrobe. Just keep reminding yourself not to buy every cute thing in sight, and you will have a happy, healthy credit card as well as a trendy, smart baby at the end of the spree.

1. Babygros
A bit like boiler-suits but with feet too, they're what all my babies used to sleep in. During the day it's nice to change them into something slightly more interesting, if only for something to do. They don't actually need anything else, but it's a very un-funky baby who lives in babygros. Check regularly that your baby hasn't grown so that her toes are getting squashed at the bottom. If this happens you can always just cut the ends off (without your baby in it) until you get some new ones.

2. Bodies
Buy loads of these. Bodies, whether long- or short-sleeved, are the staple of every baby's wardrobe. Every time I think I have enough bodies to clothe all the babies in Northern Europe, a combination of a poo disaster, some painting, splashing and a particularly messy eating session render every one filthy, wet and useless, and I wish I had even more.

3. Footwear
If Jimmy Choo made shoes for the under-threes, he would be a very distressed, but even richer man: babies and toddlers wreck shoes almost as quickly as you can work out how to put them on properly. All that crawling, falling over, sliding, splashing in mud and puddles and general carelessness means beautiful baby shoes are left grubby, scuffed, torn and holey within weeks. Unfortunately, baby footwear

is insanely expensive considering how quickly they grow out of their shoes or just destroy them, but it's the one area where spending money on good quality and a good fit is essential – as Topsy and Tim learned early on, your toes grow crooked if your shoes are too tight, and when she does come to trying on her first pair of those Choos, she will thank you for having bought some good baby shoes. For early crawling, just some soft 'padders' are fine, but as soon as your baby is sturdy on her feet then try to get some stronger shoes with good ankle support. This is also a good place to add some junior street-style – I was won over by a pair of baby Nike trainers, and had one seriously cool baby boy for a few months.

Don't get shoes with laces – Velcro is much easier, and it's too far away from their fingers for them to pull open all the time. Shoes with thick, heavy soles are a bad idea as it makes them walk badly and puts strain on their back and neck. In the winter, look for a pair which are either warm and padded already or which have enough room for thick tights and socks – baby feet get cold very quickly, and you'll be back indoors before you know it. For the summer months, lighter sandals are a good idea, but for crawlers make sure their toes are covered: if not they will scrape all the skin off the top of their toes and feet, which is probably fairly unpleasant.

And finally, **check that your baby's shoes still fit** about twice as often as you think you should: many times I've been horrified that I hadn't noticed my children were in shoes about two sizes too small – they just grow so fast!! (I notice this section is miles longer than any other. Maybe I do have a shoe obsession after all?)

4. Headgear

In the summer, a hat with a brim is essential, and you can go the whole ray-banishing hog by getting one with flaps down the back and sides of the neck. They look really silly but are probably the best way of preventing sunburn. Hats are a real battleground, because all babies and toddlers want to do is pull them off. My solution has been to buy summer hats which tie on, and balaclavas for the winter. Try getting *that* off, young man.

5. Baby sleeping bags

A friend of mine showed me her baby's one recently, and now I wish I had known about them earlier. As babies kick their blankets over their heads within 30 seconds of being tucked in, it's very hard to keep them all snuggly and warm while they are lying down. Baby sleeping bags cleverly do up over the shoulders like a vest, so there's no way of crawling out of them. They keep your baby's temperature constant, and there are no arms, thus avoiding any restriction to all the essential hand- and arm-waving and chewing involved with being a baby. As I watched this contented baby play in her baby gym, neatly contained in her pink and white cocoon, I kicked myself for not having thought of this for mine. Maybe for the next one…

6. The rest

Long-sleeved Ts, a couple of shirts, trousers, a jumper or two, tights, socks (lots of these), and a seasonally appropriate coat, and you're good to go anywhere in comfortable, practical style.

Where to Get Your Yummy Baby Clothes

Budget: stylish, affordable babywear

As Mother's Luck would have it, cutting down the price does not mean compromising on style: baby clothes available on the high street are more beautiful, practical and stylish than they have ever been, and you don't have to re-mortgage your house to have a funky baby.

Here are some of the shops whose kids' ranges you will get to know very, very well in the next few years:

☆ Baby Gap   ☆ Petit Bateau
☆ George at Asda   ☆ Caramel
☆ Tesco   ☆ Mini Boden
☆ Monsoon Baby   ☆ Junior Jigsaw
☆ Next   ☆ Boots
☆ Mothercare   ☆ Gymboree

Finally, never forget hand-me-downs from kind, stylish friends, and never be too proud to buy baby clothes from car boot or jumble sales. At 20p for a T-shirt, who cares if it's been through a few washes already? Charity shops are a must, and I have so far found Paul Smith, Kenzo, DKNY and Ralph Lauren kids' clothes for almost nothing. With the money I save, I can splash out on something special and not feel the pinch.

Blow-out: Gucci, Pucci, Choo: the ultimate, luxury babywear

I have to put my tongue firmly in my cheek as I write this list, because some of the baby clothes available are just too fantastic and luxurious to be taken seriously. Baby Dolce & Gabbana? True. Completely ridiculous, but completely true, and completely something to put on your 'I don't expect to get this, but I'll ask anyway, because you never know' Christmas wish-list.

These clothes are the best quality a ton of money can buy, and having felt the difference between high street and designer, I know what I would buy if I could afford it. If you can, or even if you just can't quite, but deserve a treat, then add a little glamour to your baby's wardrobe. *They* won't care, but you will glow with pride. Here are just some of the Yummiest names to choose from:

- ☆ Kenzo
- ☆ Versace
- ☆ Dolce & Gabbana
- ☆ Paul Smith
- ☆ Paul and Joe
- ☆ Temperley for Little People
- ☆ Tigerlily
- ☆ Burberry

- ☆ Séraphine
- ☆ Little Darlings
- ☆ Joseph Baby
- ☆ Simonetta Tiny
- ☆ Baby Graziella
- ☆ Christian Lacroix
- ☆ Baby Dior
- ☆ Ralph Lauren

PART SEVEN

Your First Few Months

With the immediate shock of the birth and the lack of leg-waxing opportunity now hopefully subsided, you can start to face the next few months of Yummy Mummyhood. What's really important to remember at all times is that there is no reason AT ALL why things should start to feel easy or manageable during this period. A few months is *almost* long enough to get used to a new DVD player or a new car, but it is certainly *nowhere near* the length of time required to get used to being a mum, or learning how to be responsible for a child.

I have no idea how long that takes, as I haven't got there yet, but you should treat the first few months with a baby as one long test of your endurance and adaptability. You *will* manage, but anyone who suggests you should be cruising along with your eyes closed by now is just being an insensitive prat.

I Just Don't Have a *Thing* to Wear!!

If, like me, you spent the last four months of your pregnancy stroking and drooling over the beautiful, slimline, totally unsqueeze-into-able contents of your wardrobe, then you probably also looked forward to swanning about in some of these garments soon after the huge lump was removed from your abdomen.

Somewhat cruelly, it doesn't work like this. Firstly, even *you* won't bounce straight back into your pre-pregnancy dresses, and secondly, babies are terribly philistine in their lack of understanding and care for how a lady looks and feels about herself, especially if the lady in question is their own mother. This will all change during their teenage years, when what you wear will become paramount to their 'cred' and social acceptability, but that's a long way off: the focus here is on new babies, who play almost as much havoc with your wardrobe as unborn ones.

The Problem: Breastfeeding

Actually, breastfeeding should never, EVER be seen as a problem. But it does have the following impact on what you can (and should) wear:

☆ **Dresses are out!** In order to breastfeed you need to be able to get a breast (or at least a nipple) to your baby, and this is impossible in a dress without virtually stripping from either the neck down or the hem up. Everyone convinces themselves that it *is* possible only once (usually when there's a wedding or a summer party to go to, and there's a neglected designer number just crying out for an airing). Unless you are into public nudity, you will learn from the humiliating and frustrating incident and stick to separates in future.

☆ **Separates are in.** Anything which can easily be hoiked up to breast-height without ripping, stretching or looking dishevelled is what you're after. Keep tops loose, but NOT baggy: we're going for shape not cover-up now the pregnancy's over, remember.

☆ **Banish all black.** This was the hardest one for me: I *love* black, and everyone knows it's the best colour for helping the 'slimline' look but milk, whether breast or bottle, is **white**. This means that any clothes which are darker than pale cream will show tons of white marks, and should either be avoided altogether, or never *ever* worn without a large cloth over your shoulder. This looks pretty stupid, but will ensure a blemish-free outfit, should it suddenly be needed. Hey presto!

☆ **Shirts.** This is a tricky one: shirts are great for reducing the 'I look like Pamela Anderson' problem, as they lengthen your neck and streamline everything. BUT, unless they are loose enough to be lifted UP to breastfeed (and shirts which are that loose tend to look like sacks), then you will have to *unbutton* them to your midriff and feed that way, which leaves you very exposed across your whole front. Up to you, but it's not the most subtle option.

☆ **Clinging on.** I didn't know this, but when you are breastfeeding you can't go anywhere without wearing breast pads. These are *essential* if you want to avoid the appearance of two dark wet patches where your nipples are, and for emergency wiping during feeds. Unfortunately, breast pads are quite thick, and they show through thin tops. Much like the double-bump caused by an ill-fitting bra, so walking about with two discs protruding through your skinny T-shirt is not a look to covet. Look in the mirror before you go out, and throw a cardigan, gilet or wrap over the top if you spy any sign of padding or it's less a case of 'headlights' and more a case of 'full beam'.

TOP TIP: *ALWAYS put a couple of spare breast pads in your handbag when you go out. Have spares dotted around in useful places, like the car's glove compartment (beside the scraps of tissue, cracked CD covers and mouldy apple cores), your wallet, the baby's changing bag, every coat pocket, including your husband's, every bag you own and might ever take out with you. I have been caught short hundreds of times, and it is always horribly embarrassing. And always dispose of them carefully: my best friend's boyfriend still blushes when he sees me, having woken up on his sofa with one of my old breast pads stuck to his cheek. I did* mean *to throw it in the bin. I just forgot.*

The Problem: I'm Just Not Quite the Shape I Used to Be

Not yet, but you will be soon if you want to be and work at it. In the meantime, if you've been a good girl throughout your pregnancy and if your baby has been kind to you, you should only look marginally different from how you looked before, except that several bits will remain **larger** for a while, in particular your tummy, bum and boobs. Not much then!

Many women enjoy their new, more curvaceous shape, as it feels nice and feminine, but it does mean that what you wear needs a little more consideration than usual.

The Problem: Crawling About on Your Knees

I always forget about this bit, until it's too late and my best trousers are ruined: when you have a new baby you will spend *loads* of time either kneeling down to change them, sitting cross-legged on the floor gazing at them, or generally doing things which are bad for your trousers. Wear a pair that you don't care too much about when you're at home, and keep your Jigsaw best for out on the town. But do NOT fall into the trap of wearing tracksuit trousers all the time – this is so easy to do, but will leave you feeling as frumpy as a big, fat frumpy blob, and you will start to slide down the slippery slope towards grey underwear and unwashed hair. It's also great fun to dress up from head to toe once every week or so. You will feel lovely and grown-up again, and believe that the future bears some glamorous days if you can just hang in there!

Makeover Magic: Time-efficient Beauty Tips

Nobody has a greater need to feel beautiful than you, a New Yummy Mummy: months of maternity clothes, swollen ankles and free-for-all discussions about parts of your body most civilised people have the decency to keep quiet about, have passed, only to be replaced by relentless sleep-deprivation, a baby requiring 24-hour attention, and a neglected, unfamiliar body.

Under such circumstances, a severe self-esteem boost is called for, and the most effective remedy is a little body pampering and some glow-enhancing make-up.

But here's the rub: looking good when you've just had a baby is not as simple as it used to be. 'Me-time' is reduced to a fraction of what it was, your bathroom is now littered with plastic bath toys instead of aromatherapy candles, and when you do locate some miracle-working make-up, you will soon find that applying it with a wriggly baby on one hip is virtually impossible. To cap it all, your skin will probably have changed a fair bit, and now needs a whole new range of products.

Do not despair! There are simple ways to make the whole 'beauty routine' thing a lot easier and more successful. You just need to adapt to your new physical and practical situation, and you will soon feel and look fabulous again.

Beauty is Only Skin Deep

The massive changes you experience during pregnancy and giving birth can leave your skin in pretty rough condition. Yippee. Here are some things you should look out for:

☆ **Hyper-pigmentation.** After the birth, keep using your lightening products, because they will carry on removing old skin cells and increasing the production of new, un-marked ones. Stick to the high-factor sunscreen and wear some fashionable head-gear.

☆ **Dry skin.** The simple solution is to drink lots more water, but you should also invest in a super-hydrating day moisturiser and avoid too much washing and scrubbing, which just dries your skin out even more.

☆ **Shadows under your eyes.** No new mother should be without the best eye-cream she can afford and an under-eye skin-brightening product. I always had a spare in my handbag for those 'I'm coping really well' emergencies when bumping into other mothers in the park. *Tired? Moi?* Treat yourself to a really good eye-mask, and an eye-cream specifically made to refresh, tighten and brighten.

☆ **Stretch marks.** Keep up the crunches and sit-ups, and keep massaging your specifically designed stretch-mark products onto the affected area. If you're not feeling flush, then stick to pure Vitamin E oil and lots of hope.

☆ **Skin on the rest of your body.** This may feel a little under par too: a bit dry, hairy, pale and saggy. All of this can be helped with the fabulous products available these days. Try not to neglect your normal hair removal (sleek legs are a great way to start looking better), never forget how much a fake tan improves your mood, and keep slathering on the moisturising body lotions to finish the lovely look. Many now contain skin-tightening ingredients, which claim to make everything a little perkier – I have tried and tested many, and I actually think they work! Try to help the stretched skin on your breasts (an area often ignored, but very important) by continuing to apply your bust-firming creams if possible, and by doing some upper-body exercises if you can remember to.

☆ **Your legs.** They will be feeling heavy and tired from all the baby-carrying, so invest in a leg-reviving product to lift away the miles and miles of buggy-pushing, and don't forget regular feet treats and occasional pedicures to perk you up.

Top Beauty Products for New Yummy Mummies

Face

☆ **Origins Modern Friction**, for the gentlest microdermabrasion there is.

☆ **Clarins Beauty Flash Balm:** found in more bathrooms than almost any other product. What a start to the day! Try M&S Instant Beauty Lift for a cheaper alternative.

☆ **A firming day cream**, like **M&S Ceramide Formula** or one which combats pigmentation marks, like **Olay's Total Effects Anti-Ageing and Blemish Care**.

☆ **Elizabeth Arden's Eight-Hour Cream** should be in every mum's handbag, as it provides a lasting moisture surge for lips, hands and anywhere else.

☆ **Spot combater: Doctor Burt's Herbal Blemish Stick** can also be popped into your handbag and applied whenever spots dare to show signs of appearing – and they will…. **Origins Spot Remover** is also tiny and very effective.

☆ **Sun cream.** At least SPF30, at least one layer, and at least once a day. I *will* convince you to stay away from the Evil Rays.

☆ **The best night cream** you can afford, to mend all the damage done during each tiring day.

Eyes

- ☆ **Clarins Eye Revive Beauty Flash.** Same again, but for the eyes now – too kind!
- ☆ **Crabtree & Evelyn's Eye Gel Mask** is fantastic for relieving tired eyes, especially if you pop it in the fridge for a while beforehand.
- ☆ **Olay Total Effects Eye Transforming Cream** gives an immediate radiant glow.
- ☆ **Stila Eye Concealer.** What the creams don't manage to repair, this product will conceal instead. *Et voilà!*

Legs and feet

Please don't neglect your feet – it only takes a minute every day, and you will be so happy when you look down. Get a really good emery board for sanding away the dead skin, and a deeply moisturising leg and foot cream or gel with menthol to cool and refresh. **L'Occitane Exfoliating Foot Care** helps to prevent calluses which you will be more prone to with all the added walking about.

Fake tan

This is the final step in the total body gorgeous-making. Good old **St Tropez** still works brilliantly, and makes you look like you've been there for a week. The new breed of day-tanning creams make a honey-glow possible if you can't be bothered with the full 'disposable gloves and brown stains in the bathroom' charade.

Origins Let it Show can be applied as you walk out the door for an almost instant glow, and if you want a golden sheen as well then stock up on **Nuxe's Huile Prodigieuse Or**. It makes you shimmer and gleam like a model. Lovely.

Body

- ☆ **Dermalogica: The Ultimate Buffing Cloth.** My skin is as smooth as silk thanks to this miracle skin-sloughing cloth – it's the simplest start to achieving your new, glowing body.
- ☆ **Dove:** the **Firming Lotion and Intensive Firming Gel Cream** are the best value firming products I've found, and **Bliss Lemon and Sage Body Butter** keeps the driest, flakiest postnatal skin super-smooth and moisturised.

Don't forget to keep hair-free. Whether you're a shaver, a waxer or a creamer, this tiny detail makes a massive difference to your overall look and confidence. Veet home waxing strips are brilliant, and they also do some fab depilatory creams, which actually smell nice, and a hair minimising moisturiser which means you don't have to worry about these bits so often.

Hands

If you find your hands are looking a little neglected, treat them to a quick home manicure, or a special treat like **Elemis' Intensive Hand Repair.** Leave on overnight in some thin gloves for a mega-moisture boost. If you're short on time, **Crabtree & Evelyn's 60-Second Fix** smoothes and nourishes hands in one minute. **Cutex Hand and Nail** cream is cheap and very effective and **Olay's Total Effects Hand Treatment** combats age spots too. Treat your hands to a weekly exfoliation and deep moisturising mask to really make a difference, and always use a hand cream with SPF, to prevent age spots forming, as your skin may be more prone to them now.

New Mum, New Make-Up

When it comes to post-baby make-up there is one golden rule: **keep it simple**. Something strange happens to our brains after we give birth, which can make us do the most peculiar things and severely clouds our judgement. If you didn't suit blue mascara before you were pregnant, then you probably don't suit it now so stick with what you know. I honestly believed that my post-baby pink lip-gloss made me look healthy and sexy at the time, but looking at photographs of it now makes me wince.

Lipstick is a really bad idea with a baby anyway because if like me, you are constantly kissing them, they will look like they've got smallpox most of the time. Vaseline and Eight-Hour cream are perfect for adding shine and moisture at the same time.

Perfume should also be avoided for a few months after your baby is born, because babies use your smell to bond with and recognise you. If Mummy smells like Chanel No. 5, then every other woman out there wearing Chanel No. 5 will smell like Mummy as well. Very confusing. (NB: If you start to pong, reach straight for the nearest bottle of eau de toilette and apply liberally: baby-bonding doesn't give you the right to smell offensive.)

Top Make-up Tips for New Mums from Jeanine Lobell, founder of Stila Cosmetics

If you only have five minutes to get ready, apply a little under-eye concealer. This little step makes a huge difference.

Counteract any dullness with an illuminating foundation. For dark pigmentation, camouflage only where you need it using a concealer, either alone or over a light, tinted moisturiser.

Multi-use products are key and anything which can be blended with fingers saves a lot of hassle.

What suits you can change after you have a baby, so don't hold on to the same foundation you've used since school. Chances are your skin has changed a lot and it no longer disappears onto your skin. Having a baby is a great time to let go of old ideas and move on to something better.

Several tiny make-ups bags, rather than one big one, keep things tidier, and it means you only carry the one or two products you actually need throughout the day.

On the practical front, having a baby in tow while you are trying to apply make-up can be tricky. We've all done passenger-seat mascara-applying, but this is a whole new ball game: I've ended up with more foundation on my shirt than my face in the past, as tiny baby fingers have managed to find their way into the bottle and smear at will. If you don't want to make a complete mess of it:

☆ Give yourself plenty of extra time so that you're not hurrying, and try to do it when your baby is asleep. Alternatively…

☆ Pop your baby in a bouncy chair and show her the way it's done. It's never too early to teach the importance of blending.

☆ Choosing a colour palette also makes things simpler, because everything is already co-ordinated for you, so it takes the decisions out of your busy hands.

Hair

Hair can take a battering in the first few months: tiredness makes hair look lank and dull, and it can start to fall out in handfuls. I sweated like mad every night for a few months, leaving my hair greasy as well. Mmmmm, lovely. Luckily, with minimal effort, your hair can look lovely again, and it's one of the best ways to give yourself a polished 'I'm a Wonder-Mum' look.

Top Yummy Mummy Hair Tips from Daniel Galvin Senior and Lino Carbosiero

Let your body settle down after the birth and wait a few months before you have a re-style.

After the birth your moods may be going up and down a lot - keeping your hair in top condition and regularly having it cared for will help to keep you looking great and feeling better.

A wash and blow-dry is a new mum's quickest, most effective pick-me-up.

Try a daily supplement of Vitamin B complex, with added ascorbic acid. It can help to make healthier hair and nails.

Tiredness and stress can make your hair goes dry, so try these home remedies: apply over-ripe avocado pear, or wash hair with egg yolk, leave for an hour and then wash and condition as normal.

Busy mums need a style which is easy to manage, and which can look great just by running some product through the hair. Long hair is ideal, as it can quickly be tied back into a pretty, relaxed ponytail.

Never forget that your hair is your ultimate beauty asset: it should be treated like your best cashmere sweater, and never taken for granted.

Some women experience very pronounced hair loss after having a baby, which often becomes distressing and can have a negative psychological effect. The new Philip Kingsley Post Partum Hair Management service gives an analysis of your scalp and hair, and offers advice on encouraging growth, diet, and improving hair condition. Or you could just ask your own hairdresser to take a look at the amount of hair you are losing, and see if she can suggest anything to help.

Yes, But How and *When?*

If you are starting to wonder how you will ever manage to find the *time* to do all of this, then wonder no more: you will make some.

Noella Gabriel, Director of Product and Treatment Development at Elemis

When you have a new baby, it's quality not quantity which counts. You have so much less time, but it's vital for your health and wellbeing to make time for yourself and to treat your body and mind. Too many women deprive themselves of any comforts and luxuries because of their anxieties about the baby.

Well said. If you want to find ten minutes to have a relaxing bath or to apply a fake tan, you will find those ten minutes. If you invest in a personal favourite pampering product, even if it means splashing out, this will be your big treat, and you won't feel hard-done-by at the end of a long day with your baby. You have earned it!

Oh, and don't even *think* about pampering yourself if your baby is awake. The whole point is to relax, and this is impossible if you are listening out for baby noises, or trying to play peek-a-boo with a face-pack on. Wait until the all-clear and indulge properly.

And finally, **don't give up making an effort**. You may feel pretty rough for a while, but by spending even the smallest amount of time making yourself look and feel more beautiful, your self-esteem will get the boost it needs, and those early months will feel much better. And you are *so* worth it.

Sexy Mama: Getting That Body Back in Order

One thing you will notice after your have your baby is that you still look fairly pregnant for a good few weeks, or even months. This is infuriating, especially as everyone you talk to looks straight at your stomach, to see how things are shaping up. I made almost the worst error any woman can ever make by asking a mum at the school gates how many weeks she had to go until her baby was born. It turned out she had given birth four weeks ago. Ouch!

The encouraging news is that you can *start* to get your body back into something resembling normal from the word 'go'. If you take it very slowly, and keep your Sensible, Intelligent Woman hat on, you shouldn't have any trouble at all.

Before we start, some things we need to get clear:

☆ Your 'in order' might not be the same as my 'in order', but we should agree that **you do not have to turn into a big blob** when you become a mother.

☆ **You will *never* go back to your exact former shape and size.** Pregnancy makes your actual body size change (I mean in terms of bone structure, etc.) and trying to fight this is futile and silly.

☆ **Do not expect quick results.** Many Yummy Mummies look at least five months pregnant for a few weeks after the birth, and it's not because they don't care, it's because they've just had a baby.

☆ **No pain, no gain**. That is our mantra, and if you want to have a toned, fit body again, you will have to work even harder at it than you did before. Sorry, but it's true.

☆ **You may like your new shape.** For many of us, having a baby makes us look at our bodies in a new way, and we suddenly discover that being more 'womanly' is a good thing. If this is you, then hooray! You probably won't want to lose a whole lot of weight, but you *will* still need some firming up to feel strong and sexy again.

☆ **Check with your doctor or midwife** if you are not sure whether to get the trainers out yet.

In the first weeks after the birth you will still be in recovery so doing lots of exercise is a Bad Plan.

A Good Plan is to treat these first weeks as a warm-up for what's to come by going for short hobbles (walking hurts a bit for a few days), followed by longer, brisker, pain-free walks, to get some cornering practice in with your new, shiny pram. As with exercising in pregnancy, *you* know your own body and its limitations better than anyone, so **do what feels OK to you, and stop if you feel bad.**

You will hear about the six-week check, which is basically a final 'Off You Go Now' from your doctor, because by this stage most stitches, problems, stretching and general post-birth carnage has sorted itself out. If you want to wait until you've had your six-week check then do, but if you are feeling confident and want to get going sooner, then book yourself a doctor's appointment earlier and get toning!

Here are some tried and tested ways of losing the post-baby wobble. Most are fairly obvious, but it's amazing how much of getting fit *is* obvious: we just need someone to tell us what we already know and make us get out there and sort it out.

1. Tummy
Let's start where it shows most. Looking at your post-baby tummy will not make you very happy, especially if you had something more along the Gwen Stefani lines in mind. Fear not: a washboard is yours for the taking if you are prepared to work at it.

WARNING: Pregnancy can cause your abdominal muscles to separate, resulting in back pain and damage to your abdomen if you strain them. Before doing any crunches or sit-ups check that these muscles are coming back together by lying on your back, putting your fingers above your tummy button, and lifting your head and shoulders up using your abs. If you can feel a gap of more than three fingers between the left and right abdominal muscles, then you should stick to pelvic tilts and transversus abdominus exercises. Once there is only a gap of one finger, you can go on to more exciting stuff.

Pelvic tilts

Very sexy move, this. Lie on your back with your knees bent. As you breathe out, pull your abs in, and try to flatten the small of your back down towards the floor and hold for three. Oooh, baby.

Transversus abdominus

This is the deepest layer of muscle in the tummy zone. It's also a bit of Latin for you. Kneel on all fours. Now stop laughing, and just kneel on all fours, and, with your back flat, pull your tummy in towards your spine, hold, and release. If you keep laughing it won't work at all.

Crunches

Before you go for the full sit-ups, try doing small but effective stomach crunches every day. Get on your back again, hands behind your head (or by your side if you're not strong enough yet), legs bent, and squeeze your abs to lift your head and shoulders an inch or so off the floor. Hold for three, slowly go back down, and then do it as many times as you can, even if you need to fart a lot. Three sets of ten should do for starters. Don't use your arms or back to lift yourself up, just feel your stomach muscles doing all the work.

Sit-ups

If you are really sure you are ready, then go for the full monty. Watching people try to do sit-ups in a gym is depressing, because 90% of them are doing it wrong and ruining their back and having absolutely no effect on their stomach muscles at all. When you do sit-ups, the only muscles which should be working are your abs. If you are jerking up and down, using your arms, back, legs and neck to get you up there, then you will do yourself an injury, and your stomach muscles will be no stronger. Concentrate really hard on only using your abs, do sit-ups slowly and in a controlled way, and don't feel you need to sit right up: just raising your head and shoulders to 45 degrees is plenty. Keeping your back straight and your eyes and head looking upwards will also make the exercise more effective. If you are doing sit-ups and you can't feel your stomach muscles working hard, then you are not doing them properly. It's not how many you do, but how effective each one is. No slacking, in other words.

2. Running

For busy Yummy Mummies, running is the best exercise there is, because it tones your entire body up without wasting any time getting to a gym and you get some fresh air. Change, run, stretch, job done. This is where your pre-pregnancy work will really show, because if you put the work in before, you may be able to run within about six weeks of the birth (if you get the all-clear).

There are a couple of problems with running, though:

☆ **Breasts:** These are now very big and heavy if you are breastfeeding, and you may have to wear not just one sports bra, but several. I used to run in three bras (bloody hell!) which must have looked dreadful, but it worked.
☆ **Leakage** (down below): Even if you have been doing your pelvic-floors as regularly as a supermodel does her eyebrows, you will leak as you run. As in wee yourself, yes, and possibly bleed a fair bit too. I know it's not nice, but it's true, so never go running without a maternity pad in place, and you might even think about taking a spare one with you in case, like me, you leak through one on your way around the park. This is all very unglamorous – I'm so sorry.
☆ **Timing feeds:** Not your own, although that helps, but the breastfeeds. Running just after you've fed is the best time, because your breasts are empty and therefore lighter. I remember feeding Charlie two minutes before the Tesco Race for Life kicked off, and getting straight back for another feed the minute I'd got my breath back. He probably just got a mouthful of endorphins and some sweat, but he seemed very happy with his lot.

3. Swimming

You might not be able to swim for several weeks after the birth because of stitches, leakage, infections, or dread at having to reveal your post-birth tummy to the attendants, so check with your doctor. If you've spent the best part of your pregnancy flopping about in a pool, then you probably want to keep as far away from the place as possible. If not, then swimming is a very good way to get back in shape, because it doesn't bash your body about, and it tones all of your muscles. Get a gorgeous new swimming costume, though – nobody deserves it more, and you'll be so happy to throw your stretched maternity one away.

4. Pilates

If ever a form of exercise were tailor-made for Yummy Mummies, it's Pilates:

☆ It sounds kind of groovy (Pi-laaa-tes, daaahling) and separates out those who can say it properly from those who can't (I do hope your tongue is still glued to the inside of your cheek, by the way – remember what I said about keeping a sense of humour?).
☆ It works all the parts which pregnancy so effectively messes up.
☆ It's low-impact, which is good for bouncing boobs.
☆ It makes your muscles longer and leaner-looking, rather than shorter and squatter, *and*
☆ You can wear some extremely gorgeous clothes while you're toning and honing.

If you didn't do any Pilates during your pregnancy or before, then find a teacher who knows about postnatal issues, and who can take a bit more time to help you out. I know to my shame that all the 'lying on the floor and barely moving at all' is *much* more strenuous than it looks, and if your abs have been on extended leave since you were fifteen, you won't be able to do half of it without looking like an idiot and hurting yourself (as happened to me). With time, you can increase the amount you do, and soon you will have a strong back and abdomen once more.

5. Weights

This is something you can do almost immediately, because there is no jumping involved, and if you have been doing weights all the way through your pregnancy anyway, your body will be used to it. Doing weights also increases your metabolism so you can burn calories in your sleep.

WARNING: All your joints and ligaments are still very soft, thanks to all the hormone relaxin, so don't over-strain yourself.

6. Walking

Sounds stupid, I know, but don't underestimate the belly-shifting potential of pushing a pram around for miles. Add a baby and lots of heavy shopping, and you are getting a fantastic aerobic workout. Try not to do too much of this when your baby is awake – I imagine it's quite boring for her – but if she nods off on the way into town, take the chance to go for a half-hour speed-walk, and watch those legs shape up.

Jeanine Lobell, founder of Stila Cosmetics

I feel more beautiful in a way, because I realise what my body is capable of now. I could live without the stretch marks, but I would never trade them to go back to the old me: I love this life!

I Need a Personal Trainer

No you absolutely do *not*. I know lots of body-beautiful actresses and television celebrities have personal trainers to help them tone up the post-baby wobble, but these people also have somebody to shop, clean, cook, look after the kids and co-ordinate their soft-furnishings for them. (Or so I've read, so it must be true.)

If you don't employ all of the above, then you don't need somebody to tell you how to get back into shape either. *You* are the best personal trainer you can get, so get some self-motivation sorted out, be honest with yourself and remember: if you want to get back into shape, you will. If Davina McCall had sat on the sofa for six months drinking cups of tea, she wouldn't look like the super-babe Yummy Mummy she is, so think of that when you're about to give up again. How many sit-ups have you done? Well, do twenty more.

Exactly *When* Am I Supposed to Fit All This Exercise In?

Now here you *do* have a good point. Finding the time to do any exercise is the trickiest part once you have a baby: they are awake well before the day starts, when they do sleep during the day you feel you ought to rest (or sort out some of the washing, empty the dishwasher, and put the first two hundred baby photos in an album), and by the time the evening comes, doing any more physical exercise feels almost impossible. But find the time you will, if you try some of these suggestions:

☆ **Join a gym with a crèche.** More and more gyms are cottoning on to the fact that 'mothers with babies' is one of their biggest target markets, and are opening crèches on site. Find one you like, be brave, and spend an hour in the morning burning fat with other mums. I met some of my best Mummy friends in the gym.

☆ **Swap babysitting times with your Mummy friends.** There are probably lots of other mums near you who are also desperate to get out for an hour and work up a pound-shifting sweat. See if you can set up an exercise swap so you can both benefit. This is particularly true if you are bringing up baby alone, or if your partner is away a lot. It does take time to find somebody you know and trust well enough to look after your most precious of preciouses, but within a few months you should be getting there...

☆ **Go whenever you can.** I used to go for a run horribly early in the morning before my husband went to work, or the minute he got home in the evenings. It was usually dark and cold at both of these times, and it took a very strong will to drag me out of bed, but if that's the only time you have then use it.

☆ **Schedule it in the diary.** If your exercise time is given the same weight (sorry) as his after-work meetings or doing the weekly shop, then it won't get squeezed out. If it's in the calendar, you might find it harder to get out of.

☆ **Use the weekends.** Here is the perfect opportunity for him to spend time bonding, and for you to spend time burning.

TOP TIP: *Enter a short, manageable running race. One of the best is the Race for Life, which is a women-only five-kilometre run, held all over the country to raise money for breast cancer. To call it a race is overstating it a little: there are women walking, jogging, sprinting, pushing buggies, puffing and panting all over the place, and the atmosphere at such events is always exhilarating. Once you've entered, you will have something to work towards. Even if you don't finish, at least you've tried, and you've helped to tone up your wobbly bits for a good cause.*

Check out www.runningdiary.co.uk to find a short race you might like to work towards.

Postnatal Depression

23 March

I've had enough. I don't want to do this any more. I hate every day. I'm so tired and bored of it all, and all I can see is another day, another week, and then week after week of the same, same, same stuff. And I'm so tired. I stand in the playground falling asleep on my feet, so blank and numb that I hardly know whether Phoebe is there or not. I'm no good for her. I'm no good for Emily either because I'm too sad all the time and it's affecting her, and I'm no good for H because I'm so awful to be around and all I do is complain and be miserable. He must hate me. I hate myself. But I can't help it and I want it all to stop. I want to stop. I often think it would be better for them all if I went away. Just went off one day and never came back, and they wouldn't even notice and they could all be happy and have fun again without this leaden, distant, irritable mother dragging herself about the place and making them all miserable too. It's my fault. I know I should just get it together and be stronger. Be a better mother and do my bit to look after the family and keep everyone happy. But I can't. I can't even do that and I don't think I ever will. I feel so guilty, and the longer it goes on, the worse I feel. I'm sorry, Emily. I'm sorry, Phoebe. I'm sorry, Harry. I'm a useless mother, and I don't want to do it any more.

Postnatal Depression is such an over-used and misunderstood expression that I'm always very cautious about using it. Nowadays, if you don't suffer PND at *some* point you could almost be excused for feeling short-changed: *every* Yummy Mummy worth her Louis Vuitton baby-bottle case (and all the rest of us who are at least aware of the existence of such luxuries, but can't afford them so have to make do with a free *Marie Claire* bag instead) gets postnatally depressed if she's doing it right, and coping without some sort of breakdown is just not playing the game properly.

This is lunacy. There is a *huge* difference between being exhausted and emotional, and suffering from depression. To worry about Postnatal Depression before you've even found a suitable mate is completely mad and unnecessary. It's far more likely that you'll be a bit grumpy and tearful for a while than that you'll need psychiatric help. And women are often grumpy and tearful anyway, so it's not such a big shock.

However, **it's wise to know what to look out for.** You probably don't have postnatal depression if you are:

☆ extremely tired
☆ sad quite a lot
☆ forgetful
☆ emotional
☆ frustrated
☆ totally uninterested in sex
☆ annoyed at being a dress-size too big

All of these are just perfectly normal human reactions to the massive change which has recently occurred in your life, and to the fact that your level of sleep-deprivation would be considered off-limits in most torture chambers. Of course you are exhausted, moody, weepy and confused. You've just had a baby – what did anyone expect?! Most of these symptoms will pass within a few months as you begin to get some regular (if still woefully inadequate) sleep, and as you adjust to your new life and role.

You *might* have Postnatal Depression if you:

☆ are not coping *at all* with the daily routines of looking after a baby.
☆ often feel very negatively towards your baby or yourself.
☆ cannot get through a single day without crying.
☆ are unable to see the funny side of anything. Even elbow skin.
☆ don't ever want to leave the house.
☆ stop caring: about your appearance, about the state of your home, about your baby, or that you are still a dress-size too big.
☆ have a complete change of character.
☆ feel detached from reality.
☆ don't feel in control of the way you feel or behave much of the time
☆ have any of the above and have suffered from depression before.

Postnatal Depression is not to be confused with Postnatal Exhaustion and Shock (trademark). The latter is to be expected; the former is not. If you feel overwhelmed, overloaded and under-rested, then try to get some sleep and some help around the house, and wait for it to pass. But if you feel that you are completely losing track of reality, if you have stopped being able to make rational, sensible decisions, if you cannot get through a day without wishing it were over, if you have stopped living in a normal, safe way, or if your moods or behaviour frighten you then you need to get some help. If we call every difficult or sad day 'Postnatal Depression', it will make it a lot harder for those who really suffer to be taken seriously and given the help they need.

It's also useful to know that **PND doesn't necessarily strike immediately after you have a baby**. Lots of Yummy Mummies cruise along happily for months before things fall apart quite suddenly.

This is what happened to me after my second pregnancy: I was back to normal within days after the birth, cooking, cleaning, running, shopping, refusing all help and dismissing my friends' and family's suggestions that I was doing too much. I convinced myself that getting straight back into my normal routines would make the transition easier, and that I knew how to do it all now. Everything was great for about six months, and I was just patting myself on the back for being the most fabulous, capable Yummy Mummy on Earth, when my world fell apart, I realised I was deluding myself, and I had to accept defeat. Drat.

It's Good to Talk

By the time I had my second bout of PND I was much more ready to talk to other women about what I was going through, and I was amazed, and guiltily relieved, to learn that quite a few of them had had a similar experience. Yummy Mummies are brilliant at supporting one another, and it's also reassuring to know that people are looking out for you, and making sure you're OK.

Antidepressants

I was strongly against these 'pills for people who aren't as hard as nails' before I first took them, believing them to be for weak-minded losers who couldn't pull their socks up and get on with it. This reaction to a somewhat hard-nosed upbringing came to an abrupt halt when, on the advice of my doctor, I took my first dose of Prozac in 2001, while suffering from Postnatal Depression:

25 August, 2001

I feel like I am slightly drunk all the time. Things don't bother me so much and I feel really laid-back and relaxed. Had a BBQ with David and Caroline, and despite this being very boring, and the kids being quite a handful, I found it totally unstressful. I even caught myself smiling this evening, which was weird. I suddenly feel able to let things take their course rather than needing to control everything. The children are noticeably happier and are being lovely. It's like being on holiday from everything, and I love it.

From the moment I started taking the stuff our lives improved fantastically: I was happier and less volatile; we started spending more time as a family doing fun things; I was less rushed, obsessive and hyperactive; I didn't mind all the hitherto frustrating aspects of motherhood; and I could feel my whole body and mind slowing down and becoming more balanced. It felt as though a huge PAUSE button had been pressed, and we could all enjoy what we had at last. I took the antidepressants for a year, and I don't regret it at all. I wouldn't like to do it again, because I'm always wary of putting chemicals into my body, but under the circumstances it was worth it.

WARNING: the attitude towards antidepressants in this country is still fairly negative, and you may feel guilty or inadequate if you decide to take them. You shouldn't. If you break your leg, nobody chastises you for getting a plaster cast and some crutches, but if your *head* is a little out of sorts you're expected to stiffen that upper lip and soldier on. Now *that's* madness. Talk to your doctor, talk to people who have tried it, and make up your own mind whether it's worth a go or not. You should be aware, though, that antidepressants aren't intended as a quick-fix temporary solution to your problems.

☆ Most doctors recommend you take them for at least a year.
☆ They can have some unpleasant side-effects (headaches, trembling, dizziness among other things).
☆ They may make you feel worse.
☆ They may not work.
☆ They can be hard to come off unless you do it carefully and slowly.
☆ It's wise to use them in conjunction with some psychotherapy or counselling.

On balance, I suppose it's probably better *not* to mess with the neuro-chemical messengers in your brain, but if doing so makes the difference between a life which has become unbearable and one which is stable and enjoyable, then give me the little pills every time.

Counselling/Psychotherapy

'A shrink? *Moi*? I don't need to lie on a leather couch once a week talking to a complete stranger about whether I enjoy sex any more to get by', is what you might say. You might also say that you are coping fine and would rather go through the birth again than get some psycho-crappo-mumbo-jumbo-load-of-bollockso THERAPY!! (This is concrete proof that you do need some help by the way – go through birth again *already*? No, no and no.)

Well, this was pretty much my attitude when counselling was first suggested to me by my GP, and the first few weeks were a complete farce: I refused to co-operate by lying through my teeth, and she refused to give up by trying to make me co-operate. Finally, though, I realised how useful the 'complete stranger' element was: I could tell her anything without any preconceptions or judgements on her part. She just listened, understood and suggested ways of improving things.

The first and most useful challenge she set me, I shall pass on to you:

1. Tip all the baby's toys, books, puzzles and clothes on the floor, and sit in the middle of this bombsite without worrying about the mess and becoming frantic with unfulfilled desire to tidy it all up again immediately.
2. Leave it like this *all day*, so that you get used to the feeling of living beyond your control and in a complete pigsty.

The result was amazing: I was less stifled by all the baby-clutter within 24 hours, and could almost accept that my house would look nothing remotely like a *Vogue* interiors feature from now on.

Of course, you'll be back to tidying up and restoring some sense of style and order within weeks, but if you learn to chill out and cope with most of the mess, even for a while, it will help you enormously.

So, you see, counselling has its benefits, there is nothing to scoff about, and if you find one you like, as I did (she is still a good friend) it can make the difference between sinking or swimming. Talk to your doctor or midwife who should be able to suggest therapists in your area.

Yummy Mummy Clobber

It's not only your baby who needs a whole lot of new, shiny stuff: we get some goodies too!

1. Handbags

If you've already had a glance at the 'Popping Out' chapter, you will be primed for what I'm about to tell you: Yummy Mummies have to carry around a lot of stuff. Not only that, but your hands will be so full of all this stuff and your baby, that having everything in a disorganised mess will make your life impossible as well as stressful. This is where a well-chosen handbag comes to the rescue. It can also be the item which makes a somewhat haphazard clothing situation come together and look like boho chic, so choose that hold-all with care, and get something totally Yummy.

Top Handbag Tips from Anya Hindmarch, designer

Get a bag that is for your children's stuff and one for you. NEVER share. After a day with my children, my bag is mostly full of Action Men's arms and biscuit crumbs (mine).

Every new mother should have wipes, muslin, dummies, formula and gin in her handbag.

All busy Yummy Mummy handbags should have loose pockets – one for food in (all feeding equipment) and one for food out (all nappy stuff).

- ☆ Size matters. If it can't hold everything you need for a day out with your baby, it's too small. I know it's beautiful, but it's too small, so move on...
- ☆ Shouldering the burden. If you can't throw your bag over your shoulder to leave both hands free, get another one. Carrying a heavy baby requires two arms.
- ☆ Organisation and compartmentalisation is key. My old bag had no internal compartments: it was just one big hole, and consequently was completely useless. Don't believe me? Here's what I found at the bottom of it last night:

2 suede gloves covered in crumbs
1 Baby Gap sock
3 blunt pencils
5 packets of Sweetener
2 Rennies and 4 loose Strepsils
1 nail buffer with no cover
1 old, dry baby wipe (used?)
Emily's spelling test
Eight-Hour Cream (open)
I Caffe Nero take-away lid
1 apple with a bite taken out
2 breast pads and 1 nappy (must re-stock)
1 lipstick, no lid
Half a granola bar
1 tube of hand cream
1 soft toy dog
1 hairbrush, full of hair
1 old hairclip and 7 (!!) hair bands
12 pieces of tissue paper
1 lovely picture by Phoebe
1 Mr Incredible figurine
1 small bag of mouldy duck bread
1 Bobbi Brown foundation stick
1 overdue *Motorcycle Diaries* DVD

By contrast, on a work day, my bag looks more like this:

Make-up bag
Vogue
Wallet
Eight-Hour cream
Lipstick with lid
1 apple
1 notebook and pen
Bottle of Evian
Appointments diary
Mobile

So you see, if your handbag has no separate compartments it will be a disaster. Last week I bought a new bag with eight separate sections, and I am sooooo happy with it. It still has bits of tissue floating around, but if I need a wipe super-quick, I'm there before the snot has reached his upper lip. Fabulous. And it looks the biz, too. Don't wait seven years to sort your life out like I did – get a proper bag *now*.

Empty it out several times a week, put everything back where it should be, and hit the next day in organised style. Make your handbag a child-free zone: no little fingers are allowed in my bag, which has helped to keep it free of marbles and less sticky.

2. New Shoes

If you haven't got one already, then get a pair of very comfortable shoes which can withstand a lot of wear. I reckon I walk at least four miles a day, every day, and that doesn't include all the running back to retrieve things I've dropped, climbing on climbing frames and chasing children around supermarkets. Not ugly and comfortable, but lovely and comfortable, obviously. If you find some you love to bits, buy two pairs, because you will wear them out quite quickly.

Top Shoe Tips from Tamara Mellon, President of Jimmy Choo

A good pair of shoes makes an outfit! I always believe that if you have a wonderful pair it adds that touch of glamour which will perk you up when you're pregnant. You can still wear heels but I personally found flats more comfortable. Treating yourself once in a while to a pedicure and foot massage keeps your feet beautiful and ache-free.

3. Pillows
If you're going to spend so many hours in your bed feeding, or trying to get some rest, you'd better make the experience as comfortable and sensual as possible. Lots of pillows covered in the most beautiful linen you can find will see you through the long nights with a smile on your face. Possibly...

4. Relaxing Scents
Stock up on scented candles, linen spray and aromatherapy bath oils. When everything seems difficult and exhausting, being surrounded by a comforting, relaxing smell can really help. It also helps to hide any less-than-pleasant aromas coming from your baby – or partner.

L'Occitane do a lovely Lavender Linen Water to make your bed smell good enough to get back into *again*. Jo Malone's Orange Blossom scented candles freshen the grimiest of living rooms (and look fabulous too), and The White Company is also a great place to look for fabulous candles and linen spray. If you can't afford the time or money on such luxuries, then a trip around Tesco's should help: I have their vanilla candles everywhere, and The Body Shop has a good range of burning oils.

5. Blindfold and Earplugs
These will enable you to catch forty winks during the day, or at night when your baby is awake and Daddy is trying to settle her. The more beautiful the blindfold the better, because then you can really let loose with it when your libido returns. One day. Agent Provocateur do the sexiest ones I've seen, Bombay Duck has an excellent selection too or hang on to long-haul airline ones if you're not that fussed.

Reality Check: How Are You Doing So Far?
Well? How *are* you doing so far? And how far is 'so far'? It's a good idea to take stock of things about a month or two down the road, and look back at what has just happened, how you have changed, how much your baby has become a part of your lives, and how

amazingly you have managed to learn a billion new skills.

I always find that the first six months, and more truthfully the first year, feels like living in a tunnel, and I just hang in there until I come out at the far end on my baby's first birthday to a world of more sleep, better routines, more confidence and my old life starting to creep back in again. It feels wonderful, and this is always the point at which amnesia kicks in, and I decide I want another one. Duh, Liz!

Obviously the first year is also a fantastic time, when your baby begins to be a person, you get to know each other, you find games to play, ways to make each other laugh, and you just live in wonder at the speed with which they learn. Last week she could barely sit up, and now she's crawling off to pop Lego in the CD player the moment your back's turned! There are millions of fantastic moments, but enjoying them all can be really hard if part of you is still missing your old life and wondering just *how* long it will be until you can stop wearing maternity bras. Give it another six months if you can.

This tunnel-living is not common to all the Yummy Mummies I know, and an impressive number of them find the first six months or more to be just maternal bliss. If you feel like you're struggling, and you find the first year of adjustment difficult, then the only way is UP, and things can only get better and better. Every cloud... *That's enough thank you, David Brent.*

While you're at it, **this is also a good time to check how you and your partner are getting on.** Too often, all the new baby obsession can mean that you two barely exchange insults let alone loving words. This is a very slippery slope, and just *assuming* that everything will get back to normal soon is a bit like *assuming* there will be toilet paper in Starbucks. It's this sort of sloppiness that leads to relationship breakdowns, terrible stress wrinkles, and global warming. Probably.

Here's a checklist to cheer yourself up. If you can tick just three of these things, you are a Wonder Yummy Mummy, and you deserve a big kiss from someone over the age of six months:

☆ Can you change a nappy? In less than five minutes?
☆ Can you dress your baby without breaking both her arms?
☆ Have you managed to get out of the house with your baby yet?
☆ Have you had a deep, hot, aromatherapy bath?
☆ Are you managing to feed your baby?
☆ Can you fold a buggy?
☆ Have you had an uninterrupted meal with your partner?
☆ Have you visited a café, and stayed there long enough to have a coffee?
☆ Have you got through a day without crying at all?
☆ Are your nails still looking good?
☆ Do you still *care* about your nails looking good?

See? Who said you weren't coping? Six months ago you wouldn't have believed you would be able to do so many baby-related things and now look at you. Sure, you're not perfect, and there's a long way to go before you have it all under control, but for now console yourself with the fact that you are in a very hard phase of your life, and if you're staying afloat at all you are doing very, very well. Nobody else will tell you this, so repeat it several times a day. **YOU ARE DOING VERY, VERY WELL.**

Incidentally, if you answered 'no' to the last question you are in danger of losing your grip on what's really important (well, important-ish, anyway), so take a few minutes to remember what your life used to be like, to remind yourself how much looking good perks you up, and to look at some pictures of the world's Frumpiest Mothers. That should make you dig out the emery boards pretty sharpish.

Yes, But What Do I *Do* With It?

This must seem like such a stupid question to anyone who has never sat at home for fourteen hours with a tiny person who can't do *any* of things that all their other human friends can do perfectly well.

But if you've tried it, you will know that it's NOT a stupid question. If you feel stupid or worried because you don't have a clue what you are supposed to do with a baby, then don't. Why should you know? Who has ever told you? If, like me, the first new baby you ever see is your own, then how can you have any idea what to expect to be doing with it all day long? Playing charades? Watching *The Office* repeats? Putting up shelves?

Everyone from distant aunts to the local milkman is happy to dole out advice about how to conceive (rather a lot of help offered from the milkman here), grow, deliver and raise your children, but there's barely a mention anywhere of what they like to do in terms of activities, games and so on. Not everyone finds this part of being a mother either instinctive or easy, and it's no slight on your maternal capabilities if you struggle with it.

At the Third Stroke: How to Fill Those Long, Long Days

A day with a baby is a very, very long day: it usually starts somewhere between 'Far too early for *my* skin to look half decent' and 'Oh, you are taking the piss', and it finishes – well, it doesn't really matter when it finishes, because you are beyond caring by that point. Let's just say that you can easily be looking at thirteen or fourteen hours of daytime to fill. With *what?*

Well, probably not with playing charades, watching *The Office* repeats or putting up shelves. Babies are hopeless at DIY.

Here are some tried and tested ideas to keep you going for quite a while, courtesy of my good Yummy Mummy friends and my own years of playing. I wish I had known about some of these when I first started.

New babies

Eat, sleep, poo. There's quite a lot of this for the first six months, and it can use up a huge chunk of your day. New babies can eat every four hours or so, and usually do; they can sleep a lot, and usually do except when they are eating; and they can poo, which they do both during and in between the first two activities. Eat, sleep and poo. Eat, sleep and poo.

While They are Sleeping

All of the sleeping in the early weeks is a great opportunity to get a few things done, because once your baby stays awake for most of the day you will never be able to get anything done ever again in a non-frazzled way.

☆ **Go shopping.** You NEED new clothes more than ever right now, and it will be very difficult to shop once your baby has his own opinions on things. Looking at beautiful new things makes post-natal women happy, and buying them is even better. Everybody knows that, and anyone who claims it is untrue has never had a baby. If the shops are too far away, see if some cyber-shopping has the same effect. Then you get the added bonus of a package arriving a few days later – double hurray!

☆ **Get your hair sorted out.** A new baby can easily sleep through a cut, colour and blow-dry, so pamper your head and walk out looking like one of those models in the adverts who shake their hair about a lot and have bouncy breasts. You may not *feel* like that, but your hair can tell great lies.

☆ **Sit in cafés** reading, and looking at people who look much nicer than you. Hurrah for the coffee culture which has (finally) invaded our country. The reason most cafés look like crèches is because all new Yummy Mummies need to get out of the house, do some reading, drink coffee and feel a part of the world again. It can reaffirm your fading belief that life really does go on, and that you have some lovely days to look forward to. The third bar stool on the right in Cambridge's Caffè Nero saw me through some diffi-cult times after my babies were born, and I owe it one. Actually, no I don't – I practically *own* it now with the number of coffees I've bought. Come to think of it, they should put up a plaque.

☆ **Go to the cinema.** A wonderful way to escape for a couple of hours, but it's worth checking you can bring a baby before you go. I went about twice a week for the first six months, and my baby just slept, except for one time when he was lucky enough to open his eyes and catch a few minutes of a debauched party scene in *Bright Young Things*, but I just fed him and he dropped off for the rest of it. Another advantage of breastfeeding.

☆ **Do something creative at home.** If you are a crafty lady, this is the only chance you will get to use those creative skills because glue, paint, sandpaper or staple guns + *awake* newborns = trip to A&E.

☆ **Go to the dentist.** It's still free!

☆ **Use your brain.** Read, learn Italian, do the crossword, write a poem, sort out your tax return – whatever it takes. That brain is desperate to be used for anything which doesn't involve babies.

☆ **Get a passport.** Zipping off for a week in the sun might not seem very likely right now, but you might as well get this boring piece of admin sorted out now while your baby still sleeps so much. This especially applies if you have family abroad whom you might like to visit soon, because all children, including newborn babies, now need to have their own passport. The person who decided that this was a sensible idea had obviously never tried to take a passport-approved photograph of a six-week-old baby. It is almost impossible, and you should allow a few extra days for it to go wrong several times. The photograph has to be taken against a white background, there can be no hands in view (so you can't just hold your baby up in front of the camera) and – get this – your baby's eyes must be open! I prodded and poked mine for five minutes with no success, and when she finally did wake up she cried so much that I had to feed her, and then she went back to sleep again. Mission utterly unaccomplished.

While They Are Awake

More complicated.

☆ **Stimulation**. Babies have very sensitive eyes, ears and mouths, and they love having these senses stimulated. Looking at coloured lights, sunshine flickering on a wall, light streaming through coloured glass, twinkling lights in shops, reflections, mirrors and so on will delight your new baby. The same is true of sounds, especially delicate ones: bells, rustling paper, splashing water and so on. You get the idea.

☆ **Peek-a-Boo.** I always thought I'd get bored of this after a month or two, but seven years of peek-a-boo later I'm still delighted every time by the giggles and smiles it produces. Maybe that says something about my mental regression... It's a great game for teaching babies about prediction too, which is key to their development. Sadly it's only prediction on the scale of 'mummy's face will pop out from behind her hands *again*', and not 'the FTSE 100 is about to crash', but it's a step in the right direction.

☆ **Repetition.** Again, not the most mentally taxing activity for you, but it is fantastic to watch your baby learn something new just by repeating a series of actions, words or sounds. You can almost *see* the connections forming in your baby's brain, and they can make astonishing progress this way. It can be as simple as putting a ball under a cup and letting your baby lift the cup off again and again and again. Avoid doing what I do, which is to teach them to say very silly things, such as 'Bless my soul' or 'Daddy's got love handles!' They will say it, it's very funny, but you can't un-teach it.

☆ **Reading.** DO IT. From the day they are born, DO IT. Prop your baby up on your lap facing a bright picture book and read to her every single day as though her life depended on it. Yes, you will feel like a complete idiot: a new baby can barely understand more than ten words, and has no idea what the pictures and symbols in the books are all about. But reading to a child does such magical and wonderful things that feeling like a complete idiot is well worth it.

You may gather that I feel quite strongly about this. You betcha! But why?! Why spend so much time reading to a baby – sometimes the same book over and over again - who cannot understand a word? Because one day it will. In fact, a baby can probably understand a heck of a lot more than you think it can, even at a very early age. Reading the same words, making those same sounds over and over and over again becomes like music to them. They hear that music, they remember it, and then they start to copy it. And that's how they start to speak.

This is all just another of Liz's theories, by the way, but my evidence strongly supports it, and all of my kids have been very early talkers. (Though I suspect that is mainly because they had to be to get me to shut up.) And anyway, reading is a lovely, cuddly activity: it calms children down, and it's a good excuse to actually sit down for a while rather than tear around the house picking all the toys up again. A very good tip, which I'm sure you know already but here it is anyway, is 'don't just read the printed words'. They are usually achingly dull for a baby, and paraphrasing wildly, adding adjectives, questions, exclamations and embarrassing noises is far more entertaining for both of you.

☆ **All singing, all dancing.** Having a good boogy to your favourite songs with your baby is a brilliant 'bonding' thing, and music is fantastic for babies' development, apparently. Particular favourites in my family were the soundtracks to all the Tarantino movies, which I took to indicate good cinematic taste rather than a propensity for bloodbaths and class-A drugs. Only time will tell. Dancing also sheds a few baby pounds, which can't be bad, and it can really cheer you up if things are getting on top of you. Hold your baby tight, turn the music up nice and loud and shake that funky thing. Make sure nobody can see in, though: my postman thinks I'm really weird since he witnessed me teaching Phoebe my 'Uma Thurman doing Mrs Mia Wallace in Jack Rabbit Slim's Twist Contest' impersonation.

The singing part can be a bit tricky if you only know 'Twinkle Twinkle Little Star' and 'Baa Baa Black Sheep', and it becomes very embarrassing when you find yourself in a playgroup, fluffing the lines to 'Incy Wincy Spider'. The thing that saved me was being given a *huge* book of nursery rhymes, and practising them when nobody was looking. Get one with big, bright pictures, and your baby might even enjoy it too. Oh, and if you really can't sing, then don't. Get a CD instead and mime.

☆ **Park Life**. As soon as your baby can hold his head up himself, he is ready to check out the local talent in the playground. This is a godsend for you, because it means playing out of the house for a change, and you also have a good chance of bumping into other Yummy Mummies with the same idea.

I used to pad a baby swing with a couple of huge blankets, or even a pillow – how sad am I to carry a *pillow* to the playground? – and pop my babies in when they were not much more than a month old, and they seemed to love it. Either that or they were so terrified they couldn't even cry, but I'm choosing to believe that they loved it. Slides are great at a very early age too if you hold them, but most other things need six months or more before your baby is ready. Precocious he may be, but he can't go on the monkey bars before he can walk.

From six months

This is a whole new ball game. Six-month-old babies can sit up or even crawl around, get their hands into all sorts of places they shouldn't be, laugh their little heads off, and understand loads of words and concepts; and they are tons of fun to play with.

As with all stages of Yummy Mummyhood, there is no reason you should instinctively know what to do with a slightly older baby. I had no idea at all, and spent far too much time wondering if I was doing the right thing for a baby of that age, until I met my first Mummy friend Sarah, and she introduced me to a world which would be my lifeline for the next – well, still counting the years, actually. It was the world of PLAYGROUPS.

There is never a safe time to walk into your first playgroup, and it will scare the living shit out of you whenever you take the plunge. There's much more about this in Part Eleven, but for the moment we are only concerned with the things playgroups will teach you about what to do with your growing baby.

Playgroups are a mine of useful information and ideas for how to amuse, stimulate and teach Mini-Me. Here are just some of the gazillion things you will get up to:

☆ **Playdough.** Remember this stuff? It's fantastic, and whether your baby plays with it or not doesn't actually matter, because the healing power of squishing it between your fingers is better than several trips to see an acupuncturist. Babies can't *do* much with playdough, but even prodding, squeezing, rolling and eating it is something new for them to try. After a year or so you will be a dab hand at mini sausages, peas, kumquats, or whatever delicacies your angel eats.

HOME-MADE PLAYDOUGH RECIPE

Shop-bought playdough goes hard in about two weeks, even if you are super-careful like me, and wrap it up in clingfilm after every play. If you want soft, gooey dough which lasts for years and is dead easy to make, then try this. I didn't believe it would work either, but it does:

☆ *1 cup of plain flour*
☆ *¹/₂ cup of salt*
☆ *4 teaspoons of cream of tartar (NOT tartare sauce, as I discovered!)*
☆ *2 tablespoons of cooking oil*
☆ *1 cup of water*
☆ *food colouring*

Mix it all up in a bowl, microwave for four minutes, stirring well after each minute. Knead well to finish. Ta-da!

☆ **Finger painting.** Cover the entire room in plastic – this is going to be very messy, but it's worth the huge hassle and stress, because babies *love* seeing all the bright marks they have made with the paint on the paper, table, sofa and kitchen walls. Paintbrushes are useless to begin with, because babies just wave them wildly about above their heads and in your face, and refuse to let go their iron grip. Cotton buds, bits of sponge or fingers are much better for the first year or so. Avoid pouring loads of paint out: your baby will get bored after about three minutes and you'll just wash it all down the sink.
☆ **Duplo.** Lego's big brother, and much more suitable for tiny mouths than the original. Hopefully you'll inherit a bucket-load of this stuff, because it costs a fortune and you cannot *not* have Duplo in your house. Where will tomorrow's architects come from without Duplo farmyards, towers, and more towers?
☆ **Train sets.** Ditto the inheritance thing, but you could always put this down as a first birthday request. It's bulky to store, it covers

your entire living room floor, and your baby will get annoyed when it keeps coming apart, but train sets can pass many hours away very happily.

☆ **Sticking.** By now you must be thinking that I am determined to trash your house, what with all my handy paint, Duplo and play-dough advice, and glue will surely be the final nail in your immaculate home's coffin. The best plan is to do all the gluing yourself to start with, and just let them slap down the colourful scraps of paper you've saved from various bits of junk mail. They feel very clever, and have something to show Daddy at the end of the day.

☆ **Music.** Not listening to it this time, but making some, using drums, bells, rattles, xylophones, recorders and so on. Empty bottles with popcorn kernels in are just as effective, but make sure the lid is very well attached, and un-removable by determined fingers.

☆ **Puzzles.** Once you've mastered 'attaching the raincover', the next puzzles to turn your attention to are those wooden ones with the pictures which lift out. Babies who are good at puzzles are more likely to be the problem-solvers of tomorrow. I think.

☆ **Kissing.** My all-time favourite. Perhaps I'm strange, but I would happily spend a good hour a day just playing kissing games (you kiss me, I'll kiss you, and so on) with all of my babies. Let's face it, by the time they're five they will be so über-cool that they won't let you anywhere *near* them, so you should grab all the kissing opportunities you can before they begin to protest.

☆ **Splashing.** Put several towels on the floor wherever you do this, because however carefully you swear you'll watch the proceedings, water will get right down your child's front and onto the floor *somehow*. Excellent fun, though, and quite therapeutic in an 'Oh shit there's water everywhere, but, oooh, isn't water calming' sort of way.

☆ **Swimming.** Once your baby has had all his inoculations (and probably before, but if it's your first baby you will be over-cautious about gross swimming-pool germs) you can take your baby swimming. Or, rather, bobbing about looking cold and a bit bewildered. Ten minutes is quite long enough for me in a pool these days and luckily that's the same for babies. But swimming is meant to be very good for them, and holding on to your baby in the water is the most gorgeous feeling.

☆ **Soft play areas.** Another godsend, if fairly noisy, often dirty and always expensive. Soft play areas are huge padded rooms with ball-pools, slides, pretend kitchens, ride-on toys, things to bash and throw and generally get as much aggression out with as your baby can before it's back to Mummy's nice furniture. If there isn't one near you, then drive as far as it takes and make a day of it. Go with Yummy Mummy friends, pretend you're having a nice time, realise you *are* having a nice time, buy some lousy coffee and unhealthy food, and come home knowing you've made a big effort, and have done a Good Mothering Job today.

Doing Too Much

There is such a thing as over-stimulation, and this can lead to terrible trouble getting Junior to go to sleep. Filling your baby's day with lots of activities, indoor and outdoor time and new experiences is a great thing, but if there's no 'down time', such as reading together, having a short nap and so on, babies and toddlers can get so over-loaded that they can't switch off at all. I guess it's a bit like taking lots of speed, washing it down with coffee and watching a fast-paced action movie. Hardly the stuff of peaceful nights.

There. This should all see you well on your way into the first stage of Yummy Mummyhood. Nothing, as ever, is gospel: you can do whatever suits you and your baby best, but hopefully some of it will be helpful, and reassure you that nobody has a clue what they are doing to begin with, and it takes time to learn all the new skills you need. Evolution has been slow indeed on the Instruction Manual front.

PART EIGHT

The First Year

With the total confusion, chaos and exhaustion of the first few months over, you can start to settle into you new lives together. I'm not suggesting that it gets a whole lot easier, but there will definitely be something resembling a pattern, or a routine, and all of the very basic tasks will seem much less taxing.

Unfortunately, there are a whole load of new things to get used to, so here is a look at some of the hurdles which are lurking within the first year of motherhood.

Popping Out: In Memoriam

'Popping out' is a highly undervalued luxury of the childless. I used to love popping out. I'd pop out for an emergency pint of milk. I'd pop out to return an overdue DVD. I'd pop out just to see that the world was still there, and if Office still has those brown boots in my size in the sale.

Just like that. Out I'd pop.

Alas, with the arrival of a baby (a quite different and more painful form of popping out), this relaxed, spontaneous activity was lain to rest, alongside morning sex, sitting down to eat, and sleeping well.

Here's how it should be:

One quiet morning, a young woman decides she needs a magazine fix.

She slips on her shoes and a jacket, grabs her phone, cash and keys to the flat, and walks out of the door.

She has just 'popped out'.

Here's how it is with a baby thrown into the mix:

A young, exasperated, sleep-deprived woman decides she needs to get herself and her baby out of the house before she goes mad. She spends the next twenty minutes trying to find small socks and shoes, preferably matching, but whatever presents itself first, trying to put both these items and also a jumper, coat and hat on a very wriggly child, finding her own shoes and coat, putting the shoes back on the now over-heated child who has kicked them off, searching for her keys which have been hidden somewhere by the child, panicking when she realises her wallet is in the changing bag and has had yesterday's milk spilled all over it, catching a glimpse of her face in the mirror and realising she has a visible foundation tide-mark on her left cheek, unfolding a buggy which doesn't want to unfold, and so on, and so on.

Eventually she leaves the house, a trail of toys and biscuit crumbs in her wake, not noticing that she never did manage to find her keys, or that she also forgot her phone. Or that her tights are laddered.

She has no idea why she is going out any more, and is certainly not 'popping out'.

The Good News

While you will never go back to those crazy, heady days of being able to pop out with only a moment's notice, there are ways to make leaving the house a good deal easier, and to be prepared for almost any eventuality when you are actually out and about. (Having a baby means you will be faced with just about every eventuality at some point, so preparation is key.)

Leaving the House with a Baby

Don't leave home without:

☆ **nappies**
☆ **wipes**
☆ **dummy** (if you use one. Thanks, Liz, we worked that out ourselves.)
☆ **blanket or muslin square** (even if it's sunny, you need *something* to cover their legs, and make them feel more snuggly and secure)

You should probably also take:

☆ **bib** for wiping and catching all manner of unsightly spillages
☆ **rattle/soft toy/baby book/hard toy** for teething babies to chew
☆ **cloth** for more drastic spillages
☆ **change of clothes** for baby
☆ **bottle** of baby's milk and water
☆ **rusks/biscuits**
☆ **raincover** or **sun-shade.**

And if you really must:

☆ **change of clothes for you**, especially a clean top – spillages can be quite severe
☆ **bottle of water and a snack for you** (childcare is hungry, thirsty work, and playgrounds don't generally come with a coffee shop as standard!)
☆ **portable changing mat** (not essential, but very handy if the facilities are a little, er, grim)

If you can make sure that the 'baby's bag' is ALWAYS ready for action, with enough nappies, wipes, toys, spare clothes, breast pads and snack food to keep a baby happy for a while, you should always be able to dash out at very short notice. Regular cleaning out also means you shouldn't find a three-month-old bottle of milk and a rotten satsuma at the bottom of it.

Spontaneity (the shortest section in this book)

When you become a parent, any attempt at being spontaneous, off-the-cuff, last-minute, a bit crazy or just free to do what you like, when you like, will vanish.

It's tragic, and I still miss my 'Oh what the hell – let's go out for some drinks' life. You get used to it, but it's still a bit sad. Well worth it for the lovely kids you get, but sad nevertheless.

Eating Out

Straight in with some great news for new Yummy Mummies:

Eating out with a newborn is easy-peasy, lemon squeezy and you can still enjoy it.

After that it's a little more complicated, but don't worry about that yet. Use the first few months to go out at every opportunity, because your baby will sleep and sleep and sleep, and you can always sneak in an unscheduled feed if there's any stirring before the coffee arrives. It also makes the transition into your new role as Yummy Mummy a little gentler, because you are still out there in the real world, doing what you used to do.

It can feel quite stupid to go out so much when all you really want to do is sleep but trust me: you will regret it soooo much if you hide at home every evening. As soon as you've had enough of your four walls, your baby will have had enough of sleeping so much, and eating out will become much more tricky, though still very possible and necessary for an occasional dip into the Other World outside your home.

I like to see taking young children to restaurants as a vital part of their education rather than as a frivolous, self-indulgent, social faux-pas. Getting them used to the environment and some basic etiquette from the earliest age is all part of the exercise.

There are some good tips to think about before you go, however, which are intended to help *everyone* have a much better time:

☆ **Take something for your baby to do.** To expect your baby to sit quietly and contentedly while you sip fine wine and appreciate the subtle flavours of your antipasto is, frankly, ridiculous. Always bring a favourite pram toy and a few books, and if you've left everything behind, use your imagination with what's on offer at your table: hiding things under napkins or taking the sugar sachets out of the pot and putting them back in again can keep a baby happy throughout a main course.

☆ **Don't expect to sit at the table the whole time.** In between courses or while you're waiting for the drinks, take your baby for a walk around: show him the lights, the chef, what's outside – anything to change the scene and make him happier to get back to the table again.

☆ **Bring some jars of baby food and milk.** You may both love oysters, but little Olivia doesn't.

☆ **Check whether babies are allowed** in your chosen eatery: many restaurants don't have licenses for under 18s, and this includes the teetotaller in the buggy. It's mad, but it's the law, so check.

☆ **Find out if they have high chairs.** If you are feeling very organised, you could bring a small portable one, but it's quite a hassle if you don't need to.

☆ **Ask to sit in a corner**, as far away from everyone else as possible, and move all the condiments, vases and expensive-looking crockery out of your baby's reach before you sit down. Pizza Express still hasn't forgiven Emily for chipping their marble table-top with a knife handle, but they were very gracious about it. Babies are strong!

☆ **If you are ordering food for your baby, ask for it to be put on a cold plate**, and to be brought as soon as possible. It usually takes five minutes to cool down enough, and babies do not like to be kept waiting for food.

☆ **If you want to breastfeed**, check out the general scene, and if you *really* don't feel comfortable then ask if there's a quiet room somewhere you could feed in. But whenever possible, be brave and do what's natural. People have got to get used to it somehow.

☆ **Ask your waiter if the chef can adapt a meal to suit your baby better.** If it's just a case of leaving out the basil or chilli in the pasta sauce, they can usually oblige.

☆ **Don't be scared to ask for a doggy bag.** I am always slightly embarrassed to do this, but when tomorrow lunchtime comes and I have a full plate of spaghetti alla carbonara in the fridge, I congratulate myself on my shrewdness.

☆ **Think of the other people in the restaurant.** I know you will, but it's amazing how many people are happy to let their kids shout, bang things and even have a tantrum in the middle of a restaurant or café without making the slightest effort to apologise or stop the disturbance. Yummy Mummies have a duty to make their babies welcomed in society, not be seen as a new breed of super-bug.

☆ **Know when it's time to leave.** Much as you may wish to sample the mango sorbet, if it's time to go, it's time to go NOW. Leave a decent tip to ensure you are welcomed back and make for the door.

Child-friendly Restaurants:

☆ **Pizza Express** (or Pizza Stress, as it's known in our house. Provides crayons, and sometimes balloons, and your baby will love watching the chef activity in the background.

☆ **Brown's.** Kids are very welcomed here, with crayons and paper as the norm, and all manner of antisocial baby behaviour tolerated. I've done enough waitressing there in the past to know! Please tip well…

☆ **Most noodle bars and sushi restaurants.** These generally have a very chilled-out atmosphere, and the small portions are ideal for children.

☆ **Tex Mex places** (Old Orleans, Nandos and so on). Not the most glamorous eateries, but they are great for babies because of all the background noise.

☆ **Curry restaurants.** Now we're talking. Naan bread is the perfect finger-food for older babies, and most curry houses are less formal and stuffy than smart French restaurants. The earlier you get your baby into the delights of curry the better – think of it as vital preparation for university.

Are We Nearly There Yet?

Travelling With Babies

Grenada. 8 September. Emily eight months old.

We've arrived! Emily was a dream on the flight, despite our six-hour delay at Birmingham airport, which could have been awful. She played with her pop-up castle, listened to stories and pretended to feed her panda bear for an hour on the plane, and spent the rest of the time being carried around the cabin making friends with everybody along the way. She was quite a celebrity by the end of it! She slept for three hours, because we had managed to tire her out so well, and she doesn't seem to be affected by the time difference much at all.

The biggest problem so far is the heat – I am worried that she is dehydrating with all the sweating she's doing, but hopefully we can keep her topped up with water. I am so happy that we've come away. It was a huge hassle packing and coping with Emily on the journey, but now we are here I know it will do us all a world of good to get away from normal life and routines.

How much or even *whether* you manage to hit the road, sea or sky with your new arrival depends very much on how much travelling you've done before. If a week in Wales is as brave as it's got, then a trip to visit the in-laws round the corner (round the *corner*?! Move immediately!) might be as much as you want to attempt. For those like me who live to travel, having a baby means you either learn how to travel with a baby in tow, or you stop living.

Taking the former as the preferred option, we have hauled our kids all over the world with varied success, and have brought our battered suitcases back aching with helpful tips for making the journey, and the holiday itself, more bearable. Allow me to empty the sandy, dirty, badly folded contents onto your lap.

WARNING: There is one thing you have to get firmly imbedded in your head before you even *think* about going on holiday with your baby:

YOU ARE NOT GOING ON HOLIDAY.

What you are doing is **SURVIVING IN A DIFFERENT PLACE FOR A WHILE**, and this brings me neatly to my number one travelling tip for all Yummy Mummies:

Lower your expectations
If your plans for the holiday involve *any* of the following words, then you may be in for a disappointment:

☆ rest
☆ relaxation
☆ culture
☆ in-flight movies
☆ romance
☆ people-watching

Instead, you should lower your expectations to sound more like this:

If we manage to get there, see anything beautiful at all, have one 'wow, I'm on holiday' moment and get back without losing more than three crucial things, filing for divorce or contracting more than five foreign illnesses, it will be a successful trip.

Once you have accepted that you will not read a book on the plane, or wander aimlessly around the departure lounge trying on perfume and buying 3-for-2 paperbacks, chocolate supplies and mini toiletries, you are in a much better mental state to cope with what's to come. If you can really leave with such dire hopes for the trip, you will have a fantastic time because it will, of course, be a lot better than this.

The world is still your oyster – just remember the travel wipes...

Never be in a hurry
While this applies to any type of travelling, it does so a thousand times more where children are involved. Last-minute toilet stops, refusals to get into the buggy, emergency nappy-changes, lost toys, escalator traumas and juice spillages are just a few of the myriad obstacles which will slow your progress down.

If you're **going by air** then allow *at least* the recommended two hours before departure and then add an hour – there may be a bus to transfer you to the terminal, a train to transfer you to the gate and several flights of stairs or escalators to negotiate. Once you've added time for folding and unfolding a buggy, strapping and unstrapping a child into the buggy, double-checking you still have six bags, one baby (preferably your own) and a partner in tow, and walking miles to find the nearest baby-change, then you really are getting close to departure time. Much better to have an hour to kill in the toy shops than to be the one dragging a screaming toddler towards final call at Gate 63.

Car journeys can be enormously lengthened by extra stops for nappy-changing, feeding and sick-wiping. If having an extra twenty minutes chasing ducks at the Westmoreland service station means a happy (and sleepy) baby for the next three-hour leg, then better to have the spare time.

Pack beautifully

Does Victoria Beckham arrive at Gatwick with her family and seven hundred carrier bags of 'stuff'? No, she doesn't. She arrives with matching suitcases and a clean T-shirt. You may not have the entourage to make this happen, but packing beautifully is the only way to travel in style when you have a baby with you. Do you care that the inside of your matching suitcases are full of dripping bottles of Calpol, bits of jigsaw puzzles and yoghurt-stained babygros? No. If it looks good on the outside, I am prepared to believe that this Yummy Mummy has it all covered.

Pack cleverly

When a Wet Wipe is required, you'd better be able to put your hand on one fast. Bags within bags is a good way to overcome this problem: have separate bags for snacks, drinks, toys, wipes and nappies, books, and so on. Put all the baby-related stuff in a separate, pretty 'baby's bag' so that whoever is left holding the baby has everything they need to hand. Many is the time I've gone to change a baby, only to realise that I have the toys and drinks bag, but the nappies are with my husband, who is browsing the latest releases in the 'Far Too Thick For My Hand-Luggage' section of Books Etc. And when I say 'put things in bags', I don't mean plastic carrier bags, of course. All those free make-up and toiletry bags you've accumulated from magazine and cosmetics promotions over the years come into their own when you travel with a baby.

Finally, every time you put something back in a bag, make SURE it goes in the right place. The more anal you are about this, the easier your trip will be.

Time the sleeps carefully

You want your baby to sleep during the actual journey as much as possible, believe me. So leave as much time for running around beforehand as possible, and never give your baby anything containing sugar or caffeine within an hour of your journey. I spent a night in a Eurostar carriage with three children who were drinking caffeine-filled fizzy drinks out of baby bottles. Never mind the tooth decay, obesity and brain rot which would result – I wanted some kip! (Disclaimer: fizzy drinks don't rot your brain. Geez…)

Most babies fall asleep after a good feed, so if you can hold the next one off, even just for twenty minutes longer, and deliver the slumber-inducing goods as the train pulls out of the station, then you will create your first reading, sleeping, snogging etc opportunity. You will also look much more on top of things, and everybody travelling with you will love you that little bit more.

TOP TIP for flights: *Babies get terrible earache during take-off and landing because their ears are a funny shape inside. True. They can't tell you what's wrong, but the deafening screams will let most of the cabin know that something isn't feeling so good. Giving them a milk feed, or even a drink of water at these times, can really help. I'm not sure if it does anything for the earache, but it's a lot harder to scream if there's a nipple in your mouth.*

What to pack for the journey

If you are a lady who packs straightening irons, a leather jacket and eight pairs of shoes for a week in Goa, then this section is for you. Print it out, and stick it to the inside of your suitcase.

We used to take everything with us. Really, almost everything we used for the baby on a daily basis at home would come along in the most humungously ginormous (sic) baby bag in the world.

We have now learned that most of what you 'need' for the baby at home, you either don't *need* at all and can do without for a week, or you can buy over there, thus saving vital space for those straightening irons.

Do pack:
☆ Wet Wipes. At least three packets.
☆ Tissues.
☆ Several dummies. Even if you never use one, this could be the time you start.
☆ Twice the number of nappies you think you'll need for the journey, and buy the rest there.
☆ Bottle of water with a teat and a lid. My babies always need extra water when they are travelling.
☆ A couple of baby books; preferably not the thick, board-book kind as they take up too much room.
☆ Dry snacks (breadsticks, dried apricots, rice cakes, etc.).
☆ Emergency ready-made milk carton, and a jar of baby food in case of delays.
☆ Tiny toys. One small car, a soft ball or some plastic farm animals can make a three-hour delay much more bearable. The more the merrier, but think small, packable, and multi-purpose.
☆ A couple of Calpol sachets, in case of bizarre, travel-related fever or pain. They like to test you out, you know.
☆ A clean top-half for you, because the one you wore on the flight will be ruined by the time you land, and one for your baby too.

Do not pack:
☆ Boxes of drink with straws. Can't close, shouldn't bring.

☆ Messy food. Rusks are one of the worst: they paste all over everything, and are impossible to wipe off.
☆ Big, bulky toys. You can live without them, and there's no stylish way to carry a Fisher Price pop-up castle off a plane. I tried.
☆ Special things. You can lose a lot on a journey, and anything with special meaning is bound to be the first to go, closely followed by library books – ooops.
☆ Musical instruments. Infernal tootling on recorders and the shaking of bells and rattles is more likely to cause air-rage than a standing ovation.

What you'll need at the other end

If you're in an all-inclusive, super-duper, lovely, child-friendly, your-wish-is-our-command kind of a place, then this list is very short. A favourite cuddly toy and the right bottles and teats should see you through nicely.

For all other trips away, you might need any or all of the following, depending on whether it's camping in France (???!! With a new baby!) or a weekend in London:

☆ Travel cot.
☆ Light-weight, foldable buggy.
☆ Raincover or sunshade, depending on what's in store.
☆ Bibs.
☆ Baby food: for travelling we always take the powdered variety, as it's lighter, but a few emergency jars are a good idea. If you're going anywhere in the developed world, you should be able to buy baby food there, so taking half a ton of milk powder, baby jars and favourite biscuits is just silly. It's a great opportunity to introduce your baby to some exotic cuisine as well – we discovered that French babies are being fed on jars of asparagus with roasted butternut squash, and Charlie particularly enjoyed the creamed artichoke. Beats mashed-up turkey twizzlers any day – *bon appétit!*
☆ Nappies. Again, you can buy nappies almost everywhere now. They are usually just the same as at home, except there are some

great comedy names going (Dodots in Spain, and baby wipes are known as Swippies in Italy). Love it.

MAKE IT EASY ON YOURSELF. If you are keen to have a *break* in between all the baby-chasing, foreign-changing-mat-using and immediate restaurant-vacating, then do some research into baby-friendly companies. Some airlines are more baby-friendly than others: BA has a fantastic reputation, Virgin Atlantic provides baby food and nappies, and most Asian-based airlines are very baby-attentive, e.g. Singapore, Thai and Malaysia airlines. I have heard that Gulf Pacific beats everyone else hands down, thanks to their Sky Nanny service (yes please!) and there are travel companies which will tailor everything to your specific requirements, and will help you find hotels with crèches, baby-sitting facilities, high-chairs and good-quality cots (www.babyworld.co.uk has a good list). For an eco-friendly holiday, try www.responsibletravel.com, who will also help with family-friendly services.

Spending time on these details can mean the difference between a moderately relaxing day or two and a completely exhausting week.

Top Hotels for Babies and Parents
There are more of these springing up every year, but here are some to get you started:

☆ **The Grove Hotel, Hertfordshire:** Has an Ofsted nursery at weekends where you can leave babies aged from 3 months while you try out the Sequoia Spa treatments.
☆ **Woolley Grange, near Bath:** You can leave babies from newborn upwards in the Woolley Bears Den, open all day every day. The hotel also provides changing mats, sterilisers and almost anything else you might want – as well as babysitters.
☆ **The Ickworth Hotel, Suffolk:** Surrounded by 1,800 acres of parkland, this hotel also has a crèche taking babies from newborn, leaving you to enjoy the stunning scenery sans pram, or to sleep.

When in Rome

Different countries have very different attitudes to babies and young children, and unless you want to make the English even more unpopular abroad, it's best to check the local etiquette before going. In the hot southern-European countries there's a very relaxed attitude to children, so long as they behave well, and they are welcomed almost everywhere. In France, this welcome usually means, 'so long as Maman and Papa can still look absolutely divine, and eat their meal slowly, and in peace'. Restaurants in France, Spain, Italy or Greece rarely have high-chairs in my experience, but this is made up for by the fact that people there love babies so much and will offer to cart them off to the kitchen while you eat your meal. Very unnerving, but greatly appreciated. *Grazie!*

In other countries the tolerance threshold is a good deal lower, and we've found this to be particularly true in the new East European countries. In the Czech Republic, children are expected to behave impeccably, dress as smartly as they can, and there is no place for grotty hands or snotty noses. My mother is Czech and still won't let up.

Breastfeeding is another potential social stumbling block: in many forward-thinking European countries, breastfeeding in public is still as shameful as letting rip in a library, and you may find it even more awkward than usual. I'm afraid this is the only thing I will not adjust my habits to. If Europe wants to be considered the cultural, fashion and intellectual capital of the universe (which I think it does, and should), then the sooner it cottons on to the idea of feeding a baby naturally, the better. Why is it OK for Italian women to dress provocatively, but not to use their assets for anything constructive? Maybe because D&G corsets don't allow much room for breast pads… Yes, that'll be it.

Very, Very Long Haul

You will never complain about long, boring flights again after you have made a ten-hour plane journey with a baby. Anyone without kids who moans about 'all that tiring air travel' they have to do for work will be in for a serious beating. The chance to sit down, watch a film, be served food and drink, and talk to nobody for ten hours – yes pleeeaaase!

Long haul is very brave, but again, totally possible, and not half as bad as you might expect. Bring even more food and milk than for short trips, but don't bother about bringing more toys: you won't need them all, and your baby will be just as happy being adored by the cabin crew and being carried up and down the aisle seven hundred times. You might annoy everybody else on the flight, but you won't get deep-vein thrombosis, that's for sure.

Ideally, you want your baby to sleep as much as possible, so flying at night is brilliant. My brother and sister-in-law come over from New Zealand with their young girls every year, and swear by doping them with a sleeping potion that is said to be safe for kids. I wouldn't, but they do and have never had any trouble with it. Ask your doctor. An alternative, suggested by a very travel-y Yummy Mummy friend, is to give your baby cold camomile tea in a sucky cup. Weird.

Hot Places

Babies are not really made to cope well with extremes of temperature, so if you can leave Antigua until next year and stick to Majorca instead, that is the best plan. If you just need your heat, then there are some things you should know about:

☆ **Dehydration.** Babies dehydrate very quickly, and they will need a LOT more fluid in the heat. This should not only come from the normal milk feeds, but also from extra top-ups with cooled, boiled water. If your baby is not drinking from a bottle at all, then try spooning it in, with a teaspoon. It's very fiddly, but any fluid is better than none.

It's a good idea to know how to say 'cooled, boiled water' in the necessary language. I remember trying to order some from a lovely waiter in Venice, who brought us fizzy water, cold water, iced water, boiling water, but not cooled, boiled water. Poor man – he was really trying, but so were we.

TOP TIP: *To see whether your baby is dehydrated, feel the soft, diamond-shaped fontanelle at the top of her head (where the skull bones haven't joined up yet). If it dips in, your baby needs more fluid. A bulging fontanelle can be a sign of meningitis, so keep an eye on this area.*

☆ **No Fun in the Sun.** Never put your baby in the sun. Never, never, never. If you do, you are mad and a Very Bad Mummy. Their skin is not at all ready for so much UV, they get heat-stroke really quickly, and a baby with a tan should be unthinkable. Use the highest-factor sunblock you can find for children – even if it's cloudy – cover their limbs in thin cotton, use a hat, and keep them in the shade. Watch out for burned tops of feet and backs of hands, and if you can get some mini sunglasses with 100% UV protection then so much the better. Or you could just go to Cornwall instead.

☆ **Overheating.** Babies can overheat unbelievably fast, so keep checking how many layers they are wearing, and keep them well hydrated and cool.

Cold Places

Again, if you can avoid extremes, so much the better. We took our baby skiing last year, and spent at least 50% of the holiday putting on and taking off layers of thick baby clothes. He hated every minute of it, and we spent a fortune on baby mountaineering gear. Madness.

☆ **Extremities.** The story in my family goes that when I was 18 months old, my parents took me on a 10km sledge ride in Moravia, for the entire duration of which I screamed my head off. It wasn't until we got home three hours later that some bright spark noticed my hands and feet had turned blue. Well spotted, guys. The moral of this cold tale is that babies' hands and feet get very cold, even if they are wrapped up to the eyeballs in sheepskin.

☆ **Dehydration.** Just as above. Cold air is often dry, and you will need to offer extra fluids.
☆ **Head case.** Have you also heard that we lose 30% of our body heat through our heads? Well, if it's true, then your baby had better have a good hat. Earmuffs are also a good idea because they look very cute, and babies are often prone to earache.
☆ **Overheating.** Why is it that in very cold countries the local inhabitants feel the need to overcompensate wildly, and heat all their houses, shops and cafés to an unbearable temperature? It's very annoying because you have to strip every time you go indoors, and it also means your baby will overheat before you've even looked at the menu. Be aware of this, and get ready to take tiny layers off quickly.

In conclusion: travelling with a baby is fine. It's very easy if you plan it well, and prepare for a complete disaster. It gets you away from the daily routine at home, and your new companion can break a lot of ice with foreign waiters who would otherwise peer down their noses at you. Many of my Yummy Mummy friends have found that they travel *more* after they have a baby, because they need the change of scene more, and they want to show Baby Phileas what is out in the big wide world.

The Most Yummy Travel Items: for Utterly Glamorous Breaks:

☆ **Jo Malone In-flight Bag** looks unbelievably chic and contains everything you will need to survive the flight looking fresh and Yummy.
☆ **Molton Brown New Age Traveller Kit** fits ten heavenly-scented products into a leather bag.
☆ **Prada's Reviving Travel Programme** is a minimalist's treat, and houses just four bare essentials rather beautifully.
☆ **Storksak Weekend Sak:** Very Louis Vuitton in design, this elegant bag has a leather trim and comes with a changing mat, an insulated bottle holder and a long, detachable strap. Checking in has never looked so good.
☆ **Cashmere socks and blanket.** Get matching ones for you and your baby to really look the co-ordinated part.

PART NINE

You

Who Am I?

SOUND THE HORN! RING THE BELL! Roll out the red carpet and give your armpits a quick sniff, because here we are at last. Ladies, prepare yourselves to alight in considerable style, at what I consider to be the crux of the matter. This is the most fundamental, and infuriatingly baffling question, which every mother faces time and time again, and whether you survive Yummy Mummy-hood or not depends on your finding an answer to it:

Who The Fuck Am I?

Right now, at this stage in your life, who are you? **Are you the same person *now* as you were before you had a baby,** or have you left that person behind and become somebody new? *Really?*

Let's try to sort this little dilemma out. On the couch, please, and let's take a look. You probably feel, at various times, like any one or more of the following:

☆ a wife/partner
☆ a daughter
☆ a mother

☆ a colleague
☆ a girl
☆ a friend
☆ a woman
☆ a Sex Goddess (if you read it, you might believe it)

You may not feel like *all* of those things, but even if you can tick four or five of the boxes, that's a whole lot of different sides of your personality to keep an eye on. Not only that, but each one can contain enough sub-personalities to confuse the most highly skilled impressionist. For example:

Girl	= shopaholic, man-hunter, stationery collector, rock chick, glamour-puss, room re-organiser, brain box, lousy thrower (ouch!), butt-toner, hair-flicker, list-writer…
Daughter	= friend, moody cow, carer, mother's pride and joy, source of grey hairs…
Friend	= confidante, boyfriend-vetter, style advisor, honest-opinion-giver, tactful liar, listener, clothes-lender, sentence-finisher….
Colleague	= gossip-monger, tea-maker, boredom-breaker, daily lunch date…
Wife	= cook, cleaner, shopper, whore, nanny, decorator, friend, nagger, money-spender, money-earner, pants and socks buyer, dandruff-checker…

…and so very on. Trying to keep track of all of these sides of all of your characters requires the mental agility of a chess supremo, and getting them mixed up could leave you doing such unthinkable things as shopping with your husband, shagging your mother or telling your boss she has a huge bum in that skirt.

The addition of a new personality, a new part of you, is always traumatic and confusing, because whatever *form* the New You takes, it never occurs alone: there are always knock-on effects on all the other 'you's, and the key, in my most non-expert, non-psycho-analytically trained opinion, is to work out how all the 'you's can live together. Not how to *replace* one with another, but how to keep as many of them going as you can, and switch between them.

And that, my gorgeous friend, is what I think the hardest part of becoming a mother is. It's not the nappy changing, the lack of sleep, the peculiar breasts or the responsibility. It's not missing out on hen weekends, having to wear practical clothing or negotiating a pram around Sainsbury's.

Coming to terms with the fact that you – YOU! – are a now a mother, can be very hard, and it takes a long time. It doesn't mean you have to *feel* like a mother the whole time, but you are, nevertheless, on some level and forever, a mother. Learning how to fit this in with all your other roles and personalities is your key to survival in the first year. Even though you are a long way away from somebody actually *calling* you Mummy (which is, incidentally, the most fantastic, *fantastic* feeling), the very idea can be enough to send a lot of Yummy Mummies into shock for several months, and this is often a big factor in the postnatal slump.

Chrissie Rucker, founder of The White Company
Since becoming a mum, I often ask myself 'Where is the girl I used to be?' My life is no longer my own – I wake up and think about others before me. All the priorities in my life have changed, at home as well as at work. But it's the only way I'd have it!

How to Cope with the New You

For me, the most successful method of adjusting to Motherhood has been to keep as many of the Old Me parts going as possible, within my new role as a Mummy. As soon as I realised that I could be a mummy and *still* be a friend, a girl, a lover, a colleague and a woman, I felt much happier with the idea. I stopped feeling that I should give up all the things I used to enjoy. The Old Me was still very much alive and kicking, and I had to learn not to neglect her. Quickly.

Here are some things which might help:

☆ **Keep as many 'normal' rituals going as possible:** the Sunday-night soak, the weekly takeaway, having friends round for a drink, sorting out your wardrobe, and so on. Keeping as many things the same as they were before you had the baby lessens the perceived impact on your life.

☆ **Tell friends you want to keep conversations as they used to be.** The temptation to talk about babies all the time is almost irresistible, but this means your old relationship will die completely. You still need to talk about what's good to read, who's having an affair with whom, where to buy the best jeans and what's coming out at the cinema too, you know.

☆ **Ask your friends how they feel about you now.** Often, it *feels* as though there's suddenly a deep gorge between you and your old friends, as you all struggle to learn how to talk about babies instead of which actress has had Botox. If you do ask, it usually turns out that they are cool with it, love seeing you in this new light, and are in complete awe of what you've achieved. And then you can get back to music, books and attractive colleagues again.

☆ **Force yourself not to talk about baby things with your partner.** If you guys stop talking about anything other than number of poos, length of feeds or the latest cute faces, you will lose what you had together before your baby came. Even if you really couldn't be less interested, try talking about his work, politics, sport, last night's documentary about Roman bathing rituals or whatever. Anything but parenthood and babies will do.

☆ **Get time away from your baby.** When you are breastfeeding, this can't be for more than a couple of hours to begin with, but even if you can only get away for twenty minutes, grab every opportunity. Wander about looking at un-baby-related things, feel free of all maternal responsibility, meet up with a friend for a quick chat and a giggle (don't talk about babies!), buy something lovely for yourself (not your baby!), flick through books, go for a walk – anything, *anything* which takes you away from your 'Mummy' character, and lets you be 'Old You' again. Not only do you get to feel normal for a while, but you will run back to your baby, swear you'll never leave her again, and enjoy being back in Mummy Mode. Until next week.

☆ **Start a new hobby, or join a class:** If you already take adult Italian classes, Iyengar yoga and Dressmaking for Beginners, then you might not have time to start something new. In fact, you won't have time to go to half of these classes for six months or so, but if you can keep at least *one* of them going it will give you a fantastic opportunity to slip out of your Mummy role, and back into your 'designer of the year' fantasy for a couple of hours. The great thing about joining a new class is that nobody knows anything about you, and you don't come with a 'Mummy' label attached to your forehead. You are free of all nappy and vomiting talk, and can adopt a new personality for the evening. I joined a ballet class last year, and they still think I am single and I work in an interior design shop. It's heaven.

If you have trouble adjusting to motherhood don't feel guilty and don't worry: you are perfectly normal, and it's vital not to ignore how you are feeling.

Remember that it takes time to adjust to being a Mummy. You may love it some days and hate it other days, but if you can carry on being the Old You as much as possible, you should survive the change a lot better.

I Am Turning Into My Mother

This one can creep up on you and strike very early on in Yummy Mummyhood, and it's deeply unnerving. (It's especially alarming for me, because I have given my husband unquestionable grounds for divorce should I turn into my mother.)

Happily, I can reassure you that you are not necessarily morphing into your *own* mother, but into a mother in general. It only feels peculiar because you are more likely to repeat things said and done by your Mum than those said by, say, Lizzie Jagger's mum, just as you are more likely to inherit your mum's legs than Jerry Hall's. Damn.

Here are some things I do that make me feel worryingly like my mother:

☆ Spitting on a handkerchief, and wiping it around my baby's mouth (I hate that I do this, but it cleans things up nicely).
☆ Constantly tucking my daughters' hair behind their ears.
☆ Saying 'laaaast mouthful…' and 'If you throw that spoon again, it's back in the stocks for you, young lady.' (Not really.)
☆ Frequently dusting down crumbs, dry paint or whatever from my toddler's clothes. Oh get off, Mum.
☆ Fussing.
☆ Talking to my baby about somebody who is right in front of me, in the third person.

As the months and years go by, the number of things you'll repeat from your parents will go up exponentially (we're currently on 'I don't *care* what Hannah Morris's mummy lets her do: I'm *your* mother, and I say *no* crisps in your packed lunch!' Sigh.) Of even more concern, is that this sort of copycat behaviour applies to the way you talk to your partner as well. The day you find yourself muttering 'Oh never mind, *I'll* change her' or 'The dinner didn't cook *itself*, you know' just as your mother may have done to your father, is the day you realise how she felt after a long day looking after you. Slippery. Slope.

The only survival strategy I have found is to go with the flow, enjoy rediscovering some of the old habits and sayings, and make up some brilliant new one-liners for your own children to hate. If you still feel that you are turning into your mother, then do something she would never have done and reassert your uniqueness. In my case, anything self-indulgent will do, which suits me perfectly.

Coping – Or Not...

November 2004. Charlie five months old.

This week is a total disaster. I haven't managed to cook anything decent for anyone, put any of the washing away, play any fun games or raise a smile all week. Everywhere I go there's more mess and jobs and stuff to do which I'll never get round to, and which drives me nuts. I hate all the clutter and mess, and every time I try to tidy something away, Charlie starts to cry, so I have to abandon yet another job and go back to dangling shiny objects in front of his nose. This weekend we're off to H's parents, so I won't get the chance to get on top of things, and on Monday morning I'll be back in the piles of mess again. And I'm supposed to be writing a column every month about how to be a good mother. I haven't got a clue what to write these days, and I would give that up as well, if it weren't the only thing which keeps my brain going, and brings in some cash. Not coping at all!!

In general, I would say that I am a very good coper: very little fazes me, I'm much more likely to say 'I can' than 'I can't', and as Life continues to throw one mini-disaster after another at me, I tend to just knuckle down and get on with it.

But I absolutely cannot cope with everything which is required of me in my multiple roles of Mummy, wife and writer all of the time, and I'm not at all ashamed to admit it. There are days and weeks when everything is going well: the children are happy, I am happy, my husband appears to be happy, and we all live in a Happy Home. Then there are days, even weeks, when I feel like I'm drowning: I hate all of it, I can't cope at all and I turn into a miserable, grouchy, mean, shouty old hag. During these stages, I find it impossible to imagine how I will ever get back on top of things again, and I begin to descend into a downward spiral of doom and despair. This almost always coincides with somebody I know and don't like very much getting a huge pay-rise or inheriting a villa in Tuscany.

To haul myself out of this self-pitying vortex, and back onto the Coping track, I rely on my carefully selected support network, and every Yummy Mummy I know does exactly the same thing. You should start developing your own morale-boosting strategies as soon as you can, and prepare to turn to them at regular intervals.

☆ **Mummy friends:** It takes a long time to find Yummy Mummy friends you really trust and can confess your non-coping to. When you find one (and it may only ever be one), then count yourself lucky, and handle this relationship with kid gloves – you will both need it to get through the gloomy days. Most of the time I feel so much better just for having *told* someone about my struggles that I cheer myself up. And most of the time my friends are going through something worse, and I end up cheering *them* up and being glad I'm only dealing with a baby who refuses to sit in his high chair, and not one who kicks, spits and bites.

☆ **Family:** This is often more tricky than friends, because there is more history and baggage in the relationship, and we are more likely to become defensive of other people's suggestions. However, family should be the best place to get help and support, and I think many grandparents just love feeling that they have a useful, advisory role to play again.

☆ **Babysitters:** I'm not suggesting that you get a babysitter round just so that you can tell her how hard things have been this week, and how many times you have wanted to throw your baby out of the third-floor window (Never, *ever* tell a babysitter this, unless you want to explain it to the Social Services lady). But when you don't feel that you can cope any more without going mad, get a babysitter and take yourself out of the house, away from your baby, and back into the world of non-puking, continent, walking, talking people. That excludes pubs after closing time, then. Just an hour or two away can put everything in a better, happier, clearer light, and you'll wonder what the big problem was…

☆ **Old friends:** This can work very well if you only treat seeing old friends as an opportunity to get away from your 'Mummy' life for an evening. If you are hoping for some helpful support and sympathy, then you're barking up the wrong tree: childless people can't understand even one *iota* of what you are going through, and they will also probably find you very boring if you go on about how hard parenting is. Leave the details of your breast-engorgement and possetting baby to those who know and can empathise.

Knowing When to Get Help

Every Yummy Mummy goes through periods of not coping very well, and scaring herself and her partner silly. Most of the time it lasts for a few days, and whatever it was that was causing the distress just peters out for a short while, before something worse comes along. This is normal.

But if you ever feel that you can't cope a day longer without something going seriously wrong for you, your baby or the Habitat sideplates, then get yourself to a doctor, midwife or health visitor as soon as you can and see what advice they can offer. It does *not* mean you are a failure.

Babysitters

Yet another big mistake we made with our first baby, which I hope you will be clever enough not to repeat, was not getting a babysitter for the first year at least, for fear that this would somehow damage her emotionally. (Our baby, not the babysitter.) The result was that we barely exchanged words for this entire period, except for baby-related chit-chat, and we completely forgot who we used to be. A recipe for disaster, I think you'll agree.

Not all babysitters are child-abusing, baby-shaking drunks who bring their greasy boyfriends with them and indulge in clumsy sofa sex the second you leave the house, with *EastEnders* blaring in the background to drown out the noises of your baby crying in her cot. Most babysitters you will use are very kind, competent, trustworthy, experienced child-carers who will look after your baby as well as you do. We now get a babysitter every few weeks, but we stick to one hard and fast rule where our youngest is concerned: **we only ever ask somebody he is very familiar with**. Older children probably don't mind too much if so-and-so's Lithuanian au pair comes round for the occasional evening because you can explain it to them, and bribe them with the promise of watching a whole DVD while you're out. Young babies, on the other hand, will be scared half to death if they wake up in the middle of the night and a complete stranger comes to tuck them in. This happened to me, apparently, and I think it might account for some trust issues I have…like I don't trust anyone, for example. Talk to your friends, or the staff at your baby's nursery, and see if there's anyone you like who would be willing to guard the blessed infant while you go off for a quick, nervous drink before rushing back to check if everything is all right. (It always is, by the way, because they phone you if not.) Spend a few weeks letting your baby get to know this person, and then just go for it. The worst that will happen is that you get 200 metres down the road and come back again. The best is that you realise how easy and liberating it is to go out of the house without your baby, to do whatever it is you used to do and to be a couple again.

TOP TIP: *Always treat and pay your babysitter well. A good, reliable babysitter is worth her weight in gold, even if she is fairly hefty, and there's no point counting every half-hour and paying exactly. Give her the extra fiver and you'll be set for months to come, and make sure you've left her some recent DVD releases, plenty of nice food and drink, and new copies of all the necessary magazines to flick through. A happy babysitter means a happy Mummy.*

What's Happened to Me?

Some very strange things can happen to your mental state in the year after you have a baby, which may take a while to become apparent, and which can be very unsettling.

I developed a new fear of flying and of heights in general after my second baby and suffered a year of debilitating anxiety attacks after my third, often triggered by worrying about having an anxiety attack. Very annoying. Some of my Mummy friends have had periods of claustrophobia, agoraphobia and several other new phobias (including one who suddenly had a terrible fear for her own life, which meant she could barely cross the road or get on a bus without panicking). These new, apparently irrational mental issues can be very frightening, frustrating and confusing. Why has your baby turned you into a paranoid hypochondriac? Why do you suddenly have panic attacks in crowded stations? Why can't you get on a train without breaking into a sweat? Why do you lose your temper with the cashier in Boots when she has no five-pound notes and gives you all your change in fifty-pence pieces? Why do you burst into tears when *The Archers* theme tune comes on?

I don't know why, but I know a huge number of previously unaffected Mummies whose emotions changed dramatically after they had their first or subsequent babies, and we all agree that it must simply be due to the massive emotional and physical change you go through when you become somebody's mother: we put ourselves under such huge pressure to get everything right all the time, to do too much without ever having a proper break, and to seem to be doing it all so well, that all of the stress and strain can take its toll on a very deep level, and manifest itself as anger, anxiety or constantly heightened emotions.

Many of my closest mummy friends now admit to having had treatment for such symptoms of stress, but none of them had talked to anybody about it before. Some had even hidden their problems from their partner. These new feelings and reactions can take a long time to come to the surface (even years), but if they do, you may worry about what is going on in your pretty head.

Don't panic – especially if you are prone to panic attacks! Talk to your doctor about it, and see if there is anything you can do to help your mind switch off and have some time out. Everybody needs it, but busy Yummy Mummies need it more than most.

Stress-busting

When it all gets too much, and you think you are about to explode, implode or lose even more hair, it's time to take some time for yourself and chill out. Spending time on relaxation and using soothing products is one of the most important things a new mother can do for herself, and if you take a bit of care on these matters you will survive a lot better.

Here are the best stress-busting products and treatments I have come across, some of which I have in my handbag at all times in case I end up bashing my head against the kitchen wall before *Woman's Hour* has started.

Bath

'There must be quite a few things that a hot bath won't cure but I don't know many of them.'

As ever, Sylvia Plath was bang on the mark with this observation, and if you want to make things even more restorative, then try popping one of the following under the running tap:

☆ **Origins Float Away Sleep-inspiring Milk Bath**
☆ **Elemis Pure Retreat Bath Soak**
☆ **This Works: Deep Calm Bath Oil**
☆ **The Body Shop Lavender Milk Bath Powder**
☆ **A few drops of pure lavender oil**
☆ **Crabtree & Evelyn Comforting Bath Milk**

Bed

☆ **Origins Sleep Perchance to Dream Pillow Mist**, and **Sleep Time On-the-spot Gel**
☆ **Jo Malone Lino nel Vento linen spray** gives your bedroom a clean, baby-free smell to retreat to.
☆ **The Body Shop Calm Water Fragrance Oil**

Handbag Essentials

☆ **Origins Peace of Mind On-the-spot Relief** or **Diffuser.** Sniff 'n' chill has never been so easy or effective.

☆ **Bach Flower Remedies:** The SOS Essence Blend can be found in handbags in every town in the country, and for good reason. Four drops under the tongue and everything looks better. For a mood booster, try Optimism which promises 'more joy when life seems at a low ebb.'

House
☆ **Jo Malone:** Spring Jasmine, Tigerlily, and Amber & Sweet Orange are especially calming and relaxing.
☆ **Diptyque:** Try the Narcissus or New Mown Hay as a pick-me-up, or the Essence of John Galliano, which is more musty and church-like, for a complete wind-down.
☆ **Arco:** True Grace candles last for 40 hours, and come in relaxing scents such as lavender, camomile, Moroccan rose and jasmine tea.
☆ **L'Occitane room spray:** All whiffs of nappies and spillages are quickly spritzed away,
☆ **The White Company:** Their Lavender and Orange scented candles are wonderfully relaxing and very chic too.

Salon Treatments for Special Days
☆ **Clarins Pro-Active Facial:** Using PRO-Formula products (i.e. very highly concentrated), combined with specific Clarins massage movements, this facial is highly effective, deeply relaxing, and includes a hand or scalp massage.
☆ **Dermalogica Facial:** This specialist facial uses only Dermalogica's miracle-working products, and your every blip and stressed-out zone will be personally treated and loved. Choose from a menu of extras to make your tailor-made treat even better. I confidently left without any make-up, and my skin looked as good as it did before three babies had left their marks.
☆ **Elemis Day Spa:** A mouth-watering list of sensory luxuries to choose from, for everything from nails to the entire body and spirit in calm, oriental surroundings.
☆ **Bliss Spa, London:** There's a huge menu of treatments to choose from at London's sleekest salon, but the Triple Oxygen treatment

is their most popular complexion reviver, and the microderma-buffing is great for pigmentation marks and lifting old, tired skin away.

If things have really built up into a nervous knot, then a full week-end, if you can somehow manage to swing it and you're not breast-feeding, is what you need. There's nothing wrong with going on your own either – I took myself off for a reviving two-day break to London recently, and spoke to nobody the whole time. It was just me, my thoughts and the world around me, and it was exactly what I needed. Try www.healthfarms-uk.co.uk for a long list of wonderful-looking places near you.

DIY Treatments

A trip to a salon is a big treat for most of us, but there's no reason why you shouldn't be able to feel (almost) like you're in a salon at home instead.

☆ Get your husband (or a friend if he's not around) to **give you a neck, shoulder and head massage**. With scented candles and dimmed lighting you will immediately forget the dozen baby bottles that need washing.

☆ Watching TV is the perfect opportunity for some **serious leg-and-foot soothing**. (Let him watch whatever he wants, and switch your mind off while he pummels the day away!)

☆ **Use bath time to transform your body from dry and neglected to gleaming and loved.** Pop some moisturising bath oils in (Bliss Lemon & Sage Softening Soak is heavenly and leaves skin glis-tening) **and scrub and buff your body** with either a scrubbing mitt with body wash, such as Dove Firming Body Wash, or just a scrubbing product alone, but one which gives added beauty benefits (try Bliss High Thighs Slimmer Scrub). Don't forget your feet – scrub all the dead skin off with a high quality foot loofah or scrubber.

☆ While you're lying there, sort your tired skin out with a **highly effective face mask**, such as Dermalogica's Multivitamin Power

Recovery Masque, Nivea Visage Pampering Honey Mask or No7 Heavenly Hydration Moisture Mask. Any of these will restore smooth, soft, glowing skin.

☆ Follow all of this with a **generous slathering of your favourite body lotion or oil**, preferably one which firms and conditions the skin too. My favourites include Dove Intensive Firming Gel-Cream and Nuxe Spa Tonific firming cream, and remember to moisturise your feet with a foot cream which works on those stubborn, hard patches of skin.

After all of this, which needn't take more than 20 minutes, you will feel incredibly relaxed (you will probably be 90% asleep actually, but that's kind of the idea), and you will look like you've just spent two hours in a beauty salon. This kind of self-indulgence is NOT a luxury – it's an absolute necessity if you are to keep feeling good about yourself, and prepare yourself for the next tiring week. Go. Indulge.

Wonder Mums: When Honesty is Not the Best Policy

At a certain point in the early days of Yummy Mummyhood, and then at regular two-week intervals until you finally see the light, you will ask yourself this question:

Why does everybody else seem to be coping better than I am?

It's a perfectly reasonable question, especially when you are feeling low, somewhat unkempt, unloved, and you can't remember the last time you found anything to be straightforward, obvious and easy. I have felt this way *so* many times, and I still kick myself for being so gullible and insecure.

The fact is that everybody else is *not* coping better than you: they just *seem* to be. This all comes back to the 'faking it' thing, which is a fantastically powerful self-confidence-boosting tool. It can also be a case of widely differing definitions, as discovered by:

The following things should help you to get through any periods of self-doubt, self-loathing and convincing-yourself-you-are-hopeless:

☆ **Lots of Yummy Mummies lie.** Not all, but lots and lots. It's not really lying, but more a case of embellishing, selecting and slightly distorting the truth. Remember this at all times, and try to picture this outwardly perfect, confident, strong woman struggling to change a nappy, and drowning in piles of laundry too.

☆ **Have a go faking it yourself.** This is not to make other Yummy Mummies feel bad, but to make yourself feel better. This is where the beauty routine, new clothes and fifty sit-ups a day come in very useful. If you look fabulous, you will feel much better, and it will appear as though you are cruising along brilliantly.

☆ **Pull your tummy in.** Even if nobody notices, you will *feel* stronger, taller, more confident and it's great for your posture.

☆ **Smile.** Again, it may fool nobody, but smiling *will* make you feel better, and you might just forget your worries for a while.

☆ **Talk to somebody about your problems.** This can feel quite risky, especially if the 'somebody' is an outwardly coping Yummy Mummy. But nine times out of ten you will find that she is feeling exactly the same way, and you will both benefit enormously from the honesty. Honestly. (See **A Problem Shared** in Part Eleven.)

Hopefully these will help you through those self-flagellation sessions. Even if you are actually *not* coping very well, and you *do* need to get some help, and you cry most days and wonder how you will ever manage to keep this fakery up, I can promise you that you are in very good company, and doing no worse than a whole lot of other Yummy Mummies.

Old Friends: Where Are They Now?

It's a sad fact that keeping up with old friends becomes very difficult when you have a baby, and even the most solid, long-term friendships can come a cropper once early nights and baby clobber are thrown in. It's not only a problem of finding the time to meet up with old friends: once you do get together there are so many baby-associated things going on, or going through your mind, that you may find it very difficult to know what to talk about. Then you suddenly realise you have become one of those boring 'parent' couples, so feared by all groovy parents and child-free people, and you want to jump in a deep pit. Keeping up with the friends you had before you became a mother is your lifeline to the world you used to know, and these friendships are too important to let waste away. The further down the Mummy road you go, the more you will need these Old Friends to take your mind away from the daily grind and to go back to being the girl you once were. Hang on to these friendships and you will survive much better.

Here are some good ways of keeping your friends united:

☆ **Don't give them up.** It's the easiest thing in the world just to accept that things will never be as they used to be between you, and to move on to pastures new. Old friends are almost always your best friends, so work at it and find the time.

☆ **Book a time to meet up well in advance.** This makes it harder to back out of, and it gives you several weeks to stock up on enough sleep to make it through an entire evening without crashing out mid-sentence.

☆ **See friends when it suits your baby and you.** We used to do the whole 'No, no, eight o'clock is fine for us. Emily doesn't have a regular pattern yet, so whenever suits you guys is fine with us' thing, which was totally untrue. It would throw her sleep pattern right out of line, making me very tense and the baby very grouchy for days. Much better to tell them when a convenient time is for *you* and have them work around it. They have no kids – they can manage!

☆ **Tell them when you want them to leave.** Any good friend will understand that new Yummy Mummies need even more beauty sleep than their friends. Sitting there yawning and wishing you could lie down is not the way to have a fun evening.

☆ **Keep to short, fun visits.** Being with a friend's new baby can be a shock for old, child-free friends. Most people love new babies for an hour or so, but after that they become less interesting, and so do you. Short and frequent is much more friend-friendly than a whole afternoon of feeding, playing, changing and cooing.

☆ **Ask if they mind you feeding in front of them.** The first time you breastfeed in front of an old friend changes that relationship forever, so make sure you are both ready for it. They will see you in a new, Motherly light, which will make picturing your drunken pole-dancing-in-the-college-bar days seem wholly inappropriate now. If they stop picturing you like that, they stop remembering the good times you had, and that can be the beginning of the end. Real old friends will be able to see past your new role and remember there's still a pub-going, dinner-party-giving, fun-loving babe in there just screaming to get out again.

☆ **If your baby poos, change him immediately.** *You* won't mind the smell, because Yummy Mummies love everything about their babies, including their snot, poo and flaky scalps. Other people will feel sick the moment the first whiff crosses the lounge. Poo can end friendships, so run for the changing-mat pronto.

☆ **Become a house-party queen.** We managed to see a lot of our old friends by organising parties at our place. Not snorting-cocaine-off-semi-naked-women type of parties, you understand, but medium-sized gatherings involving nibbles, alcohol and good company. It's often a big hassle to go to other people's houses with a new baby, so get friends round to yours.

☆ **Book a special girly day out with your best friends, as soon as you are able to leave your baby long enough** between feeds to have at least half a day out. Go to the cinema, have lunch together or treat yourselves to a really fancy afternoon tea. Basically do anything which makes you feel young and carefree again. Baby? What baby?

One of the problems I still encounter with several of the old friends I've managed to hang on to through three pregnancies is their persistence in calling me up at the last minute and inviting me out.

'*Do I want to go to the cinema? Yeah, sure. When? Now? What, as in right now? Are you mad? At what point in the last seven years did you miss the fact that I have three children and consequently cannot go anywhere without making the sort of arrangements which would make the British Olympic Committee look like a bunch of old ladies organising a WI cake stall. No I can't come out now, thanks for asking, but I do hope you all have a fantastic time, and I'll think of you as I drift off to sleep in front of ER.*'

That sort of thing. Try not to get as annoyed as I do, and remember that anyone who hasn't got kids cannot be expected to think in the same way as you do.

Another strange trait of old friends is not understanding the importance of being on time. My very best old friend is now known by all my kids as Late Marnie, because she never turns up within an hour of when she said she would. For most people this would be an endearing quirk, but when you have a baby, an hour can make the difference between a happy baby and a very miserable one. Many is the time I've got everything ready, baby fed, changed and in a good mood to coincide exactly with the time she was expected, only to have her arrive an hour later to an exasperated Liz, a hungry baby who needs a feed and then a change and is more than ready to go out for a walk in the pram for her sleep. The whole thing is a disaster, and you feel even more like a boring friend than ever.

Tell your friends how hard it is when they turn up at random times, and see if you can get the message through. (I love you, Marnie, but you are crap at keeping time.)

I Am the One and Only

If, like me, you are the first of all of your friends, peers or colleagues to have a baby, it can be even more difficult to adjust to motherhood. None of your friends can give you any advice or help from personal experience, they all find it really weird that you have a baby (despite all reassurances to the contrary) and you can feel your old friendships starting to slip away. Being the only mum in the group exacerbates the difference between the life you had and the one you have now, and it doesn't help to soften the massive blow motherhood delivers. This is where a supportive partner or an understanding parent can really help, and when staying at home on your own can be disastrous.

There is some good news, however: being the first means you will be a much-needed source of knowledge and support in the future when everyone else starts to have babies. This is where I am now, and I love being able to help my pregnant friends through their vomiting, enlarging and panicking periods. The second advantage of doing it first is that you can sit back and smile as everyone else grows out of their jeans and develops terrible haemorrhoids, while you just look back on it all with fond memories. Been there, done that. Ha!

Sex? Sex? Are you *Trying* to Make Me Angry?

12 February. Emily six weeks old.

I can't do it. I just can't do it, but I know I have to soon or it'll be too difficult to get back into it. But I know it will hurt really badly, and I will bleed, and I might rip my stitches. I am scared that H will find it too different now: I must have changed, inside, and what will happen if he doesn't like it any more, or it feels bad, or even horrible. I really want to and I really don't – oh help!

Here's a topic I've been dreading.

I've been dreading it because I promised to be ruthlessly honest with you about *every* aspect of the whole 'becoming a mother thing' but at this point I really want to lie. I want to lie, deceive you and protect you from the ugly truth.

Here are some lies I would love to tell:

☆ The pregnancy hormones coursing through your blood will send your libido through the roof.
☆ After giving birth, your sexual sensitivity quadruples, causing you to achieve earth-shattering orgasms as you walk from the cot to the laundry basket. Lactating breasts are a huge turn-on for all men, as are all the new folds of skin to be found pretty much all over your body.
☆ All that time spent resting in bed after a new baby means the opportunities for a quick shag are plentiful – hell, it's like having a second honeymoon!
☆ After a day with the kids, you will be so pleased to see an adult that keeping your hands off your partner will be practically impossible. Leave all the washing up – let's have sex, sex, sex!

Ahh, the yarns I could spin. But I shan't. Instead, I have the unenviable task of breaking this news to you: sex after childbirth is a good deal more complicated, and often less fun for a while than it was before.

As far as I can glean from my own experience, and from those of my closest Mummy friends, parenthood causes 'having sex' to plummet down the list of desirable or likely activities, to rest between 'emptying the nappy bin' and 'cleaning the mould off the bottom of the fridge'.

It's there, it's got to be done at some point (and preferably more than once a month), but you would rather find something else to do if possible. Like sleep.

Passion-killers will spring up in various guises, but here are some of the worst offenders:

1. Lack of Sleep

Sleep. Ahhh, SLEEP. Despite being fairly hardy creatures, we humans do ask for just a handful of things in order to survive. These include food, drink, handbags, sex, and SLEEP.

When you have kids, you can still eat, although this becomes more tricky and haphazard. You can, and should, drink (water and endless cups of coffee between 5 a.m. and 5 p.m., and strong alcohol after that). You *absolutely o*we it to yourself to have as many hand-bags as possible, to keep all that child-associated junk in, and you can still have sex if you really want to, or if you are hoping to make your marriage survive more than a year or two. *But you cannot sleep.* Ever again. I mean, obviously you do manage to sleep at some point, but it's never when you want to, or for long enough, and it's always broken. Now, in *this* book, broken sleep doesn't count. It's a bit like saying to someone who hasn't eaten for three weeks, 'You see this Sunday roast? Well, you can smell it, look at it and lick the gravy, but that's all you're having until some unspecified time tomorrow. Now go away!'

Sleep deprivation has several effects on humans, especially women: we become irritable, we look rough as hell, which in turn makes us even more irritable (beware the woman who has spent a fortune on looking fabulous but still looks rough as hell), our hair thins, we lose our memory and, above all, we crave sleep more than anything else. Yes, *even more than sex.* Although, come to think of it, if Clive Owen were to appear, then – oh, never mind. The point is that when you have kids you stop sleeping well and you become chronically exhausted. Anything that attempts to come between you and the faintest chance of some kip runs the risk of being annihilated by maternal wrath, and this especially applies to your sexual partner, who should bloody-well know better than to even ask.

Given this state of exhaustion, you can see how it happens, if, after twelve unbroken hours of baby-entertaining, pram-pushing, swing-swinging, baby-changing, hand-wiping, floor-sweeping, dishwasher-emptying, laundry-hanging, tantrum-calming and clothes-changing, your husband sidles over to your side of the bed and starts making suggestive movements on your thighs, you cannot help but roll your eyes to the ceiling, sigh deeply, and hope it doesn't take too long. He may be beautiful, kind and you love him to bits but you need to sleep RIGHT NOW, so hurry up!

When you feel like this, don't panic. You have not fallen out of love, or out of lust. Your marriage is not doomed, and you are still capable of lust and sexual desire. But for now, and possibly for a few years to come, you are just bloody exhausted, and really need to catch up on some sleep. OK?

2. Mental Overload

Trying to remember all the things a mother has to remember takes the brainpower of – oh, I don't know of what, but it's a heck of a lot, and it can fill your brain completely. Bearing in mind that pregnancy is said to cause your brain to shrink (no, I don't believe this either, but I've read it many times and it's a handy excuse, if you don't mind undoing all of the hard work done by the women's liberation movement) it's understandable if you sometimes have trouble remembering everything, resort to writing lists of lists of lists, and talk to yourself occasionally.

Unfortunately, I find it very hard to stop going through all the things I have to remember, and I have been known to take my lists to bed with me. Forget 'She'll be wearing pink pyjamas': I'm more a case of 'She'll be writing a mental shopping list and trying to remember whether she has prepared the night-time milk bottle when she comes.' Hardly makes a man feel special, does it?

Again, I think this is perfectly understandable, and you should not feel at all guilty or concerned if you find yourself crying out the name of your baby's health visitor during a rare moment of passion. If, on the other hand, your husband cries out the name of your baby's (now you come to think of it, very attractive) health visitor, then it's an entirely different matter and you should make enquiries immediately.

3. 'Down There'

Oh God, how can I put this? OK, imagine a perfectly crafted Burberry trench coat with its neatly covered buttons down the front. Now picture (if you can bear it) pushing a ping-pong ball slowly through one of the buttonholes. Quite a squeeze, I know, but it *will* fit if you push hard enough.

When you've recovered, try to imagine how the buttonhole looks now. It's not quite as tightly closed as it was before, is it? Well, so it is with you 'down there'. No matter how many pelvic-floor exercises you do, or promise yourself you will do, your vagina will never be quite as tightly closed as it was before three and a half kilos of baby squeezed its way through a hole which should be no bigger than, well, closed, actually. Sorry again, but it's best you realise this now.

To make matters worse, there is an even bigger psychological hurdle to overcome. What was once such a sexual, personal and pleasurable place has now acquired a new, *functional* role that is very hard to ignore. Added to this is the scary fact that in many cases your lover has watched a child's head emerge from this private sanctuary, and he is very unlikely to forget the image easily. This can be quite intimidating and unsettling and may prompt many questions: Will he ever look at me again without picturing that grim, bloody, wholly un-dignified scene? How can I ever look alluring or sensuous to him again? Can I ever go back to seeing my body as a sexual thing, and not as an extra in *Men in Black*?

And let's not forget about breasts, while we're at it (or not, which is precisely the problem). Breasts quickly come to represent nothing more than milking machines (I used to dread any fondling, sucking or tweaking, in case of unwanted spraying). When the feeding stops, your luvverly juvverlies end up being so floppy and small that getting a handful must feel to him like trying to scrape a sandcastle out of very fine, dry sand: let go for a second and they just run away, under your armpits again (assuming you're lying down).

I'm probably alarming you now, which is not the idea at all. I'm only telling you all of this because nobody told me, and I wish I had known that other people have these worries and feelings too, and that it's perfectly normal. Over a couple of bottles of wine with my best Mummy friends, I discovered that most, if not all of them, still worry about their sex lives since becoming parents years ago.

Maria, mother of Jack, four, and Chloe, two

Sex? What's that? Our sex life has completely changed since having children – it's not my extra flabby bits which has made the difference, it's just the sheer exhaustion of looking after the kids. We do get round to it, and it's lovely, but we have to go to bed as soon as the kids do and just go for it!

Sophie, mother of Georgia, three, and Toby, ten months

We have a new rule now, which is 'No Foreplay'! With such limited time and opportunity, we have to go straight to it or I fall asleep. Occasionally, though, we ignore the rule and spend a bit more time, which feels really special.

This last point will ring true with almost every set of parents throughout the land. We do exactly the same thing, and a 'wham bam thank you ma'am' is the best way to ensure you get some regular sex. And when push comes to shove (so to speak) most people would rather just get on with it than take an hour to get the juices flowing. Which parent has the time or energy for *that*? In, out, job done. Good night.

In contrast, many of us also agreed that sex can become much more meaningful and more special than it was before. It can even feel better, more intense, and more pleasurable. Good news at last! On balance, we concluded that it's probably a good idea to talk about these things with your partner, if they are concerning you. It may turn out, as it did for most of us, that all is groovy and still *very* attractive down there, thanks for asking, love. It's just different. And, believe it or not, the whole 'Wow, you are amazing, because you gave birth to our child' thing, does, just possibly, make him a more considerate lover.

It may not happen very often, it may not happen the way it used to, but sex after childbirth is definitely still *there*. One day you *will* get some sleep, you will drink enough Sauvignon Blanc to believe you are Sienna Miller, and for him to believe you are Angelina Jolie, and you will both have the best night of sex you can imagine. Promise. In the meantime:

TOP TIPS for surviving sex after childbirth:

☆ **Do it as soon as you feel ready.** Some midwives advise waiting for your six-week check, but if you feel ready, for God's sake go for it!

☆ **Use a lubricant.** Breastfeeding, hormone changes and exhaustion can leave things a little drier than either of you might like.

☆ **Protect the mattress.** There might still be some peculiar extra bits which want to leak out while you're trying not to look.

☆ **Don't delay.** Seven hours of tantric sex may well have been your norm in years gone by but these days, at the first sign you are nearing the end, make for the finishing line like Frankie Dettori at the Grand National. If you delay even a couple of minutes, your baby is guaranteed to wake up, leaving you both frustrated. This does nothing for the 'rekindling our sex life' part of the exercise.

☆ **STOP if it hurts too much.** Having sex after childbirth can be very painful. How painful is *too* painful depends on your particular pain threshold (and after birth, yours will be much higher than it was before), but if you feel that it's not worth it to carry on, just say so, and leave it a few more days.

☆ **Be brave.** Putting off sex until you really feel like it is a terrible idea. It could take a year or more to *really* feel like it again, by which time you will have learned how to live without it. It's worth forcing yourself to have a go regularly, just to keep things alive, and because one time it might suddenly feel fantastic again.

☆ **Free your mind.** 90% of sex happens in your mind so this is a great opportunity to forget you are a mother, and go back to being sexy, hot, young you again for a short while. A very short while, but it's the best therapy.

Contraception

This may be the last thing on your mind when you've recently given birth, but it's vital that you sort some GOOD contraception out as soon as you can. Never believe that breastfeeding is an effective contraceptive: lots of my Mummy friends are currently looking after the results of such false information. You can be extremely fertile from the moment you give birth, so talk to your health visitor about the best ways to avoid going through it all again in forty weeks' time! And one last thing – your periods may take many months or even years to get back to normal again. Mine never came back at all between my first two (proving that just because you don't *think* you can get pregnant, you can) and took about a year to re-appear after my third.

Square One: Where You'll Be At the End of Every Day

14 December. Charlie six months old.

This is so ridiculous. I have worked really hard all day, the only time I sat down was when we cycled to the park, I have hardly had a second to eat properly or think at all, my legs are aching, my head is spinning from the constant multi-tasking and relentless Charlie-watching, and now, after the final clear-up, I can't see any evidence at all that I did anything today. Nothing. The whole house looks exactly as it did yesterday, and it'll be the same again tomorrow. I want to see what I've achieved. I want a tick in a box, a star on a chart, or a pay a cheque into my bank. I'm right back to square one again, and I hate it. There's no reward, and no sense of achievement at all.

One of the hardest things to adjust to when you become a mother is the fact that you never seem to *achieve* anything. Even though you know perfectly well that you're achieving lots, by helping your baby, being a good mother, keeping the house resembling a home rather than a bomb-site, cooking meals and probably doing a million other domestic jobs, you will still *feel* as though you are achieving nothing.

At the end of the day, when you've put away all the toys, cleared up the kitchen, wiped the high-chair down, swept most of your baby's dinner off the floor, cleaned out all the bottles, prepared the next feed, emptied the bin, folded away tiny items of clothing, hung out the next load of tiny items of clothing, sterilised anything which needs it and cleaned out the baby's day bag, where are you? Where has all of this hard work got you? Precisely nowhere, apart from one day further along the line. You are back to square one yet again, and it can feel really, really bad. Human beings are simple creatures at heart, and we like a reward for our efforts. Most of us like to feel that if we work hard to achieve something we will get some kind of reward for our efforts. This reward could come in the form of a pay cheque every month, a promotion at work, a bonus, a compliment, a word of thanks, or even just some recognition of our effort and appreciation of what we've done.

Far too often for mothers, this recognition never comes, and we are left feeling tired, unappreciated and depressed. I'm painting a bleak picture here because when you find yourself back at square one for the hundredth time it can be very hard to convince yourself, as friends and family may try to do for you, that you have achieved something, that you *are* appreciated and that you are doing a great job.

This is just a reality of Yummy Mummyhood, and I think it has been made worse in recent years by the number of us who have become used to having fulfilling jobs with tangible rewards and clear levels of progress. Going from this set-up to the occasional 'Thanks for dinner', and the seemingly endless, repetitive and thankless task of looking after a baby can be a huge shock, and to pretend it's not affecting you is to pave the way for a big crash further down the line.

If you are feeling unappreciated and worthless, talk to your partner about it, and see if he can help to make your work feel more valued and recognised. He probably just hasn't realised how low you are feeling, being the perceptive male of the species that he is, and will be very happy to help out now you've come to mention it. But remember, no matter how many times *somebody else* tells you that you are doing a fantastic job, that you *are* appreciated and that all your effort *is* worth it, if you don't feel that way it will be a very difficult time for you. You are not alone – it happens to all of us many times, and you just have to try to convince yourself that you are wonderful, useful and absolutely gorgeous.

But I'm a control freak...
We are all control freaks nowadays – I wasn't actually around in other days, but from what I hear from the older generation, this control-freakishness is a new phenomenon, associated with double-tall, dry, skinny, extra-hot vanilla lattes and suchlike.

One of the seismic shifts you will have to get to grips with when you become a Yummy Mummy is that you cannot be in control all the time any more. You have to let go. Chill out, relax, go with the flow, take it eeeeaasy, and see where the day takes you.

If you can already do this, and you're happy to drink the full-fat, extra-shot hazelnut frappuccino they give you by mistake then you won't have such a fight on your hands. If, like I did, you like things 'just so', and find coping with 'whatever comes' very difficult, then you are heading for a very challenging year, and you might like to start practising how to take life as it comes a little now.

Here are some things that will interfere with your Mission Control:

☆ Babies do things when *they* want to, not when you want them to. It is pointless trying to keep to a tight schedule – sudden nappy changes, feeds, screaming fits and throwing-up sessions will throw everything off course.
☆ Everything takes longer than you think: carrying a buggy up steps, going back half a mile to pick up one baby shoe, which has been kicked off, and so on.
☆ A baby will always poo when you are just about to leave the house and are late already.
☆ You have to work around your baby's needs, not the other way around.
☆ Your chosen outfit may not make it past 9 a.m. before it is vomited on.

All of this centres around the main point, which is that you never know what will happen in the next couple of hours, and you have to be ready to change your plans at a moment's notice. If this is stressful for you, then learning some techniques to cope with it will be a huge help. Otherwise you will end up literally pulling your hair out and bashing your head against the Winnie the Pooh wallpaper as yet another plan goes out of the window and you find yourself exploding with frustration.

Learning to let go a little is one of the best lessons that having a baby teaches us. If more of us could handle it when our plane is delayed for three hours, they run out of bread in Tesco or the programme we stayed up late to watch is suddenly scrapped in favour of *TV's Scariest Cop Chases Ever 8!*, our lives would be so much healthier and more relaxed. In my opinion…

Survival Strategies for Coping with Complete Loss of Control

☆ Set yourself **very low targets** for the day.
☆ **See every 'plan' as a *potential* plan.** If it happens, it's a bonus. If it doesn't, it's not a big deal.
☆ **Practise sitting in clutter** for a short while every day, to get used to the feeling of defeat. It's horrible, but you *have* to readjust your 'acceptable levels of mess' threshold.
☆ Take some time out every day to **relax and de-clutter** your brain. This could be the trusted hot, calming bath, or a 20-minute run, some yoga, or just listening to some music. So long as it's your choice of music, and you can sit where you choose, with the volume at *your* favourite level, it's having the desired effect.
☆ **Practise counting to five when things don't go as you'd planned**, *again*. As you watch the number seventeen bus pull away, which you missed because the elastic part of the stupid raincover got caught in the pram wheels and you had to stop to dislodge it, try to stand up straight, close your eyes, count to at least five, breathe slowly and remember how cute your baby is. Having a screaming fit every time will give you a nervous breakdown within three months.

Life is a Rollercoaster, Baby

The Yummy Mummy rollercoaster puts anything at Alton Towers to shame. Forget the familiar female mood swings: your Mummy moods will be riding the white-knuckle Oblivion for the first year or two. And there's an extra twist: this ride keeps you in the dark most of the time, so you don't know what's around the next bend. It wraps you up in cosy layers of 'coping' and maternal bliss, and makes you feel absolutely on top of it all.

Yummy Mummies can go for weeks, even months, with no problems or worries at all. These are the Good Times. These are the best times you will ever have in your life, when everything is pink and shiny and sweet and wonderful. Your baby is wonderful, your life is perfect, the sky is bluer, the air is cleaner (unless you live in a city in which case it's still fairly dirty), you feel complete and settled and bursting with happiness and love. And then it happens. Your rollercoaster turns a corner and the ground disappears from under your feet. Suddenly everything which was so rosy yesterday seems hopeless, miserable, ugly, irritating and interminable. The rosy glow evaporates and you feel like you just can't go on. Just like that. These, as you will so cleverly have deduced, are the Bad Times. They don't usually last for more than a few days, or a few weeks, but if you're in a trough for more than that you really should get some help.

The only reason I mention all of this is because I, and many of my Yummy Mummy friends, have been caught out so many times by the sudden appearance of the Bad Times, and we were never properly warned about it. Every mother should expect to feel a bit 'blue' occasionally: it's hardly surprising when you never sleep, your body is swamped with mood-altering, bottom-enlarging hormones, and you stop being able to wear cashmere for a year. But it's very confusing when things seem to be going well, and you think you've cracked it, only to find yourself in a pit of despair again for no apparent reason.

Another thing you should know is that this can go on for years and it gets no less surprising. Babies go through hundreds of phases, and just because Tinkerbell has started sleeping through the night does NOT mean she will continue to do this for long. Just when you thought starting to watch a DVD after eight o'clock at night was looking possible again, Tinkerbell will decide she doesn't need so much sleep after all, thanks very much, and you'll be back to lights out before the watershed. What brought about this change you'll never know, but it will pass and things will be good again soon. You won't know when, but it will be at some point dictated by the youngest member of the family.

Laura Bailey, model

I've loved every moment with Luc but if I'm honest, it was at about five or six months that I fell head over heels in love and suddenly everything made sense. I stopped trying so hard and relaxed into my new life.

PART TEN

Baby Things

Medical Matters

Baby's Medical Kit

Babies get ill all the time. You name it, their immune systems have to deal with it: coughs, colds, flu, diarrhoea, fever, rashes, constipation, ear infections, chest infections, eczema, asthma, conjunctivitis and just about every other '-itis' you care to mention. Consequently, not only do you have to take a medical degree in your (non-existent) spare time, but you also have to buy a fantastic array of medicines and potions to treat all the ailments.

Now, depending on how much of a bug-fearing hypochondriac you are, your baby's medical kit could contain anything from a box of Band-Aid to a fully fledged mini-pharmacy. It's up to you.

To ease the strain, here are some basic essentials which every Yummy bathroom cabinet should house:

1. Calpol

Aka 'the magic potion'. Every type of pain and fever, from teething to the after-effect of vaccinations, can be relieved by this sweet, sticky, purple goo. Most kids love it, but trying to administer the stuff to a baby who doesn't want it is almost impossible. Have a cloth ready to wipe up all the spillages, and if possible get someone else to give them the medicine while you hold their thrashing arms and head still. You'll just have to find a method which works for you – good luck!

Calpol is very mild, and if you give your baby a bit too much then don't do what I did and call your GP in a huge flap. That said, I have heard awful stories of parents using Calpol as a method of getting their baby to sleep better and longer, because it makes them a bit drowsy. This is a very, very bad idea. Paracetamol is a nasty chemical, the more you use it, the less effective it becomes, and it's probably not doing your baby's liver any good.

2. Thermometer

You will need to measure your baby's temperature fairly often, but the crazy old-fashioned piece-of-glass-with-some-mercury-in-it is not really appropriate here. (Is it ever appropriate anywhere, I ask myself?)

The best option is probably to get an electronic one, which goes in your baby's ear and beeps. Strip thermometers are also handy, but I find them almost impossible to read accurately: is it browny-green or greeny-brown? Or do I detect a hint of the dreaded *blue* in there? No idea. Best to worry, just in case.

3. Nappy rash cream

Not sure where the phrase 'smooth as a baby's bottom' comes from, but in my experience babies' bums are rarely smooth. They are more usually slightly spotty, with red patches and occasional eczema thrown in for good measure. Nappy rash looks very sore and it can cause days of a grisly, grumpy, crying baby. I've found that constantly slathering cream on thickly can make it worse. Instead, changing your baby's nappy as soon as the smell has reached you and not 'in a minute', leaving the nappy off for a few minutes after each change to let some fresh air dry the rash out, and applying cream sparingly, seemed to work better for me. No, not for me, for my babies. My bottom is lovely, thanks very much, though a little orange-peely in places. Too much information.

4. A snot sucker

A what? A snot sucker. If your baby gets a blocked nose (as it will, occasionally), she won't be able to drink any milk, take a dummy or sleep. Which means she will be very, very miserable, and so will you. The only solution I have found is to – wait for it – suck the snot out of your baby's nose. You won't believe yourself capable of doing such a gross thing until your baby has gone without food, and you without sleep, for two days. A snot sucker is an ingenious device which lets you perform this hideous act without getting any slime near your mouth. Horrid, horrid, but absolutely essential!

Other Items for Baby's Bathroom Kit

☆ **Baby lotion.** For wiping your baby's skin clean, and keeping it moisturised if necessary. Also a great moisturiser for your own dry skin.

☆ **Baby massage oil.** See **Baby Basics** in Part Six.

☆ **Baby bath bubbles or body wash.** Choose an organic one (if you choose one at all – babies don't *need* soaps yet, but the bubbles are fun) like the Little Me Baby Organics range which have aromatherapy oils in them too.

☆ **Mini scissors.** Babies' nails are very sharp and they grow amazingly fast. I always used to cut my babies' nails by biting them for the first few months, and then started using little scissors as they got stronger and I was less terrified of chopping any miniature digits off.

☆ **Teething gel.** Again, this can mean the difference between a night of hell and a good five hours' sleep. Bonjela is too strong, but any baby teething gel will do.

☆ **E45 cream.** Great for any signs of eczema, or just very dry skin, When you stop getting your prescriptions free then just buy it from Boots. It's cheaper.

TOP TIP: *Babies often get sticky eyes, as some annoying piece of dust or dirt gets in there. It really bothers them and it looks horrible. The best way I've found of treating this is to wash the affected*

eye with some of your breast milk as often as you can. It's hard to get it in there, and you feel very unglamorous trying to poke your nipple in your baby's eye, but it works. If it doesn't, then apologies for the embarrassment, and maybe a doctor will be more helpful. If you are not breastfeeding, use a cotton wool ball dipped in cooled, boiled water – use a separate one for each eye!

Do I Worry Too Much About My Baby's Health?

'Too much' implies there is an acceptable amount of worry you should have. There isn't. **It is completely normal to worry about your baby's health.** You are not mad, but simply doing what every mother naturally does. Babies are tiny, helpless, delicate and vulnerable, and they are exposed to millions of bacteria, viruses and other yukky invaders every day. (Usually borne by some not-at-all-Yummy Mummy's snotty, rash-covered, sneezing, wheezing baby, who should be at home.) The good news is that, given all this potential for illness, **babies are much more resilient than you might fear,** and can usually conquer whatever it is that's making them fevered or grouchy within a few days. As time goes by you will learn to recognise when it's just time for some Calpol and an extra sleep, and when you really should go to the doctor.

NEVER FEEL BAD ABOUT TAKING YOUR BABY TO THE DOCTOR IF YOU ARE GENUINELY CONCERNED FOR HIS HEALTH. Nine times out of ten you will walk out feeling like a total idiot, as the 'life-threatening' spots you were panicking about turn out to be milk spots, caused when you didn't wipe around his mouth properly after a feed. One time out of ten your doctor will find something needing treatment, and you will be very glad you made the trip.

No matter what any well-meaning book, friend or Internet site tries to tell you, **you know your baby better than anyone else,** and if you notice a change which just doesn't seem right to you, then asking for a doctor's advice is not just understandable, it's essential. And if you don't feel happy with your doctor's diagnosis, then get another one.

Here endeth the lesson.

How Do I Know When My Baby Really is Ill?

Best to get a good medical encyclopaedia or marry a doctor to properly answer this question, but here are some good pointers to look out for:

☆ **Being out of character.** Not you. You will frequently be out of character. But your baby's general countenance, mood or look can change, and you should look out for these changes.

☆ **Dry nappies.** If your baby doesn't have a wet nappy all day, then get him checked out, and try to get him to drink some water.

☆ **Sleep.** Not sleeping, or sleeping much more than usual, can be a sign that something is up. Again, if it persists or if you are just not happy about it, seek advice.

☆ **Crying.** If your baby suddenly seems to cry more, especially if it sounds like a painful cry, then something is probably not right. Once you've checked for any stray, sharp toenail clippings that may have found their way into your baby's nappy, and when none of the usual tricks cheer him up, pop down to your GP.

Choosing a GP

I remember being stunned at the amount of time I spent in the doctor's surgery for the first year of all my babies' lives. Not because they were ill, necessarily, but for all the weighing, checking, vaccinating and general fussing that seems to be mandatory for the under-ones. All this quality time with my doctor made me realise how important it is to have **the right GP for you**. So, if you are lucky enough to have a choice of surgeries or GPs for yourself and your baby, then keep the following in mind when making a decision:

1. Do You *Like* Him or Her?

Now that you are a Mummy, detailed information about your most Yummy parts is the property of anyone who cares to ask, and a great many medical people *will* care to. If you feel uncomfortable around your GP, you're hardly going to want to discuss your holiest of holies with her, and it will all be very awkward for you. I still find it awkward, even though I really like my GP and she's seen more than I'd ever like to see down there over the last eight years!

2. Does the Surgery Have Steps to the Front Door?

Mine does, and it was a total pain for the first year, because I would have to wait patiently at the foot of the steps with a huge pram or a double buggy until some kind, Cambridge gentleman stopped and helped me haul it up to the door. As most of these gentlemen were lithe, handsome young students, it somehow felt even worse. Aaah, there was once a time....oh stop it.

3. Is it Near a Pharmacy?

The final straw after a hellish visit to the doctor is having to trek halfway across town to get whatever it is they promise will make you or your baby better. Five hundred metres is quite far enough.

4. Does it Have Toys or Books?

Babies don't like reading 10-year-old editions of *Woman's Own* magazine, and no toys means a miserable wait for everyone concerned.

What to take to the surgery

I always left at least one vital thing at home, which made my journey either totally wasted, or just more difficult than it should have been.

Here's a quick checklist:

☆ Your baby's record book, so they can check what has already been done, and mark down what they do this time.
☆ Spare nappies, so you can quickly pop a clean one on *before* your baby is weighed as well as after. Looks like you're doing a really good job that way...
☆ A change of clothes, because the inevitable always happens during the weighing process, and it's embarrassing to put your baby back into wet or dirty clothes.
☆ Food for both of you. If it's a long wait you're going to need it.
☆ A toy, in case some mean child has walked off with them all since your last visit three days ago.
☆ An air of complete confidence and competence for the waiting room, and total honesty and openness for the consulting room.

If you've got worries, then this is *the* place to share them. They won't take your baby away just because you admit to having trouble getting him to eat solid food. (Unless you are trying to feed him hash cookies or something.)

Vaccinations: What, *More*?

The first year always seems to me to consist of little more than vaccination and health check after vaccination and health check. Your baby will be pricked, jabbed and poked about frequently, but this is all very useful stuff, and vaccinations are fairly essential if you believe in disease prevention and public responsibility.

After injections, babies often develop a mild fever, so take a bottle or sachet of Calpol with you, and administer it straight away. This also makes babies drowsy, so you should be in for a nice, quiet few hours. The great thing about giving injections to a baby is that they barely notice at all. *You* get all nervous and upset, but they just grimace a little, and then get back to gurgling and burping.

And my view on MMR? Do it. I have nothing else to say on the matter, except DO IT.

Hygiene: Another Thing Not to Stress About

Why do we love to say how tough and resilient babies are, but then set about trying to protect them from every invisible microbe and potentially dirty organism known to man, woman, or Yummy Mummy?

If the *How Clean is Your House?* team were to turn up at almost any house containing a Yummy Baby, they would conclude that it was 'very, very, very clean indeed', such is the level of bug-busting that goes on (except for in my house, where it's really quite grubby in many places). WHY? Why the wiping, spraying, spit-and-polishing frenzy?

Babies need bugs. They need to be exposed to germs, bacteria, filth and grime of all kinds, because that's the only way they can develop any kind of immune system. It's one of the failings of human development that babies come out pretty badly equipped to combat many nasty things. It's only by exposure to these nasties that their bodies can learn what to expect next time, and can develop the required antibodies. If you scrub, wipe, sterilise, neutralise, kill, disinfect and eradicate every trace of dirt in your baby's environment, then one day the poor, unexposed child will come across some Grade A Muck and come a cropper. Much better to let some grubby bits get in, and kick-start some immune responses. Some studies have shown that children living in super-clean houses are more likely to develop allergies and autoimmune disorders, because their immune systems are less regularly stimulated. Bring on the muck!

Here are some other things which might make you put the Marigolds down and go for a good dirt-eating session in the local park:

Some of the chemicals in many common household disinfectants have been shown to cause vomiting, bloody diarrhoea, respiratory, circulatory or even cardiac failure, skin irritation, damage to the nervous system and kidneys, and possibly cancer. Wowzers. Clearly you have to bathe in these chemicals every night to be in serious danger, but the very fact that we are happy to spray them and wipe them all over the place is a bit worrying, I'd say.

To make long-term matters worse, widespread use of antibacterial household products could encourage bacteria to develop and spread resistance, and some scientists are worried that this may give rise to more 'superbugs'.

I turned into 'Appalled from Tunbridge Wells' when I received some chemical disinfectant in my 'free samples' pack in the hospital, advising me to spray it on all surfaces my baby might come into contact with. What, so she could fill up on carcinogenic disinfectants instead of organic, home-grown, natural bacteria? No thanks.

Also, do you know what young babies spend 90% of their awake-time doing? Not sitting neatly in their bouncy chair, playing with the newly sterilised toy you have chosen for them, but putting everything and anything they can find into their mouths. Babies are obsessed with their mouths, and nothing escapes the lick/suck/chew/slobber-all-over experience. You can spend every waking moment cleaning the place, but turn your back for a millisecond and into the mouth go those tiny fingers again, along with whatever germs they managed to pick up from the buggy, supermarket trolley, library book or Baby Gap changing mat.

Makes ya think, don't it?

Things You Probably *Should* Sterilise

☆ Baby's milk bottles before making up feeds.
☆ Dummies, but every week or so was enough for me. If they fall on the ground, just give them a good suck yourself and they're good to go again. Assuming they didn't fall into any dog poo or anything, in which case throw them away.
☆ Teething rings, every so often.
☆ Real nappies, obviously.
☆ Changing mat. If you are doing a half-decent job then there shouldn't be any nasties on the changing mat at all. But as changing a nappy requires eight arms and the manual dexterity of a couture seamstress, a few bits might sneak out of the sides, so a wipe down with something stronger than water and hope is a good idea.

Things You Don't Need to Sterilise

☆ High-chair tray. A good wash is fine, with a chemical clean every week or less.
☆ Bowls, baby spoons and beakers.
☆ Toys. If you find yourself regularly sterilising the Duplo, you must get out more. Unless your baby is sick into the storage box, or course.

Gender Bender

There seems to be a good deal of discussion in the playgroups I go to about what is suitable for which sex. Should girls play with diggers? Is it OK for Benjamin to push a doll in a buggy and bring her plates of plastic grapes? Is green a boy's or a girl's colour? Is Isabella turning into a tomboy because she likes hammers and drills?

All of this worrying and debate seems utterly ridiculous to me: Nature is stronger than nurture in this case, and no amount of gender stereotyping will make much difference at all. If Isabella wants to bash and drill things, why not let her?

I now know of loads of dads who are terrified that their darling Freddy, Billy or whatever will turn out to be (sssshhhh!) gay if he comes within a sequinned tuxedo's width of a cookery set or anything pink, and I have two comments to make on this: First of all, any man who thinks like this has some *serious* masculinity issues to deal with, because we all know that most gay men are far more beautiful, fashionable, talented and thoughtful than their macho counterparts. Secondly, he can try to toughen his son up all he likes, but if Freddy, Billy or whoever *like*s wearing dresses and brushing his hair, then that's what he likes, so leave him be.

You can't mess with Nature, so let them do whatever it is they like doing, dress them in whatever you think looks nice (while you still have some input in the matter), and don't try to force them into an outdated mould.

Such pearls and pearls and *pearls* of wisdom!

There Were Three in the Bed...

For the first month at least, your baby will probably sleep in your room, either in a Moses basket, a cot, a bottom drawer or a cardboard box. Whatever the actual container, having it in the same room as you sleep in is safest and most convenient (you can hear all the coughs, and learn how your baby wriggles around at night getting the blankets over his head). You will be up several times a night to feed and change your new baby, so having to tramp all the way over to the west wing is a real pain in the arse. Even across the hallway, as in my case, was far too far.

But after a while there comes a stage when you are fed-up with sharing your room with a snuffling, coughing, burping, wheezing night-time companion, and because you can't really ask your partner to leave, you go for the next best thing, which is your baby. Off to the newly decorated nursery for you, my sweet.

When should I move my baby out of my room?

This is completely up to you, of course, but there are some advantages of doing it sooner rather than later.

☆ Babies learn habits very quickly, and if yours learns that the room with the big shoe collection is hers, you will have a lot of trouble moving her into the room with the big rattley toy collection.

☆ The longer you leave it, the more tired you will be, and so the prospect of upsetting everything during the Big Move will become less appealing.

There is one huge advantage of having your baby in a separate room:

you sleep more.

Almost all of us worry at the idea of not being able to hear our babies at night. What if she buries herself under her blanket and suffocates? What if she removes the lining of her Moses basket and suffocates? What if she chokes on some milk and suffocates? It's all fairly suffocating-related fear, and it does you absolutely no good at all. If your baby is going to suffocate at night, you won't hear it whether she is 2 feet or 10 metres away from you. That's a very hard thing to say, and even harder to accept, but it's true and the night I moved our baby away from our room, and into her own was the night I got my first, uninterrupted five-hour sleep since her birth.

If your baby sleeps near you, you will hear every noise he makes at night, and they make one heck of a lot of noise! It's like sleeping with a room full of hamsters or something. Shuffling, snuffling, coughing…it's incredibly disturbing, you'll be up and down like a nervous Jack-in-the-Box, and there will be nothing wrong at all.

Oh, and when did I move my babies next door? At five weeks, for all of them. GO! Mummy needs her sleep!

Weaning

When, oh *When*, oh When Should You Start Weaning Your Baby?

(Weaning just means giving solid food, by the way, not teaching her to jump through hoops of fire or introducing her to suitable husbands.)

The advice and guidance on when to start on the sloppy food changes every year, and it seems to be getting later and later at a fairly alarming rate. When my first baby was born eight years ago, the recommended age for offering the first solid food was three months. By my second child we were told to wait until four months, and now babies are being asked to go for at least six months, and preferably a year, on nothing more than milk.

Nobody seems to point out the glaringly obvious, which is that **all babies are different, and they all require different things at different stages**. Where one smaller, less active baby might be happy to suck on Mummy's milk for six months and thrive perfectly well, another big whopper might need extra nutrition from solid food at only three months. It all depends on the baby and on the quality and quantity of the breast milk.

Tell-tale signs that your baby wants to start weaning:

☆ Your baby wants feeding more often than normal, or still seems hungry after a good milk feed.
☆ He stops sleeping through the night, when he normally used to.
☆ You are feeding as much as you can, but your baby stops putting on weight as normal.
☆ He starts to nick food off your plate and try to eat it. See, it's not *only* girlfriends who do that.

Another clincher for opening that first jar of baby mush is your physical state. You know by now that I am the world's greatest supporter of breastfeeding, but if you reach the point where feeding your baby is draining every last drop of energy in your body, and she *still* looks hungry, then it's time to look at some dietary extras. The important thing is that at some point your baby will need more nutrients, especially iron, from a source other than milk, in order to carry on growing properly. (And because chewing helps speech development – maybe that's why I'm such a good talker!) But exactly *when* that point is, is dictated by you and your baby. Talk to your health visitor…

The Basics

Babies need to build up to steak and chips slowly, and the first food you will offer yours will look more like porridge than anything solid. Almost everyone starts with so-called baby rice, which is a smooth, creamy-ish paste. (Actually, it's delicious, and I used to put away quite a lot of it myself.) There are tons of makes to choose from, many of which are organic, so whatever you think your gourmet baby will like best, goes.

  TOP TIPS for weaning:

☆ **Introduce new foods one at a time.** This allows any allergies to be spotted.
☆ **Feed your baby in a bouncy chair**, not a high-chair to start with.
☆ **Use a bib.** However skilled you *think* you are, the baby slop will go everywhere, and that's not allowing for spitting out, being sick and dribbling. Nice.
☆ **Use a very small teaspoon.** I used to use the rubbery ones, but my babies just chewed them until they fell apart, so I went back to metal again, but they had to be very small or it all came out of the sides of their mouths.
☆ **Allow at least twenty minutes** for a solid feed. Hurrying never helps anything, and a baby who is being forced to eat will then spend the next thirty years dealing with 'food issues'. Boring, and expensive.
☆ **Don't expect her to eat more than a teaspoonful or two** to begin with. Your baby is not going to chug the lot on her first sitting. Her mouth, throat, tummy and gut aren't used to this sort of thing, and it's a very slow process. It does mean you end up eating a lot of baby rice, though, so watch out.
☆ **Hold the teaspoon under her lower lip after the food has gone**

in, to catch all the spillages. They can just be popped back in again anyway. A bit gross at first, but your baby doesn't care.

☆ **Keep your baby sitting as upright as possible.** Can *you* eat lying down on your back without choking?

☆ **Prepare for some smelly nappies.** Anything other than breast milk makes for very smelly poos. And it only gets worse from here.

☆ **Don't wear any nice clothes**. I'm not sure how I always ended up with baby food smeared on my sleeves and in my lap.

☆ **Be prepared to abandon the attempt and try again later.** If your baby isn't interested just now, go and do something else, and try again when she should be getting hungry again. 'If she's hungry enough she'll eat anything' was my theory. Oh, I am so mean.

☆ **Don't add anything except for milk or water** to the slop. Sugar, honey, salt and vodka are absolute no-nos.

☆ **If you are preparing food from powder,** make it as runny as you think your baby likes by adding more or less milk. Don't spend hours measuring exact quantities of powder and milk – more watery is always safer than too solid, which can cause trouble in the bowel area. Ouch. Just use your own brain and work out what your baby likes.

☆ **Pureed fruit is a winner.** Healthy, tasty, soft, cheap, quick... perfect.

There's always a debate about jars versus homemade food for young babies. My parents' generation thinks jars are a ridiculous waste of money and represent the lazy, sloppy culture we live in, not to mention a lack of care for your child. This is utter nonsense. Never feel under any pressure to always prepare wholesome meals for a weaning baby yourself, instead of buying jars of prepared food, because:

☆ it takes a long time (which you may not have).

☆ you have the extra worry of wondering whether what you've made is good enough for this particular developmental stage.

☆ when your baby refuses to eat it, spits it all out, or eats it and then throws up two minutes later, you've only wasted 50p, and not two hours of hard labour.

Jars are excellent, there is a huge variety, loads of them are organic, and they don't break the bank. They are fantastic when you're on the move, and they have been carefully prepared to give your baby some excellent nutrition. Fresh is almost certainly still better, and the more often you can give home-made stuff the better: it does taste different, the texture is more like 'real' food, which your baby will move on to before too long, and you can feel very motherly and proud.

As your baby gets older (nearing nine months or so) you can get much more adventurous about what you feed her, and then the idea of doing away with jars and just sharing some of your own home-made dinner is much more bearable. At least you were going to cook it anyway, and what she doesn't eat, Daddy can polish off. To begin with, just add some baby-milk to the food and mash it up well with a fork. Gradually the lumps can get bigger as your baby's mouth gets used to the idea.

IMPORTANT: There are some foods that shouldn't be given to babies under a year old, because of the risk of allergy or intolerance. Gluten should be avoided for the first six months at least, and eggs (except for hard-boiled) should be avoided for a year because of the salmonella bacteria they can contain. Cow's milk should also be off the menu for the first year, because it doesn't contain the amount of iron your baby needs. If you are ever unsure about introducing a new food, check with your health visitor first.

After nine months or so, your baby will be off the complete mush, and experimenting with bitty foods and even finger foods. What you offer at this stage depends on how relaxed you are around a choking baby. I become hysterical the moment I hear a slight cough, but babies are remarkably good at clearing the blockage. Carrots were my biggest worry, as all my babies ever did with them was break a tiny bit off and get this lodged halfway down their throat. Rusks were the firm favourite (except that they make a phenomenal mess if pasted on clothing), with pear, melon and banana coming a close second (and third and fourth, I suppose). At this stage, making sure you always bring a jar of food with you stops being such an issue, because you can always buy a packet of breadsticks or a banana, and have a happy baby until you get home.

ANOTHER VERY IMPORTANT NOTE: **Never ever, ever, ever, ever add salt to any food** you are intending to give your baby. Babies cannot tolerate much salt at all, and what you may consider to be tasty gravy is actually enough to half kill her. Bland, tasteless and unexciting is where it's at for babies, so either prepare a separate meal for your little one, or, for those who really have better things to do, cook one meal, leave all the salt out, and just add yours when it's on your plate. You do get used to it eventually.

The Organic Baby

Whether you plump for organic baby food or not is up to you and the contents of your wallet, but there are some health issues worth noting:

☆ Babies' organs grow very quickly, and this might make them more vulnerable to toxins (e.g. pesticides) in non-organic foods.
☆ Because babies eat much more food relative to their body weight than you do – unless you are a glutton – the effects of these toxins are further magnified.
☆ Immature kidneys are not as efficient at removing toxins as our old-and-hardened ones are, so they stay in the body longer.
☆ Organic animal products tend to come from happier animals.

If you can't stretch to organic food all the time (and it is still shamefully much more expensive than mass-produced gunk), then even the odd chemical-free meal is better than nothing. The jury is still out as to whether there really are any health benefits to eating organic food, so do what you can, and don't stress about it.

The Eco Baby

Babies are lovely and cuddly, they giggle and blow bubbles, they smell gorgeous, and you can dress them up in the most adorable outfits when you go to visit friends. Unfortunately, babies also have a fairly major impact on the environment, and unless you are very careful, your gurgling bundle of Petit Bateau's finest will soon add to a whole catalogue of eco-disasters. Not Yummy at all.

While not all Yummy Mummies manage to be entirely Eco Friendly the whole time, we *do* care about the impact our lifestyles have on the Earth's future, and we all want to do our bit to help. Here's how to do *your* bit, without dedicating your entire life to the cause:

☆ **Buy second-hand clothes for your baby.** Babies don't care what they wear, washing machines are more than able to remove traces of previous accidents, and your baby will grow out of it before you can say 'Yuk, this is second-hand.' Think of it as baby vintage, if that's any help. Better still, inherit as much as you can from friends, and then pass it on when you're done. My son has lived in hand-me-downs for most of his life, thanks to a very stylish Yummy Mummy friend who kept all her son's fabulous, barely worn, perfectly clean clothes. Thank you, Vikki.

☆ **Buy organic cotton and wooden toys instead of plastic**, but avoid tropical hardwoods, and go for trees grown in sustainable forests instead.

☆ **Use re-usable nappies, of course.**

☆ **Avoid over-packaged products.**

☆ **Buy in bulk:** it cuts down on packaging, and it's cheaper. Hurrah.

☆ **Get out of your car.** It's full of biscuit crumbs, broken toys and old raisin boxes anyway, so get a child's bike seat and a helmet, cycle instead of driving, and use public transport or your legs whenever possible. It's a free workout, for goodness' sake!

☆ **Change your washing powder to a more environmentally-friendly alternative.**

☆ **Wash clothes less often, and don't use a tumble dryer.** Those horrid, clothes-wrecking things.

☆ Use baby bath and skincare products **containing only natural ingredients.**

☆ Buy clothes from **fair-trade companies**, and choose **organic cotton and natural fibres** where possible.

☆ **Paint the nursery in Green Paint:** not green paint, although that is a calming colour, but Green Paint, which contains no solvents, chemical preservatives or fungicides. If you want to use normal paint, choose water-based latex paint, which contains half the volatile organic compounds (bad stuff) of oil paints.

If you are wondering where to *get* all this planet-saving gear, here's a list of Green suppliers you might like to try:

Clothes
☆ **Eco Clothworks**
☆ **Greenfibres**
☆ **Schmidt Natural Clothing**

General
☆ **Beaming Baby**
☆ **Baby-O**
☆ **Eco-Babes**
☆ **Little Green Earthlets**
☆ **Spirit of Nature**

Paint
☆ **Ecotech Casein Paint, from Precious Earth**

Green Nappies
Much less disgusting than it sounds, Green nappies just means those which are either completely re-usable or which are still disposable but are designed with more care for the environment than traditional throw-aways.

Going Green in the nappy department used to be a complete nightmare, involving safety-pins, boiling pots of poo and a house full of drying terry towelling. Not so any more: there is a huge choice of re-usable nappies, and making the leap to these alternatives is a fantastic way of reducing environmental damage. Apparently, two trees a year are felled to provide enough pulp for each baby who wears normal disposables, and it takes hundreds of years for them to break down in landfill sites.

Here's why you should at least consider it:

☆ New designs don't leak like the old ones used to. Thank God.
☆ They don't come off, thanks to Velcro and plastic clips. Ditto.
☆ They are made of lightweight materials that wash and dry easily.
☆ There are lots of nappy laundering services, which will take all the dirty work off your hands. Apart from the actual changing part. Boo.

There are two basic types of re-usable nappy: **two-part nappies**, which have an inner nappy bit and an outer waterproof wrap, and **all-in-ones**, which are self-explanatory, I'd have thought. How many you'll need to buy is very tricky to estimate, because it all depends on how good your washing machine is, which nappies you end up using, and how active your baby's bowels are. The good news is that re-usable nappies work out as being much cheaper overall than disposables, and you'll probably only need about fifteen or twenty to see you through. That's not the end of it, though, because you will also need:

☆ Disposable nappy-liners, to catch the unmentionable in and flush away.
☆ Booster pads for extra night-time absorbency.
☆ A bucket with a lid for storing dirty nappies before washing. Better have a very good lid I should say...
☆ Plastic nappy grips, unless yours have Velcro or poppers.

This might seem like a lot of kit, but compared with all the other clobber babies need, it's not such a huge difference.

If you can't be bothered with all the washing and drying, get someone else to do it. Here's where to find a service near you:

☆ **Cotton Bottoms**
☆ **UK Nappy Line**

Laundering services are more expensive (well they would be, wouldn't they? Nobody wants to wash someone else's poo for free), but they are also hassle-free, and even more eco-friendly because the washing is done in bulk, thus using less water and detergent.

When you are travelling, or out and about a lot, resorting to disposables is almost essential. Just think about it and you'll see why. If you still can't bring yourself to use evil landfill-clogging nasties, then consider the **alternative disposables**: they avoid excessive use of gels, bleaches and plastic, and most are biodegradable.

And, finally, a huge confession: I would be more than a tad hypocritical if I just sat here telling you to use eco-friendly nappies without admitting that I don't, and never have. I feel pretty crap about it now, but I know that with the work I do, which used to involve taking my kids on the occasional shoot and travelling a lot, using anything other than the easily purchasable take-it-off-and-throw-it-away variety would have been more added stress than I needed. I do feel guilty: I wish I had bothered to check out the disposable alternatives now, having written this chapter, but I made my decision and I'll have to live with my own conscience now. So will you, so think about it…

Re-usable nappies
☆ **Tots Bots:** Velcro fastenings and elasticated legs and waist. Just like disposables, but made of soft terry towelling. Use with a polyurethane-coated or fleece wrap.
☆ **Nappy Nation:** All-in-one nappy.
☆ **Little Chicks Nappies**
☆ **The Nice Nappy Company**

Eco-Disposables
☆ **Tushies:** (Can these company names get any worse?)
☆ **Nature Boy and Girl:** (Yup.) Available from branches of Waitrose.
☆ **Moltex Oko:** Available from Little Green Earthlets.

Changes to Your Home
How simple it would be if having a baby meant just that: having a baby. Nothing else, just being who and how you were before, except

that now you have a baby. Alas, babies are far more powerful than that, and being a mother means you have to adjust almost every aspect of your life to accommodate this tiny creature, and that includes your home.

You know those *OK!* spreads showing pristine, clutter-free houses with expensive works of art on display and not a plastic toy in sight? They are staged. Nobody can live like that with a baby in the house, unless the baby is as miserable as sin or has a highly developed appreciation of modern, urban living. I'm yet to meet one which does, so I assume that behind the camera is an enormous pile of baby-associated clutter, which will be scattered over the Cath Kidston cushions as soon as the shoot is over.

The good news if that you can still have a lovely home after your baby is born, but there are certain things that need to change if you want to lessen the blow to your domestic harmony.

Needing More Space

How big is your pad? If you live in a roomy flat, or if you are even lucky enough to own a house, then you are sorted. If you don't, and you currently reside in a teeny-weeny top-floor flat, then get house-hunting right now. It doesn't matter how fantastically contemporary, stylish, co-ordinated or perfect for dinner parties it is – if it's tiny then it's too bloody small, and you won't be having any dinner parties for a while anyway. Your world is about to become more cluttered and chaotic than you can believe, and the more room you have for hiding baby clobber the better.

If you don't believe me, then look through the list of Baby Clobber again, and then try to picture your current house or flat with all that stuff in it. Now you can begin to see why you need so much more SPACE. If you don't think you can get a pram in the hallway without knocking half of the internal walls down, then it's time to think about looking for a bigger place to live.

Organisation, Compartmentalisation, Ikea-isation

If you can't actually move, then re-organising everything is the only way to survive. When things get crazy, your baby is throwing a wobbly and you need to feed him quick-smart, you won't have time to start looking for a baby bottle among all the dirty bibs and half-empty jars of baby food on the counter.

☆ **Have a massive clear-out** before you get too pregnant, try to free up some space especially for baby stuff in every room and get rid of as much junk as you can.

☆ **Make special baby-spaces:** In the kitchen, set aside a drawer only for the bottles, teats, lids, cups, plastic plates, bibs and cloths, and a cupboard for all the food things, like powder-milk tins, baby jars and so on. The more organised it is the better. In the bathroom, find a separate place to store all the bath products and bath toys, and try to store all the baby's medical kit separately from your own. That will reduce the risk of smearing Preparation H onto your baby's nappy rash or, worse still, wasting any of your most expensive age-defying beauty-restoring moisturiser on somebody who doesn't appreciate it yet.

☆ **Find somewhere to dry lots of laundry inside.** You will constantly be hanging out or folding away tiny items of clothing, and if the only place to dry it is in your bedroom then you will feel swamped and horrible a lot of the time. Keep your bedroom as baby-free as you can, so that you have somewhere for your mind to escape the clutter.

Baby-proofing Your House

I hate to say it again, but babies really have no sense at all and wouldn't survive more than a day or two in the wild. To reduce the number of trips you make to Casualty you should probably think about ways of making life a little safer for the new baby in your house.

BUT: this is a very good point to remind you about the Brain Drain issue (see Part Six). Reading some of the advice and suggestions for baby-proofing your house offered in 'Boring, Frumpy Mum' textbooks and 'Happy Baby' websites has me alternating between fits of hysterics and rage. How stupid do they really think we mothers are? To cheer you up here are some choice examples of idiotic, obvious and jaw-droppingly patronising health and safety tips. They're all perfectly *valid*, but do we really need to be told any of this?

- ☆ **Make sure your baby's cot is sturdy, and has no loose or missing hardware.** So my *Changing Rooms*-style piece of MDF with a few rods staple-gunned to it isn't good enough then?
- ☆ **Lock knives and matches away from babies.** Oops, so *that's* where her fingers keep going.
- ☆ **Keep all razor blades out of your baby's reach.** Yeah....
- ☆ **Keep doors locked at all times, to avoid fingers becoming trapped**. How would anyone manage to live in a house where all the doors were permanently locked? Even Nicole Kidman struggled in *The Others*, and she had a whole film crew to help her out.
- ☆ **Cover bathroom taps with inflatable fun covers to avoid bumps and bruises.** Or, you could just keep an eye on your baby while she's in the bath, I guess?

You get the point. No Yummy Mummy I have ever met (or at least none I have ever got on well with) has ever baby-proofed their house even a minute fraction of this amount. Babies learn pretty quickly, and while I *could* have put foam covers on *all* the corners of *all* my furniture, I figured that once my kids had bonked their heads on a sharp corner a couple of times, they would probably learn to go round in future. We had a few minor bruises, but that's what learning's all about. I have also never owned a stair gate, and have never covered any of our electrical sockets up with specially designed covers. Neither have most of my Mummy friends. I have *bought* a 'baby-proof your house' kit, but it sat on top of our fridge-freezer gathering dust for three years, and I finally got rid of it at the school jumble sale. It's hopefully gathering dust on someone else's fridge-freezer now.

Having dissed baby-proofing, I do think it's a good idea to take a look around your house and **see if there are any obvious disasters waiting to happen** – an open fire without a fireguard or a samurai sword collection near floor level are two common examples that spring to mind. If you can make some minor adjustments then do, but you don't need to go crazy. If you are near your baby and keep an eye on him, then he will be fine.

Some tips I would be brave enough to suggest are:

☆ **Don't leave your baby alone in her high chair**, whether she's eating or not. She'll either choke or fall out, and both are dangerous and embarrassing.

☆ **Tuck electrical flexes and cords away**, or try to make them shorter, because babies like to pull on dangly cords, whether there's a hot iron at the other end or not. Duh.

☆ I'm obsessed about **plastic bags** ending up on heads, but hopefully you're sensible enough to know they should always be out of reach. Thought so.

☆ **Keep pot handles turned away** from the edge of the cooker. It's that 'curious little hands' thing again.

☆ **Move all your precious objects**, video and DVD recorders, vinyl collections, trendy piles of stones and Diptyque candles up a level or two, because your baby will crawl before you know it, and wreck the lot.

☆ **Don't put your cup of tea down on the floor or on low tables.** My non-mummy friends still do this, and I have to wipe the mess up every time they come round. Always nice to see them, though!

☆ **Get wooden floors everywhere.** Even if deep-pile rugs are *the* must-have home accessory as you read this, take a nod to the Nineties and slap down some tongue and groove or get the floorboards stripped. You will be wiping more spillages than a barman working a busy shift during a televised FA cup final and there will be bits of food all over the floor. Carpet and rugs: noooooo.

If you do have to move or make major adjustments to your house, try to do it well before your baby arrives. Once they are there, even a quick painting job becomes almost impossible and pretty dangerous, as you teeter at the top of a ladder waving a paint-roller about while simultaneously trying to amuse your baby with songs and funny faces. Once they're crawling, the number of injuries and other disasters that are possible during a simple DIY job are limitless, and it's a complete waste of time.

On the other hand, doing any house-fixing work when your baby goes to bed is unlikely because you're exhausted and would rather have a long, hot soak in a bath surrounded by scented candles. When we hired a sander to strip all the wooden floors upstairs, our first baby was about nine months old, and we had to put masking tape around her bedroom door to stop any dust getting in. Stopping every couple of minutes to check if she was crying or not made an already hellish job even more so, and we vowed never to try anything like that again. Still, you live and learn.

Above all, just be sensible and think about what looks life-threatening and what just needs to have an eye kept on it. Oh, and one last thing: you can baby-proof your surroundings and take as much care and precaution as you like – your baby will get hurt at some point, usually through some fault or neglect of your own, and you will feel terrible about it. The more inquisitive and determined your child is, the worse it gets, but that's life, and as my dad always told me while we were waiting in the A&E department yet *again* after my latest cut, burn, bruise or similar injury: it's the scars which make a person beautiful. I must be one gorgeous lady!

Where's My Lovely House Gone?

Ah. This can be a problem if you've worked hard to get your place looking 'just so', and it suddenly looks 'just absolutely not so at all'. Big plastic toys are the worst offenders in my house, with stray socks and crayons coming a close second.

I spent a few years just *hating* the way my house looked after my first baby: everywhere I looked I could see some evidence of Motherhood: the shelves were lined with blue plastic Ikea boxes full of toys, paper, Lego and so on, every room had a vast piece of baby equipment in it (pram, high-chair, baby gym) and I felt completely alien in my own home. Don't do this: do what I've finally learned to do, and it's made me proud to open the front door again:

Top House Tips from Chrissie Rucker, founder of The White Company

☆ **Do your tidying little and often.** Don't expect a miracle overnight - but every little bit helps to keep on top of most of it.

☆ **A place for everything, and everything in its place is the Golden Rule:** this will save lots of time and stress searching for missing baby shoes, wipes or bottle lids.

☆ **Keep surfaces clear** - the first thing to make a house look messy is stuff on all the surfaces. If I feel things are getting on top of me, I clear the worktops, tables and shelves, and feel immediately better.

☆ **White works very well with children:** it's bright and light, and instils a sense of peace and calm. There is nothing scary about white - just be clever: get removable, machine-washable sofa and chair covers, make sure shoes are always taken straight off and put away, and get ready to wipe and re-paint occasionally. If you are using a lot of white, soften the look with a mixture of textures: a soft carpet or rug, matting, wallpaper, cushions and so on.

☆ **Baby wipes** are fantastic for cleaning marks off sofas.

☆ **Fragrance** is an incredibly powerful weapon against the stresses of motherhood. Choose your fragrance according to the time of year, as well as your mood: for Winter, use spicy and woody scents, like cinnamon, clove, orange and teak. Spring is the time for fresh and zesty grapefruit, lime, lemon and honeysuckle, and lavender is very soothing all year round.

☆ Store all the baby things in **stylish containers** that complement the rest of the décor. That way there's no intrusion or clashing, but perfect harmony everywhere. Those blue plastic boxes *were* only a pound each, but they were hideous.

☆ Get a **massive wicker basket** or other pretty container for all the living-room toys, so you can quickly chuck it all in at the end of the day and return to clutter-free living in seconds. If you can hide it *in* the furniture (e.g. in a built-in bench which opens up) that's even better.

☆ **Do this in every room**, and don't forget the bathroom: the lady in the 80s Cadbury's Flake advert didn't have water wheels and plastic ducks all over the place did she? Either store them out of sight, or in something beautiful.

☆ Try to **keep the toy boxes in a cupboard that closes**, rather than on open shelving. That way it's *really* gone from view. I spent a merry evening or two sewing little curtain-type-things, which now hang across the front of the open shelving. No, I can't sew, but somehow it worked and looks lovely.

Those minimalist, grown-up houses you may have visited, where there's not a trace of baby clobber to be found, rely on such strategies. Inside, the cupboards are crammed with plastic toys, but who cares if you can't see it? Fakery – I just love it.

In an English Urban Garden...

Gardens are just glorified, flower-ified, green baby disasters. Not only that, but they take hours and hours of work to keep pretty, which will now be impossible or far too tiring. If you have a garden with a vast lawn, miles of beds and delicate plants, consider some low-maintenance adjustments: paving half of it over to make a patio is a great idea, and covering every inch of earth with mulch will keep the weeds at bay for an extra year or more.

The first thing we did when we moved into our house was to **have the pond filled in.** (Actually, we unpacked, drank champagne and faffed about with lighting for quite a bit first, but then we addressed the pond issue pronto.) Ponds aren't a no-no *per se*, but if, as with ours, they fall in a direct line between the back door and the lawn then it's best to remove them, because that's the line your baby will take the second she can crawl.

Our next garden baby-proofing step was to dig out the huge

deadly nightshade by the front door. There are lots of plants that have poisonous parts making them dangerous to have in a garden with children, and these include:

☆ **Poisonous berries**: jasmine, mistletoe, nightshade, moonseed (what's *that*?) and red sage
☆ **Poisonous leaves**: hemlock, yew, rhododendrons, lily-of-the-valley and oleander (oh, and bleeding heart, but that goes without saying I'd imagine).

There are hundreds more, which can cause everything from diarrhoea to depression, but it's really not necessary to concrete the whole plot over: if you don't leave babies or toddlers in the garden on their own for more than a minute or so, and you haven't parked the pram under a deadly nightshade bush, you should be OK.

Finally, if your garden isn't blocked off to the outside world on all sides, your crawling baby will be off exploring the delights of your neighbourhood the minute your back is turned. Fences are the answer but hold back on the electric ones until they hit puberty.

Top Gardening Tips from Kim Wilde, gardening writer and presenter

Never let crawling babies out of your sight, especially when there is water about. It only takes a few centimetres and a split second to cause death by drowning. Even a bucket that has collected rain will be heavy enough to withstand the weight of a baby peering and falling in head first. Next door may have a pond you don't know about, so check gaps in hedges, and latches on gates.

Take care with sandpits which, if not covered, will quickly become toilets for any cats in the vicinity. Cats' faeces can carry toxoplasmosis which is dangerous to pregnant mums.

Beware of some plants that may look great, but could be extremely dangerous to your child. The common Yucca has pointed tips that could easily cause harm. Other plants I would avoid putting in a garden where babies are about include:

☆ **Daphne mezereum**…poisonous, shiny red berries look good enough to eat
☆ **Laburnum**…all parts are extremely poisonous
☆ **Aconitum**
☆ **Mistletoe**
☆ **Lily-of-the-valley**
☆ **All bulbs**
☆ **Most berries**

Plants to inspire and delight babies include one of my favourite plants, lavender. Lavender flowers can be safely rubbed between little fingers releasing its aromatic perfume: its aromatherapy benefits include inducing relaxation, perfect for naturally calming down an overexcited baby.

Cuddly plants include *Stachys byzantina* (commonly known as lamb's ears) which has soft, furry foliage that babies will love to stroke, and it's easy to grow.

Grow plants to attract butterflies such as the self-seeding perennial red valerian, buddleja, the butterfly bush and *Verbena bonariensis*, a tall, see-through perennial that also self-seeds very accommodatingly.

Changes to Your Car

Anyone who has watched *About a Boy* knows what will happen to their car when they put a baby in it. As Hugh Grant sprinkled crumbs and sprayed Ribena over a child's car seat and placed it in his otherwise pristine Audi to make it look as though he was the proud owner of a child as well as a fancy car, there were some knowing chuckles from those parents present in the cinema.

Babies and young children make a staggering amount of mess in cars so prepare to get the Hoover out regularly, or drive around in a mobile land-fill site.

Here are some things to think about doing:

☆ **Get the front passenger airbag removed or disconnected**. Babies can sit with you in the front for the first six months or more, and having an airbag smother your pride and joy would be very silly.

☆ **Check your seatbelts**. They need to be long enough, and some don't fit all the way around certain models of baby seats.

☆ **Sell the two-seater**. First of all, because there are more than two of you now (I hope), and secondly, because trying to put a car seat with a heavy baby in it into the back of a car with no rear doors will break your back.

☆ **Have a permanent selection of toys and books in the car**. Remembering to bring some toys might slip your mind in all the chaos of leaving the house, and even short journeys need some rattles, bells and board books to chew.

☆ **Have a good supply of wipes to hand**. There are enough situations which call for immediate wipe-application to fill another book. This goes for tissues as well.

☆ **Remove the headrests in the front seats**, so your baby can see better once she can sit in the back looking forwards It gives you a crooked neck, but it keeps her happier.

☆ **Buy some song tapes** to make journeys that little bit more entertaining. Who cares how stupid you look singing along to 'The Wheels on the Bus'? Your baby isn't crying and that's what matters. If you find them all too cheesy then do what I do, and make your own. It's still cheesy, but at least it's cheap.

PART ELEVEN

Life With Your Baby

You will find yourself doing lots of things you never did before, now that you have a little friend to entertain. Some of them are fun, others are very boring, and others still continue to mystify me to this day. Here are some things which will become a part of your life during the first year:

Playgroups

Entering your first toddler group or playgroup is your baptism of fire. It takes the courage of a nude catwalk model, and you are completely forgiven for getting as far as the front door and doing a sudden sharp left turn back to Costa again several times, before you make it inside.

My first, and still very special Mummy friend, Sarah, introduced me to toddler groups seven years ago, and it revolutionised my new life. The first time I went, I just stood there, wondering what had happened to me, and how on earth I had gone from an exciting job and the more than occasional night out with friends, to a room full of mums and babies doing finger-painting and story-time in the space of six months? I didn't know who I was, who any of these people were, and I certainly didn't feel like I belonged there at all.

Now I go at least twice a week to one playgroup or another, and they are what my whole 'Mummy' week is centred around. Charlie plays, learns how to get on with other kids and makes a huge mess that I don't have to clear up, and I have some adult conversation, get away from the telephone, the dishwasher and the biscuit tin.

Before you rush out to your nearest community centre for a play, bear in mind that not all of them are lovely: I've been to some truly awful toddler groups, where ill-mannered, badly dressed, snotty, spotty and violent children scream around with no parental supervision, spreading germs and beating each other up. Don't go to those ones, except for a dose of realism every so often. Ask Yummy Mummies you know where *they* go, and if you find one you like, put it in the diary: it could become the highlight of your week.

Top Tip: *Bring a jar of decaf coffee of herbal tea bags unless you want to be plied with caffeine all morning. A healthy snack is also essential if you are trying to lose an inch or two. It baffles me that, in a room full of pregnant women who shouldn't be wiring themselves sky high with the Crazy Brew, and postnatal breastfeeding women who still feel slightly overweight, there is no alternative to a cup of strong instant coffee and a fattening biscuit. Come prepared.*

Flavour of the Week

15 April 2001

Phoebe hates me. I don't know why, I can't think of anything I've done to upset her, or make her especially upset or jealous, but for the last week she done her level best to annoy and enrage me, and the second H walks through the door in the evening, she rushes over to him for a cuddle and drags him off to play in the lounge. After I've tried to please her all day! At bedtime she pushes me away and says 'No! Daddy read stories!' and I can't get near her. It's really nasty, and I'm trying to keep cool about it and not show her that she can upset me this way, but it's getting to be a bit too much now. And the most annoying thing is that at night she only wants me to comfort her when I want to sleep! I hope this is just a phase which will pass soon, because I really don't like her much at all at the moment, and I want my lovely Phoebe back. I miss her.

Sometimes 'flavour of the week' will be you, and sometimes it will be Daddy. Sometimes it may even be a granny or a nursery teacher, but definitely not you. A baby's level of commitment and fidelity to one person would give most of Hollywood's most notorious womanisers a run for their money.

You've hopefully gathered by now that each day with a baby can be quite different from the one before, and that babies go through stages as quickly as you go through expensive pairs of tights. Showing affection is just another of the ways babies can be fickle and unpredictable, and it can be really upsetting when, for no apparent reason, your baby suddenly decides that you are a fire-breathing dragon and Daddy is a saint.

When all of my babies went through phases of only wanting Daddy for cuddles, bath-time, stories and dinner times, it felt like the cruellest blow: here I was, busting a gut to feed, change, play with, love, care for and wait on them hand and foot, and they didn't want to be within a very short arm's length of me the second Wonder Dad walked through the door! The ungrateful little so-and-so's.

The temptation to storm out with a huffy 'Fine, I won't bother then' can be a very strong one, as can be the need for an extra glass or two of wine, but there is some good news: you will fall back in favour with your baby just as quickly as you fell out. Nobody will ever know why any of this happened, but it's nothing personal and your baby still adores you.

Little Friends for Little People

You are not the only one who needs new friends now. One day your baby will need another baby's face to look at, a pair of eyes to poke and hair to pull. Babies need to learn to share with other drooling types, and before you know it there will be a birthday party to organise: you'd better have some tiny companions to invite, or live with the social disgrace.

If you are planning to send your baby to a nursery during the first year or so, then this is less of an issue as she will make friends there. But, if you are doing it alone, or employ a nanny, childminder or au pair, there is less opportunity for your sproglet to do much junior networking, and you should think about ways to make some introductions.

There are too many advantages of having little playmates to list, but here are some of the main ones:

☆ Babies learn from each other. Most of it is bad, but there's the occasional gem.
☆ They can share horrible germs, which almost certainly makes them ultimately healthier.
☆ They learn to share toys as well.
☆ It teaches them how to stick up for themselves.
☆ It builds confidence.
☆ They are better socially prepared for playgroup, and, eventually, for school. *School*? Eeek.
☆ It can cure bad habits. 'Look, Alfie doesn't kick other children, does he? So you don't have to either, my sweet little angel-kins' kind of thing.

Another advantage of getting little playmates for your baby is progress-comparison: there you'll be, subtly checking to see whether Tommy over there can crawl as well as your baby yet, or being delighted when your baby wins the fight over who gets to play with the pop-up toy. It goes the other way, of course, and if you befriend a wonder-baby you will be up all night preparing tomorrow's French lesson.

The reality of baby play can take some getting used to, and watching a beefy two-year-old whack your baby's head with a metal car is more than slightly disconcerting. If you think of it as character-building on your baby's part, then it becomes a valuable life experience.

Minding Your P's and Q's

One of the things I love most about being English is our rich, precise and colourful language, and the part I love most about it is its swear words. Having lived abroad several times as a child, during which periods I became a complete native and swore in German, French and Italian with the best of them, I can conclusively report that swearing in English is by far and away the most satisfying and liberating linguistic experience there is. Saying '*Vas te faire foutre!*' is not a patch on 'Fuck you!' and '*Sheisse*' sounds more like a term of endearment than a forceful 'Shit!'. Hearing or expressing a full-blooded (but appropriate) English curse makes my day that little bit more complete, and I would encourage more people to enjoy the benefits.

Unfortunately, the same does not apply to such cussing in the pre-teen category. Hearing a four-year-old say 'Daddy is a wanker' is only funny for about one second, after which it just feels sad. What we learned very quickly is that young babies have amazingly sensitive ears, and they can learn an impressive list of blasphemous words and phrases well before they can say any of them.

Alice, mother of Jemma, three, and baby Joseph

I wanted to jump into a deep hole last week, when some very well-educated, 'smart' parents of Jemma's friend Harry came for a drink. Joseph started to cry, and Jemma said, in a piercing, clear voice, 'Oh I wish that fucking-hell-baby would go to sleep!' There was no doubt who she had picked that up from, and I turned crimson. I'm much more careful now.

The result, in our humiliating case, was an angelic, two-year-old Emily explaining to my father why I had just run down the garden hissing and throwing stones at next door's ginger tabby: 'It's OK, Grandad, Mummy has to chase the Fuckingcataway, because it poos in our garden.' Nicely put, thanks, Em.

Beware the sensitive baby ears, and make up some decent substitutes for your favourite swear words. Futtocks works for me...

Remember, Remember

From the earliest age, talking your baby through the day's enthralling activities is a really good idea. I don't know of any studies into this 'going over what we did today' theory, but we have always done it with our babies, and still do with our children, and it seems to help their memories a lot, and reinforce everything they learned that day.

Even if your baby clearly hasn't got a clue what you are talking about, just repeating the words 'we saw the *ducks*, and went in the *swing*, remember?' means their brain connections are being worked on, and before long you'll be casually strolling through the park when your super-clever baby shocks the life out of you, by making a noise which sounds suspiciously like 'duck'. He said duck! He said duck!!

Well worth the effort, I think you'll agree.

Things You Will Do and Feel (and hate yourself for)

Babies are like emotional archaeologists, but without any care, precision or tiny brushes and trowels: using their lungs, iron will and devious cunning as JCB diggers and pneumatic drills, they unearth levels of human emotion that you would rather have left buried under 20 years of denial and stiff upper lips, thanks very much. Rage, sadness, despair, ecstasy, frustration, joy, hopelessness, happiness – and of course the biggest one, love – come pouring out in newly updated levels, reminiscent of the worst American daytime soaps of the Eighties.

After only a few weeks you can find yourself in such an emotionally heightened plane that the smallest, least surprising event will trigger a truly Oscar-winning display. Cry? You'll flood the kitchen. Laugh? You'll ache for days after. Forget 'Yeah, whatever' or 'I'm not really that fussed, to be honest' – from now on you are *totally* fussed about everything, and you may find yourself feeling, doing and saying things you would rather not admit to.

It's a Love–Hate Thing

March 2002. Emily four, Phoebe two.

I can't believe what I did today. The girls have been so awful and badly behaved and difficult, stubborn, wilful, mean and generally HORRIBLE for the whole week, and the final straw came when I told Phoebe for the hundredth time not to throw her teaspoon on the floor, especially while it was full of boiled egg, and she just looked me straight in the eye, picked up her plate, and tipped it off the edge of the high-chair.

I completely flipped my lid. I shouted at her, and threw the teaspoon across the room. I walked out of the kitchen and slammed the door as hard as I could, and carried on shouting about everything the children do and say, and how they never listen.

It was so stupid, and the more I ranted on and on, the worse I felt, and the more I shouted and shouted because I was now so angry with myself. It was terrible behaviour, and an awful example to them both. The girls were shocked, I was embarrassed, and I wished I could turn back time and never have started the whole thing. My throat aches now and my eyes are red. I feel exhausted and terribly guilty.

Here are some of the things you will probably do at some point (or even many points). DO NOT beat yourself up about it. Everyone does it. You are not a monster or an unfit mother. You are a human being who is being pushed beyond the limits of human endurance, by somebody a quarter of your size, and who our society would have you believe is faultless and innocent. Pah!

1. You Will Hate

HATE. It's a very strong word, and perhaps it's even a little too strong here, but there may come a time, even for a fleeting second, when you feel that you hate your baby. I have found that a large number of my friends were shocked when they first realised they were feeling hatred towards their baby, and often worried a lot. Getting anyone to actually *admit* to this was like getting an actress to admit that she worries about her weight.

It's best to face this reality now: much as you will love, cherish and sickeningly adore your baby, there will be times when your feelings swing as strongly the other way. I have wanted to do such awful things to all three of my kids at various trying times in their early years that to write them down would probably put me at risk of having my ovaries forcibly removed.

You say you won't *now*; you don't believe you could *now*, but beware of the fledgling archaeologist in the house. Things will change. You may even tell your baby you hate her, which is a great release at the time, but it makes you feel much worse afterwards. Letting it all out is sometimes cathartic though : they won't remember a thing you say before the age of about 18 months, so why not release that frustration with a quick 'Oh you really drive me MAD sometimes, and I hate it!'

Unfortunately, having said it and felt it, you will immediately transfer all of these feelings of hatred onto yourself. This is one of the joys of being a woman and is, I believe, the result of an as-yet-unidentified gene lurking somewhere at the end of the second X-chromosome in humans. Maybe laboratory flies and worms don't have this gene, which is where scientists are going wrong. Anyway, the 'Everything is My Fault; I Am a Failure' gene is very dominant in some women, and we should be constantly on our guard against it taking over our more rational thoughts and emotions.

If you feel any hatred towards your child, ever, you are a terrible person, your children should be taken away, and you should be forced to drink rancid breast milk for three weeks. No?

Well, no, actually. If we pause for one nanosecond here, and go through just a small selection of the events which have led to this all-consuming dislike of your own flesh and blood, we see a different picture emerge.

I present the evidence for the defence:

Having woken you up every three hours, to either suck your nipples or just howl at you, this little angel's final attack was to sit on your face with a nappy full of sloppy, noxious poo. You got up to remove the offending item and invited her for a big cuddle back in Mummy's bed, despite it still being only 5.30 a.m. This kindness was repaid by her stabbing you in the eyeball with the corner of a hardback board book, pulling all the tiny hairs down the left side of your neck out, and scratching the top off a mole near your bikini-line with her toenail. No hatred yet? OK.

The breakfast cereal she absolutely *insisted* on having (believe me, even very young babies *can* insist on things) was first pasted over her face and into her fine hair, and then poured, not only down her clean clothes (which then needed changing again) but also over a large area of the kitchen floor. While you saw to this job, she hid a red felt-tip pen in the washing machine, which you didn't notice until you spotted your once-white Jigsaw shirt doing pink somersaults in the water an hour later. How are we doing now? A tad annoyed?

Fast-forward through throwing up on your shoulder (more clothes to be changed), refusing to be strapped into her buggy, and throwing your mobile phone into the toilet, all within an hour, and we reach a point where any normal person loses their rag.

And that's just the baby stage. Once they can move fast and *do* lots of things, the potential for murderous thoughts becomes enormous. When a wilful three-year-old looks you straight in the eye and pours Ribena onto the cream rug in the lounge, knowing that you are unable to move because you are currently breastfeeding her new sibling, then murder seems an attractive option. But that's a long way off for you, thank goodness!

2. You Will Shout

We have all done it, and it's not a crime. When a toddler decides he does not want to wear a coat, even though it's minus three degrees outside and snowing, he will make it very, very, very hard for you to put said garment on him. He will kick you, scream at you, push you away, and turn into a hyperactive eel.

I have seen children spit at their parents, bite them, scratch and hit them, and all to avoid having a pair of shoes or a raincoat put on. Kids save their most dramatic displays for public places, which makes the whole shouting thing even more difficult.

But shout you will, and there's no real harm done. In fact it probably makes you feel a bit better for a second. Shouting at your child *frequently* is a completely different thing, and should definitely be avoided. It makes them aggressive, they learn to shout too, and situations are rarely improved by everyone shouting at each other. But an occasional 'Will you just STOP IT!' is fine.

NB: There's never any reason to shout at a new baby, and if you find yourself actually yelling at your five-month-old then maybe you should talk to a friend about it. Young babies can't be expected to know what they're doing, and shouting at them will just frighten the life out of them, so don't. But after a year or so they are perfectly capable of doing what they are asked, and are just beginning to be 'old enough to know better'.

3. You Will Bribe

Bribery is one of the strongest tools in your box of tricks, but it loses its power faster than you can say 'If you sit down properly, I'll give you a chocolate.'

Katie, mother of James, ten months

The first time I bribed James to sit in his buggy I felt so cheap and pathetic. I said he could have a rusk if he sat down nicely, and it worked immediately. I keep it for special occasions, or when I just can't be bothered to argue!

Bribing young children into doing all the annoying things they don't want to do (getting into a buggy, finishing a meal, walking more than two paces before stopping to pick up a soggy leaf and so on) is such an easy option, and it can be very helpful. But you know very well what will happen if you use it too much, so keep on your guard, and try to keep the pay-off chocolates for rare moments of desperation. Much better to try 'If you come along quickly, we can go and see the ducks on the way home.' I know chocolate is a heck of a lot better than ducks, but you've got to try, at least.

All of this rage and irritation is all very well to have an understanding laugh about, but when you do find yourself feeling very angry, resentful, or even hateful towards your baby it is fairly unnerving. As I said, it's one of the last taboos when it comes to motherhood, and it is very difficult to admit. Unfortunately, the only way to get things back on a happy, jolly track again is to share your feelings with a friend or relative, and hope that they will understand and offer some help (like some babysitting, for example). Don't be too frightened of yourself, and please believe that **you are absolutely normal to be having these feelings**. Either that, or I seem to hang around a lot of truly awful Yummy Mummies, but I don't think that's the case.

Drawing the Line

There's enough to be written about child behaviour and manners to fill the unread sports section of the weekend papers for a year, and I'm certainly not about to tell you how to stop your baby from bashing next door's baby on the head with a plastic frying pan. How you instil some basic manners and social skills into your little one is up to you and your partner, but I will tell you how we (try to) do it, and hopefully some of this might work for your hooligan. Most of this only applies after the first nine months or so, but younger babies can start to learn 'no' when it's appropriate.

☆ **Try to explain and give a reason for everything** from the earliest age. What's the point in telling somebody to do or not do something if you give no reason for it? *I* respond very badly to that, so I guess my children will too. Even 'because it will make Mummy *sooooo* happy' is worth a shot. I think the somewhat negative 'because if you don't, Mummy will have a breakdown' is less helpful though.

☆ **Try to forewarn.** The logic of 'If...then...' is something which very young babies seem to grasp and this is invaluable for teaching when the line is about to be drawn. For example, 'If you throw that DVD in the bath, I will put you in your cot on your own, OK? OK?'. They are clever; they understand.

☆ **Execute your threats.** When the DVD *does* go in the bath, you had better be ready to put your baby in her cot for a few minutes, or all your authority will be lost forever, and that will spell carnage in 15 years' time when your baby-turned-Goth wants her equally unattractive boyfriend to stay the night.

☆ **Do all the 'telling off' or warning in as calm a way as possible.** I try *really hard* to hold my baby's hands, bend down to his level to look him in the eye, and speak in a low but firm voice when I'm annoyed with him. I do try, but sometimes I start to giggle at how stupid it is, and once I start giggling I can't stop, so he thinks it's all a lot of fun and the whole exercise is a disaster. Either that or I'm in such a bad mood by this stage that I just snap at him, and then I feel bad about it. Try. It's the least you can do.

☆ **Don't expect your baby to learn rules the first time.** I don't (I still forget to wash the bony bits of my ankles after applying fake tan), so I don't expect my children to either. But three times is enough, surely, and getting a tad peed off is then understandable.

☆ **Smacking.** Smacking is illegal in this country but even if it weren't, there is never an excuse for smacking a child under the age of one, which is what we're dealing with here. Smacking is easy and nasty. There are always better solutions than smacking, and it rarely has the desired effect anyway.

Jane Horrocks, actress

It's a hard process, trying to maintain control. My parents were into manners and respect and I've tried to instil that into my kids. I think ultimately it pays off, because you can take them anywhere without being embarrassed.

Drawing Two Lines

As our children have got older, my husband and I have had more arguments about what is and what isn't considered to be 'beyond the line'. I tend to have a much more lenient streak than him in some departments, and a much stricter one in others. Manners is a point of much debate: I am obsessive about children having good manners, and he often doesn't seem that fussed at all. We'll work it out eventually…

The potential for disagreements when it comes to what's OK for your baby to do is so huge that it's definitely best to talk these issues through as early as possible before the shit hits the fan and one of you is forced to take charge. If your Victorian principles clash with his Bohemian, laissez-faire attitude, then expect trouble in the nest before too long. If you *really* have strict Victorian principles, then perhaps you should chill out a little and get with the times.

It seems to me that one of you will always end up being the 'nice' one, and one will have to take the role of 'strict' one, and that's the end of it. When I fall into my 'strict, evil mother-from-Hell' role for a few days I really hate it, but the tables soon turn and I'm back into 'gentle and nice' mode again soon. It's just yet another thing for you to feel stressed about. Great.

Telly Tantrums

This is where I get all 'holier than thou' and make a hasty retreat to the Good Old Days of candy floss, donkey rides and hoop-and-stick.

Here goes: I don't believe that babies need to watch any television before they are a year old. There. If they do, either because there's an older sibling in the house who is watching, or because you have found something appropriate for their age, you should watch it with them, talking them through what's happening, and making sure they are sitting down and actually watching the thing.

Given my background as a television presenter, this always sounds very hypocritical, and I hate myself for be so condescending and old-fashioned. But there is surely no advantage of plopping a baby in front of a cold, two-dimensional, impersonal television set when you could just as easily be reading to him or something? And if you're using it as a distraction while you try to cook her dinner, (as we all do every so often) why not get some pens and paper out for her to be getting on with?

It's also a question of habit, and if babies know that the big black box in the corner of the room only has pretty lights in it when Mummy or Daddy is there, and then only for a short time, it can prevent a lot of writhing on the lounge carpet screaming 'I want to watch telly!' in a year's time.

Keeping a Treat a Treat

We are all absolutely terrible at keeping treats as treats. The £55 billion worth of credit-card debt in this country is a testament to this, as are the 40 pairs of shoes in your cupboard. We all *know* that the best things come to those who wait, but when Office brings out its spring collection, waiting is not the preferred option. 'The lady wants; the lady shall have right now' is today's philosophy, which is all very instantly gratifying, but it makes having a real treat very difficult.

If you think it's hard to resist things for yourself, wait until your baby looks at you with wide, imploring eyes and gestures towards the biscuit tin. Just *one* choc-chip cookie. Pleeeeaaaase. But resist you must: treats are your ticket to getting your baby to do almost anything you want it to, because if treats exists, then so does bribery. And, of course, it also means your baby can get that feeling of excitement when something special happens, instead of cruising along in the fast, spoiled lane all the time.

Unfortunately, the only person who can keep treats as treats is you, and this is where your Iron Will comes into play. If you can keep treats to a minimum, and only give them for a clear reason that your baby understands, then you still hold the trump card. If you dole out the chocolates every time Chloe finishes her baby rice, she won't have much incentive to move on to more challenging things, like sitting down at the same time. And she will get enormously fat and have rotten teeth.

We are so mean that our first baby didn't have *any* chocolate until she was 10 months old, and that was only because she got her fingers squeezed between two heavy punts and nearly broke the lot. Ooops. One piece of Happy Food was all it took to stop the screaming immediately. Magic. With subsequent children we have almost abandoned all of this self-control, and Charlie gets chocolate and other little niceties a hundred times more than his sisters did. It's not how I would like it, but we've still managed to keep even one chocolate button as a special thing, and the longer that lasts, the better for all of us.

And it leaves the rest of the packet for us to polish off when the kids aren't looking. Mmmmmm. Choc-o-late.

Sweets for My Sweet, Sugar for My Baby
Before Jamie Oliver started his (fantastic) campaign to make our children eat healthier food, a shocking number of parents up and down the fat-encrusted land were filling their kids with Heaven-only-knows-what, and wondering why these delinquents had such trouble sitting down and concentrating on anything for more than thirty seconds. Hmmmm, I wonder?

The most graphic illustration of what additives and sugar do to our behaviour is to **give your baby some artificially coloured or heavily sugared food, and watch what happens**. The first time Emily had a red-coloured ice-cream, at the age of about two, she became hyperactive for nearly three hours: she jumped and ran around, shouting, hitting, not listening to us, sweating a lot, and being very aggressive. She couldn't sit still, and when the loopiness wore off she seemed to slump into a deep sugar-low, and slept for hours. It was very disturbing, and she hasn't had a red lolly since, which causes rows every summer.

The point is that babies are very small and sensitive to whatever you put in them, and so giving a young baby lots of E numbers, sugar and chemicals is bound to have a strong, usually negative effect. Sweets are a terrible idea full-stop, as they rot your baby's teeth, contain absolutely no goodness at all, and if your baby doesn't know

about the existence of sweets she doesn't know what she's missing.
Food and drink to watch out for:

☆ **Coloured drinks.** Water is the only drink for children under two, if you can help it.
☆ **Anything containing chocolate.** Caffeine, fat and sugar for your baby? A *little* is fine, but maybe not the whole double-chocolate muffin.
☆ **Hidden sugars.** Even fruit juices contain tons of sugar, and often hidden chemicals as well. Read the label, dilute at least one part juice to three parts water for the first year, and keep it as a treat rather than let it become the norm.
☆ **Salt.** There is salt lurking almost everywhere, and as babies are incredibly sensitive to salt, try never to give them anything which has added salt in it, and never salt your food at home.
☆ **Fat.** It's just the same as for adults: babies need *some* fat, but saturated fats are a no-no, and the less active your baby is, the less fat she will need to consume. Breast milk has plenty, and when the weaning starts, most of the fat should come through the formula milk, and not in the form of deep-fried fatty sausages.

Most of this should be very obvious, as you are a Yummy Mummy and you look after you own body well. It just becomes more important to be vigilant about 'bad' food and drink where a small Yummy person is concerned.

TOP TIP: Rotate Toys. *A friend of mine suggested this simple yet brilliant idea for keeping kids interested in their toys (and unlike me she actually stuck to it for years, which I wish I'd done): rotate them. Divide them into two or three (or seven) boxes, and only bring one box out at a time. After a couple of weeks, put all those toys away, and bring out a different box. When box number one comes out once more they will seem like new toys all over again. Bingo! It takes more self-control than I've got, but it's a good plan to return to every so often when you are feeling diligent.*

He's A Genius! The Joy of Milestone Spotting

Fact: Every mother thinks her child is a genius, and likes to mention this whenever possible.

Fact: They are rarely correct.

Fact: Every mother worries, at some point, that her baby is a bit slow-on-the-uptake, and likes to keep this information to herself.

Fact: She is rarely correct either.

Your baby's physical and mental development will be something you monitor more closely than the length of your underarm hair. Barely a day will go by without you wondering whether something your baby does (or doesn't do) is normal, special or worrying. Shouldn't he be crawling yet? Is it normal to have teeth at four weeks? Is it normal *not* to have any teeth at six months? Why hasn't my baby got any hair? Did she *really* just say 'chlorofluorocarbons', or did I imagine it?

To make matters worse, every new mother is given a book containing charts of 'Milestones' your baby will pass at various stages. This is enough to send most of us into a frenzy of calendar-watching and baby-testing.

'Six weeks old today... oooh, you should be able to smile now: smile then! Come on, give us a nice smile... Look, you're six weeks old now, and it says here you can smile, so smile – *please*!' Very silly.

Every baby reaches these exciting moments at some stage in their lives but when and why that is is anybody's guess. You can try to speed things along if you really want, but a baby who decides to walk before they crawl will do so, and a bum-shuffler who refuses to stand up for a year will be hard to convince to do otherwise. *Que serra, serra*, but here is a list of things you might like to look out for. It is absolutely not a comprehensive list, but it gives you an idea of what might happen during the first year.

One Month

☆ Begins to hold her head up.

☆ Can start to track objects as you move them in front of her eyes. This provides hours of entertainment for you, but probably

annoys your baby after a short while, and gives her a headache.
☆ Likes big areas of bold pattern, and listening to music.

Two Months

☆ First real smiles (the very early smiles are said to be caused by trapped wind – I always find this a very unlikely joy-killer, and I am sure some babies do smile from very early on...)
☆ Likes to look at more detailed patterns and colours.
☆ Can grab hold of objects. Don't offer anything you mind getting slobbered all over, or which you are hoping to get back any time soon: babies don't know how to let go yet...

Three Months

☆ More regular sleep patterns. Quite a lot of babies have started to sleep for six or seven hours every night by now, but don't worry if yours doesn't: it won't last, and everyone will be back to broken nights again soon... Day sleeps can be very predictable now, though, which makes planning *your* activities a lot easier. Coffee at 11.30? No problem.
☆ Lots of words are starting to form in your baby's head now, so talk, talk, talk, and ye shall be rewarded in six months or so...
☆ Lots of gabbling and burbling happens from now on, and this is one of my favourite stages. If you pretend to understand, nod your head, smile a lot and just talk right back again, you can get some really long and varied conversations in. I'm not sure what *about*, exactly, but that's hardly the point.
☆ Knowing me, knowing you: your baby really knows who you are now, and can probably start to look at you or your partner fairly accurately when you say 'Mummy' or 'Daddy'.

Four Months

☆ Feeds less frequently (hurray!) As his stomach gets bigger, and yours gets smaller, there is more room for a decent, long-lasting feed.
☆ On a roll: sometime around now you might both get a surprise when your baby rolls from his tummy onto his back. He's not

ready to get back again, so do give him a hand, unless you think he likes playing 'upturned ladybirds' all morning.

☆ This might be the time to start dishing out the sloppy baby rice, if your baby is particularly hungry and you feel you want to top-up the milk feeds. (See **Weaning** in Part Ten.)

☆ Suck it and see: babies are very good at reaching out and grabbing objects now, so be careful what you leave within reach. Everything will go straight into the mouth, which means it's time to put your precious beads collection on a higher shelf.

☆ Baby talk. Don't get too excited, but it might not be too long until you hear your first 'ma-ma' or 'da-da'. As luck would have it, it's a whole lot easier to say 'da-da', which is completely unfair given the effort you've put in.

☆ Peek-a-boo. This is the stage they start to learn about prediction and cause and effect, so get those hands over your eyes, and start *Boo!*ing for the next year or more…

Five Months

☆ Look, no hands! The first time your baby sits up without you holding on seems miraculous. The independence this simple skill brings will make your daily life much easier, because you won't have to lug bouncy chairs and car seats everywhere if you want your baby to be upright. NB: They topple over for a least a month, until they've got the hang of it, so put loads of cushions all around her, and get ready to do some quick fielding…

☆ Small talk. You might be getting on to clearly identifiable sounds relating to specific objects, e.g. ball, duck, bus, cafetière, and so on. Or, you might not, so don't panic.

☆ Copy cat. This is a fun time to play lots of copying games, but it's risky in public: pushing a trolley around M&S making weird facial contortions looks a bit strange.

Six Months

☆ It's a rollover week! Or at least, it might be, but not in a financially exciting way. Get ready for that first complete roll. If you have a changing station, this is the time to get rid of it, or prepare to hold on at all times. And don't leave your baby lying on the floor while you go and put the kettle on, because you might come back to discover she has rolled under the sofa and you can't find her. Very scary, and potentially quite dangerous, if your sofas hide as many coins and remote-control batteries as ours do.

☆ Reading to your baby will just get better and better from now on, and all those weeks of reading to a newborn will finally seem worthwhile. Favourite pages can cause much arm- and leg-waving, and excited sounds…

Seven Months

☆ Bouncing babies. If you think your baby likes supporting a bit of weight on her legs (while you hold her, obviously), then putting her in a baby bouncer, which dangles in a doorway, can be a fantastic way of preparing her for walking, and for you to go about your jobs with a happy, upright, bouncing baby. Mine seemed to love being a part of the real world this way, and they all walked very early.

☆ Teething: if your baby starts dribbling through five bibs before lunch, stops sleeping as he used to, bites everything in sight and has red cheeks, diarrhoea and a temper to rival Gordon Ramsay, then he is probably teething. I tried teething rings (cooled in the fridge first), Calpol, old carrots and Bicki pegs, all of which helped a bit. And then the next tooth started coming – enjoy! New teeth are razor-sharp – ow! Luckily babies rarely bite while they are breastfeeding, and if they do your reaction will ensure it never happens again, promise.

☆ I want my Mummy! Separation-anxiety kicks in now, too, and it can be a difficult time to start childcare (which is just typical, because a lot of women go back to work at about this stage). You may even find it hard to walk into the next room without moans and whimpers following you. It's very sweet that they love you so much, but it can become draining.

Eight Months

☆ Crawling is something everyone looks forward to and then wishes away the second it happens. As soon as your baby can crawl, your life becomes infinitely more difficult, as every dangerous corner and unsuitable object becomes accessible to curious hands and mouths.

☆ Standing. If you are really lucky, your baby will omit the crawling stage and just get on with the real business of standing up. This prevents all the fabric on their knees from wearing through, and it also makes them a good deal less frustrated, because they can do so much more. If they do like standing up and holding onto a coffee table or whatever, then make sure you are ready to perform a quick catch when they fall, and try not to let them stand for too long: it puts pressure on their back and hips.

Nine Months

☆ Walking. Already? Well, not 'walking' exactly, but it is fairly common for babies to take a few steps on their own at this stage, and it's very exciting. You don't need to buy them shoes yet, but little non-slip 'padders' keep their feet warm and sturdy.

☆ Talking. Again, not quite *talking* yet, but the number of clearly identifiable sounds your baby can make now is huge. Nobody else can understand any of it, but you can, and that's the main thing.

☆ Mealtimes are probably getting messy enough to need a high-chair tray, so assuming your baby is happy to sit up unsupported, this might be a good time to move on up into the gleaming, new high-chair. At last your back can stop breaking every time you feed your baby solid food!

Up to One Year

☆ Testing your limits. I was apparently a whiz at this, constantly pushing the boundaries to see how far I could go before my mum went mad. (Sorry, Mum.) Your baby will probably try the same from now on, and you will need to think about ways of letting him know when he's overshot it slightly. (See **Drawing the Line.**)

☆ Year-old babies can say a lot of things, and might even be trying to combine words, although they don't realise it yet – it's just a longer series of sounds as far as they are concerned (e.g. uppa-down, eyedooit and indacar).

☆ Walking. Properly, this time. Going for walks with your baby is a new experience that involves making no actual *geographical* progress, but your baby will love it, and you will notice a great many stones, leaves, cigarette ends, crisp packets and sticks that you would otherwise have missed. Never be in a rush, and try to do as much toddling as possible – it's really good for them, and it helps you with the 'learning to do everything at a slower pace' therapy.

☆ Moody baby. Babies know exactly what they *don't* want by this stage, and are very good at letting you know. Unfortunately they often don't have a clue what they *do* want, so you'd better have got to know her pretty well by now, and be ready with some answers.

☆ Crafty baby. All of the sticking, painting, drawing and so on can really get going now, and hopefully your baby might even enjoy some of it too. Learning to chill out about the paint going everywhere except on the huge piece of paper right in front of your baby can be tricky, but once the walls have had a few smatterings of the junior artist's brush, you will stop caring so much, hopefully.

Making Conversation

I'd really rather not write this bit, because it should be so obvious, and probably does not apply to many of you. But for all the Mums out there who talk to their babies as if they are, well, babies, I say: Why? Why talk to a perfectly intelligent person in a high-pitched, super-happy voice, using grammatically incorrect language and a vocabulary of no more than twenty words? Why?

I have always talked to my babies and children in a fairly normal way, using a normal-ish voice (granted, it does get a tad squeaky and cutesy sometimes, but that's all part of the doting parent thing), proper sentences and real words. Just as 'Mummy have ball?' is not going to help your baby speak properly, neither is 'Do you think you could just gently hand the ball over to Mummy, please?'

I have really found that talking normally to babies makes them understand normal language and communication very quickly, and by the time they are 18 months or so you can have some hilarious conversations, using words like 'actually', 'sometimes', and 'maybe'. Very sweet.

These are just some of the changes you will encounter in your first year with your baby. It's an incredible amount to get your head around, and sometimes you won't get your head around it at all, but overall this first year is one of the most special you will ever have with your child. Not the best, or the happiest all the time, but very special.

The second half of the year will be so different from the first that you will look back and wonder whether it could have been so confusing after all, and what the big fuss was all about. It's often towards the end of the first year that women get very broody, as their newborn baby vanishes and they forget how tiring and uncomfortable pregnancy and birth really were. Beware!

PART TWELVE

New Relationships

With all the emphasis on the developing relationship between you and your new baby, it's easy to overlook some of the other considerable relationship changes that have occurred in your life. The way you feel towards, and communicate with, your partner has been altered forever, your old friends either don't know what to say when they come round or just stop visiting you altogether, and, in case you hadn't noticed, your own parents have become grandparents, which is a huge change in itself. Just in case you were getting complacent...

Your Partner: Do I Know You?
And Other Things You Will Ask Him...

Having a baby is equally one of the best and one of the worst things that can happen to a perfectly good relationship between two people in love.

In the BEST camp is the following:

☆ You have made a human being together, and nothing connects two people more.

That's pretty much it, but it's a biggie.

Flying the flag for the WORST camp, we have:

☆ You can love your baby more intensely than your partner.
☆ You hardly spend any time alone together any more.
☆ Sex becomes routine and rare.
☆ There are suddenly hundreds of new things to disagree on.
☆ One of you will stop work, which causes friction on both sides.
☆ *You* are much more tied to the baby to begin with.
☆ You both become obsessed with your baby, and stop being a couple obsessed with each other's fiddly bits.
☆ You become more demonstrative and cuddly with your baby than with each other.
☆ You show each other a new side of your personality, which is not necessarily very attractive.
☆ And so on.

Gaby Logan, TV presenter

You think you love your husband more than anything in the world and then this baby comes along and blows you sideways! Somehow though, I am even more in love with my husband than ever – watching him be a great dad makes my heart swell with pride.

Careful observers will note that the second list is a good deal longer than the first one. Equally clever people may deduce from this that a lot of work needs to go into your relationship now, if it's to survive longer than the socially acceptable period of time before which, if a man abandons the mother of his child, he will be branded a 'love rat'. That's about two months at the time of writing, by the way. (My husband has just read this, and says he's off – he was only hanging around because he thought it was more like two years. The bastard. I *think* he was joking...)

Joking aside, there's a good reason why so many couples split up soon after they have a baby: any two people who spend no more than an hour a week talking to one another, go out less than once every six months and only make love when there's a lunar eclipse, are doomed to become another casualty of parenthood.

It's so obvious it makes one weep, but still more and more and *more* parents are leaving each other not long after the initial 'wow' of parenthood has died away. Being moderately terrified of this outcome is very sensible. Awareness is 80% of the battle won, having sex covers another 10%, and babysitters can sort out the remaining bit for a medium-sized fee. If you know how much your baby will affect your relationship with your partner, then you can start putting the damage-limitation into practice before it's even born. (Oh, he's back. He *was* joking. Phew.)

Here are some top Yummy Parents' relationship-saving tips to try:

☆ Have a **non-baby talk every day.**
☆ **Eat dinner together**, without the baby, as often as possible. A couple of times a week shouldn't be beyond you both.
☆ **Get a babysitter** at least once a month, and do whatever you used to do before you became Yummy Parents.
☆ Get your **old friends** round regularly for a drink.
☆ **Keep up your old hobbies.** If he used to play five-a-side football once a week, make sure he carries on. Stopping him from doing so because you want a rest is being a bit mean. This also applies to him having the baby for an evening so that you can go to Pilates. If you do nothing, you'll have nothing to talk about. Except babies…
☆ **Resist the temptation to nag** the second he comes in the door. Give it half an hour or so, and you'll look less like a miserable old bat.
☆ **Don't become cohabiting babysitters.** This is a classic situation which I'm sure most couples get into at one stage or another, and it's very hard to leave. It's particularly dangerous when both of you work and you are sharing the childcare: we went through six

months of passing each other in the hallway, with just enough time to hand the baby over and relate when the last poo, feed and sleep was, how many nappies were left in the cupboard and what time to put the baby to bed. Just occasionally we would remember a quick peck on the cheek in passing. This was asking for trouble, so we sorted out some proper childcare, and developed more sensible work/family times.

☆ **Communicate about everything**, good or bad, about you, him, your baby, your mother, his mother, your friends. *Everything.* Stopping the lines of communication is the death knell for all relationships.

☆ **Have sex.** At least that's one thing he can't be pissed off about.

☆ **Don't talk to his parents about your relationship**, unless you usually do this and he's fine with it. And you are fine with the resulting interference.

If you *need* to be a statistic, why not be on the 'number of wonderful mothers per square mile' graph than on the 'number of parents who couldn't handle the adjustment to parenthood and divorced within a year' one. Easier said than done, but it's something to aspire to.

Rows You Will Have

As with the 'splitting up after the kids arrive' cliché mentioned above, the arguments you and your partner will have are so embarrassingly unoriginal that you will feel more annoyed with yourself for falling into the trap than with him for whatever it is he's done/not done this time. The reasons are just as obvious as the rows themselves: you are like all the millions of other couples who suddenly have a demanding third party to accommodate, and whose normal lives together have all but ceased to exist. We are all having the same rows, because we are all affected by roughly the same things.

Here are some clangers to beware of, and don't punish yourself too hard when the first of these slips out:

You: Why can't you put the toys away when you've finished playing with them?

Him: I will, at the end of the day. There's no point putting them away now.

(Yes there bloody well is – it looks awful in here!)

You: Why am I always the one to do all the baby stuff?

Him: Because I'm crap at that sort of thing, and you're brilliant at it.

(Good try, mate, but compliments won't help.)

You: It's all right for you – you've been out of the house all day seeing other people and using your brain. I'm going mad in here.

Him: I've been at work! It's all right for you, playing with bricks all day.

You: Look, can you change him this time: I've done the last five poos.

Him: Yeah, no problem. I don't mind doing it anyway.

(Ouch! He really didn't want to say that.)

You: Oh give it here, *I'll* do it. Have you *ever* prepared the milk bottle before?

Him: [Silence]

The thing with all of these and the gazillion (sic) other disagreements you are bound to have, is that **the moment you start one, you wish you hadn't,** because you sound like such an old nagging fishwife, you know you are both equally right and wrong, and the only way such an argument can progress is into a petty tit for tat. Except he's not getting any tit tonight, that's for sure.

You are both exhausted, and your baby has turned you into 'parents', which means you will say the sort of stupid things that all parents do. You are only doing what you think your role demands of you, but try to keep a watchful eye on the frequency of these outbursts. Three times a week is cool; three times a day is cause for some serious relationship talk, unless you *really* want him to sleep with someone less unpleasant to be around than you.

Jealousy, Resentment and Appreciation.
And Other Fun Things...

19 October 2001.

I had such a stupid, unnecessary row with H tonight, which I started, and I felt like such a bitch the whole way through. I don't even know why I did it. I'd had a lovely day with Phoebe: we went to the park, made a huge dinosaur model, painted some egg boxes and met up for a play with Daisy in the afternoon. I was happy all day, and I was just finishing off her tea when H arrived home. And then I immediately became moody and angry, and just completely pissed off with everything. I started sighing, and making a big deal about wiping the high-chair, picking up the peas off the floor and making up stories about what a hard day I'd had. It was so ridiculous, but I couldn't stop myself. I just wanted somebody to congratulate me on the long childcare day I had managed. Just a 'Well done' would have been enough, but instead I really annoyed him, we ended up arguing over who should do bath-time and who should clean the kitchen, and I said something unforgivable like, 'Oh just go and sit on the sofa and I'll do it', which was really mean. We'll talk about it later.

Over the years of petty squabbles between me and my (pretty fantastic, actually) husband, I have concluded that the causes of 90% of our arguments are **jealousy** of what the other person does during the day, and the need for some **appreciation** of what we do.

Staying at home with a new baby is a massive undertaking, with little tangible reward and no breaks. You probably gathered this already. One thing that makes it feel even harder is watching Daddy leave the house every morning for a day away from the noise, clutter and menial tasks. To your frustrated eyes, this just accentuates your 'stuck at home' status, and it's quite normal to feel a pang of jealousy.

He, by contrast, sees you spending an idyllic day with his beautiful baby, kissing, giggling and playing together, while he fights his way through the commuter rush, sits in stressful meetings all day with people he'd rather not know, and arrives home too tired to do any decent fathering activities at all, and to a wife who doesn't want to sleep with him *again*.

While Daddy comes home to a mouthful of '*I've had such a difficult day – you don't understand how hard it is looking after a baby, and now you're just going to sit there while I wash up?*', you have to expect the '*Excuse me, but I've just been at work, and I'm absolutely knackered too.*' Oh help. Both are true, but neither is helpful, constructive or supportive. Much better to both say something appreciative of the other person, and work together.

This all amounts to a glaringly obvious case of 'The Grass is Always Greener', and all parents I've ever met experience it. Unless you can see that there are plusses and minuses to what you *both* do (which you surely can?), and support each other through the minuses, there will be lots of arguments in store, which is no fun at all, for any of you.

That's Not What We Agreed...

This seems to be a very common complaint raised in playgroups I frequent, when 'Moaning about my partner' is on the agenda. Which is frequently, and I think that's an interesting discussion in itself. But for another day...

The number of mums who think they've talked everything through with their partner before the baby comes, and are heading for a cosy family life where Mummy and Daddy both participate in Baby Activities, only to wake up one morning and realise Daddy doesn't want to do anything with his baby at all, is scary. Just when we think we have moved forward, and that men are as happy to bring up a baby as women are, a guy comes along who propels us back to the nineteenth century. (Without the full-time nanny and the crazy baby attire.)

Helen, mother of Alfie, six months

I try not to think about it, and just bury my head in the daily routine and looking after Alfie, but inside I feel like I'm being ripped up. Mark and I have been together for five years, and we both wanted a baby. He seemed very excited, and talked about bonding with his son, playing footie in the park and being a bit of a super-dad. But from the day Alfie was born, he's been my domain. Mark works longer hours now, which he says is because things are hotting up at work, and he is almost never there for bedtime or breakfast. Even at weekends it's my job to do all the baby tasks, while he takes some time to 'relax' after his hard week. I am so sad for our son, and I'm falling quickly out of love with Mark. I can't believe how different it's turned out from how we discussed.

This sort of experience is terribly sad, and there is little I can offer in terms of help other than to reiterate the importance of trustworthy Yummy Mummy friends. Talk to them and you will see how many are experiencing something similar, if not quite so bad. If you want to rescue your relationship, or keep it from dissolving in the first place, then think about relationship counselling or family advice as soon as possible. Time runs by so quickly, and before you know it your 'baby' will be old enough to ask why Daddy never changes his nappy.

If you are left holding the baby 90% of the time, try to remember that what you have in your arms is the most important, precious and rewarding thing you will ever have. It won't help much when the Lego needs putting away *again*, but it's worth trying to think of the good side of all the hard work. Your baby loves you more than anyone else ever will.

Meet the Grandparents

If you think getting to know the New You is hard, then prepare yourself to meet the new grandparents. The relationship you have with your parents, and with your mother in particular, can be tested to the limit when you have a baby, and it's best to have some coping strategies in place before the bust-up.

Part of the problem is that, for the first time, **you and your parents are sharing the same role: you are all parents now**. However, this almost certainly doesn't mean that you share the same ideas about what this role requires. Add to this the fact that they have done it all before, and therefore come with some implied, superior knowledge and experience, and it's a recipe for conflict.

The next problem is the whole 'becoming a grandparent' issue, which must be something of a shock. However much they may pretend otherwise, it will shake them to the core and will require some major adjustment on their part – a new, youthful hairstyle, taking up a new, dangerous hobby and buying an impractical sports car are common examples of Yummy Grandparent reassurance measures.

Here are some changes you might experience to your relationship with your parents:

☆ **You become closer.** Lots of my Mummy friends have found their relationship with their mums has become much warmer, friendlier and more supportive since they had a baby. I have also become much closer to my mum, partly through spending more time together, partly through realising that we are both women who have gone through many of the same things, partly because we can share so many more experiences now, and partly because I have seen a caring, loving side of her I never knew existed. Oh, and partly because she buys my children lovely things all the time, and occasionally babysits. Priceless.

☆ **You are driven apart.** This is a terrible shame, but some new Mums find it impossible to get along with their parents after having a baby. Disagreements over how to raise children can develop into furious rows, and we all say hurtful things during furious rows. When it comes to matters of childcare and parenting values, these hurtful things cut too deep, and you can cause irreparable damage if you're not careful. Trying to bite your tongue off before you say 'It's none of your business. You made a complete mess of me, so let me screw up my own children *myself*!' is a very good idea.

☆ **You might appreciate what they did for you more.** Until you look after your own baby you will never appreciate how much work went into bringing *you* up. All those years of toil, dedication, love and support are thrust into the spotlight, and it can be quite an eye-opener to realise just how much your parents really did do for you, and how unappreciative you have been. Time for some fresh flowers and the best chocolates money can buy, at the least.

☆ **You might become critical of their parenting skills.** On the other hand, if you take to motherhood quite easily, and think you are doing a brilliant job of it, it's tempting to criticise the way your parents did it, and to feel hard-done-by. At this point, the wipes-all-slates-clean phrase 'They were doing their best' is a handy buffer. Never mind that 'their best' was against a backdrop of having a secure job, owning their own house, travelling around the world with you stuffed into a rucksack wearing hand-me-downs from a family with appalling taste in children's clothes, not having 150 TV channels to choose from, not leaving university with £5,000 worth of debt and not being chastised by the whole of society for leaving their baby for an evening with someone they had met briefly at a party the week before. Never mind all of that. For now, if you don't want to lose your parents forever, raise your children your own way, but try not to judge them too harshly.

7 *January.*

Mum and Dad came to see Emily for the first time today and it's left me quite confused. Mum was brilliant, and wanted to hold her, smell her, and Emily seemed really calm in her arms. But watching Dad hold my four-day-old baby was weird: I don't think he's ever held a baby before. He did seem to like holding and looking at her and he said how beautiful she is, but it did make me see for the first time how little time he spent with me when I was a baby. I'd never thought about it before, and there it was, so clearly illustrated. It's a shame I think.

Watching your parents handle and behave around your baby can open a floodgate of questions about your own childhood, which you may never have thought about before. Is that what she used to say to *me*? Did she hold *me* like that? Was *I* left to cry myself to sleep? How long was *I* breastfed for? Did *he* ever change my nappy? Did *he* read me stories, or sing to me? That sort of thing. It can be a bit upsetting, if there are unresolved issues between you already, but it can also be the start of a much happier, richer, more understanding relationship, if you all play your cards right.

I would never claim to have the perfect relationship with my parents, but I have learned a thing or two about how to all get along reasonably well, and to be able to survive Christmases together:

☆ **Give it time.** Like having a new handbag or groovy gadget, you can be especially protective and defensive over your new baby and your parenting skills in the first year. This can make getting along with your parents very tricky, if you keep snapping at them and taking offence.

☆ **Try to listen to their advice.** I've had to eat humble pie enough times to become seriously obese, as one seemingly stupid or bad piece of advice after another turned out, in time, to be absolutely spot-on. It's so annoying, and it makes your mum swell with grandmotherly 'told-you-so' pride. Grrrrrrrrrr.

☆ **Count to fifty before you criticise their suggestions.** It's far too easy to snap some harsh words at an over-enthusiastic granny who is only trying to help, when your boobs are hurting and she asks whether those are still your maternity trousers or not. They are *not*. Try, try, *try* to hold your tongue, and save it for the really bad moments when it's justified.

☆ **Show them who's in charge now.** If your parents still believe that children should be seen but not heard, refuse to own a mobile phone and think spending money on nice clothes for your baby is evil, it's quite likely that you will disagree wildly on how to look after your baby. The most important point to remember is that you are the mother, and when it comes to your baby, you have the final word.

☆ **Let them have their say.** *Then* you can completely ignore them if you want. A mother likes to pass on her advice, even if it does contrast completely with today's thinking. Listen, consider, and reject as required. Then everybody is happy.

☆ **Think of your kids.** One day your child will want to spend a lot of time with his grandparents, so getting on well with them will be really important. 'Why did Mummy call Granny an interfering old cow, Daddy?' is *not* a question you'll be happy to hear, because it's usually followed a few weeks later by 'Granny, why did Mummy call you an interfering old cow?' Ouch.

☆ **Use your partner for support.** If you are having trouble seeing eye-to-eye with your parents, make sure your partner knows this, and agree on a signal (wildly raised eyebrows and outstretched arms works for us) that means 'Help me out here – I'm going to kill someone.'

☆ **Never compare your parents with your in-laws.** In all circumstances this is a terrible idea, which leads to family feuds on a truly epic scale. As far as your parents go, *they* know better than any in-laws do how to raise a child, and any suggestion to the contrary is as fatal as suggesting your mother-in-law makes better Yorkshire puddings.

☆ **Don't use your baby as a way to snap at your parents.** I know you don't *think* you would, but when you're pushed to the limit by interfering (sorry, helpful) parents, a curt 'Come on, sweetie, Granny's in a bad mood *again*' can spill out when you're not looking. It's a terrible tactic, it leaves you feeling cheap and dirty, and children don't forget a *thing*. Even babies.

☆ **Talk about when you were a baby.** This can be a great way to learn things from your parents indirectly, and talking about how sweet you were can bring you all closer together too.

Through several fraught years, and now some very happy, peaceful ones, I have concluded that it all comes down to two things: **TRUST and LOVE**. If you trust and love each other, there are no issues about who's in control, who has the power and who needs to feel under attack. Having mutual trust means you never have to feel defensive of any criticisms or suggestions, and you both understand where you fit in the new relationship. They should trust you to do it your own way, and you should trust them to make constructive criticisms. Unfortunately, these feelings should have developed by now, and if they are still not there you could be in for a prickly ride.

Finally, it can be great fun learning how to be a Yummy Mummy in front of your own, possibly Yummy parents: it's a lovely, mushy Circle of Life thing, which can make your relationship much deeper and more rewarding. Yuk. But true.

Darcey Bussell, prima ballerina

Have a spare grandmother on hand and never run out of nibbles. Always have a contingency plan.

In-laws

Oh, in-laws. Possibly the most tricky relationship in any family, because in-laws fall into that awful middle ground between, 'You are the nicest people in the world, and I wish you could be my parents instead', and 'My life is nothing to do with you, so butt out.' Actually inhabiting either of these spaces would hurt somebody very badly, and so in-laws float around in between, moving from one end of the love-hate scale to the other depending on how well things are going with your own parents.

Here are some truths about your in-laws, which could help smooth the path to family bliss:

☆ In-Laws often take second place: most of my Yummy Mummy friends have found that the fact that she gave birth puts *her* parents in a slightly superior position when it comes to baby advice. It sounds ridiculous, but that seems to be most often the case, and Daddy's parents can feel a bit left out, or unsure of where they fit in. That's why they buy so many presents, which is a fantastic by-product of their insecurity.

☆ Your in-laws may well be Grandparents in *exactly* the same way that your parents are, but the bottom line is that they are NOT your parents, and that's where the difficulty can lie. Offending your mum is one thing, but having a maternal rant at your father-in-law is quite another. Obviously the 'you didn't buy me a Tiny Tears when I was a baby, and I'm still scarred' bit is irrelevant here, but this can easily be adjusted to 'Your son doesn't even pick his pants off the floor after two *weeks*, so don't tell *me* how to feed a baby!' Beware of such outbursts – everyone is a bit sensitive at this time, and you almost certainly don't mean it.

☆ When it comes to your baby, everything which applies to your parents goes double for your partner's parents, because there's always the background hum of 'What business is it of yours?' to get in the way. Try to drown this out with the fact that these kind people really want to help you, and would also like to be as close to their grandchild as possible. You are hormonally challenged, that's all.

I have the best in-laws in the world (no, really: they are absolutely wonderful, generous, sensitive, kind and supportive, and they have the best taste in children's clothes of any over 50-year-olds I've ever met), but we have had some tricky moments concerning child-rearing. Treat this relationship with kid gloves, and you will be very grateful in years to come when offers of babysitting make long weekends in Barcelona, *sans* toddler, a distinct possibility.

Keeping It in the Family
When you think of it, bringing two families together, whether through marriage or just by two people shacking up together for years, is a terrible idea. Families are like vast, sprawling, highly

guarded clubs, with intricate rules, codes, principles and systems. Worse still, they have a history, which shapes and influences everything the next generation does. Trying to merge two such organisations is bound to produce some fallout, and there will be redundancies before the financial year is done.

One of the first things to go are any incompatible family habits and traditions, and the sooner you can deal with these, the more harmonious everything will be. Hopefully you have spent enough time in each other's extended families to know what sort of merger is on the cards: are we dealing with different religions (potentially big problem) or is it just that you come from a strict, rules-based family, while his is more relaxed? (Small problem: you win. You gave birth.)

If you can't agree on how to do things it can be difficult, and it's the last thing you need as you struggle to adjust to your new life. It can also drive you apart extremely quickly, because we all get very defensive about how we want to raise our own children. Avoid getting into long-term rows about these disagreements, and try to sort them out early.

It's helpful to remember that you three are now a new family, and you can have your own rules and ways of doing things. If neither of you were allowed to open any Christmas presents until after dinner, then now's your chance to change all that, and to start ripping the paper as soon as you get your dressing gown on. (Which will be at about 5 a.m. for the next four years or so.) If you were both made to finish everything on your plate before getting down from the table, then maybe a more relaxed approach could be introduced for the next generation. It's up to you.

All your new rules can come under considerable scrutiny at big family gatherings, but if you can stick to your guns, and if you have mature-enough relations to accept that what you do is your business and should be respected, then you will be able to do your new *thang* without too much trouble. And if Grandpa still winds the baby up with exciting music before bed, then the threat of never bringing his grandchild back *ever* again, or just bursting into tears, can prove very effective. Not that I would know...

Other Yummy Mummies

I have to be a little careful about what I write here, because most of my friends now *are* other mothers, and so to say something like 'hanging around a load of boring, old, frumpy, overweight women who talk about kids all day long is the worst aspect of being a Yummy Mummy' will not make me popular in the playground.

Nor would any of it be true.

What is true is that when you become a mum you will have to make friends with other mums, unless you want to be very lonely and miserable. But, if to you the word 'friend' conjures up memories of sharing a villa in France, shopping sprees, long, boozy lunches, boyfriend comparisons, and evenings out at the pub, then you will be very resistant to the idea of befriending what, to you, is still an alien species. *Mothers.*

Just because you are a mother doesn't mean you *feel* like one for quite a while after the birth. It takes time to wear in your new, flat, Mummy shoes, and your resistance can be very strong. I went for eight months before I befriended a single other parent, because I just couldn't accept that I was one of them as well. Looking back, I realise what a waste of friend-making time this was, but it felt so wrong at the time!

If, like me, you have a baby in your early twenties, this hanging out with Mummies is made even harder by the fact that you are about ten years younger than every other Yummy Mummy within four million miles, and talking to 'really old' thirty-somethings feels too strange. It's also more difficult if all your old friends are living it up in the city, forging on with their careers, and jetting off to Paris on a whim.

If you have waited until the more normal thirty to thirty-five bracket, you will be in fine company, and should have no trouble finding similar-minded women to share coffee and baby tips with. But there is the central dilemma – right there: **sharing coffee and baby tips.** Who, you? Share baby tips? Is that what you do now? Do you sit in people's front rooms discussing the merits of Calpol sachets over the traditional bottles and fiddly spoons? Well, not entirely, but it's helpful to accept that baby talk is now quite a large part of your life, and the best people to talk about babies with are other mothers in the same position as you.

Here are some reasons to make lots of Yummy Mummy friends:

☆ **You need the company.** Playing with a train set at home is much more dreary than playing with one at somebody else's house. Now leave it alone and let the babies have a go.

☆ **It's a fantastic support network**. When you're feeling down, visiting a Mummy friend can be the miracle cure. She will either cheer you up or show you how hard she is finding it all too, which has the same effect. Yummy Mummies help each other out, understand exactly what's needed, and never bear a grudge.

☆ **You will learn tons.** Other people always have different toys, ways to feed their baby, favourite baby foods and so on. Watch and learn.

☆ **They will have lots of good ideas** of places to go, baby classes to try out, successful dieting tips, best airlines for babies and so on. There's a Yummy Mummy information super-highway in every playground in the land.

☆ **You can help each other out with babysitting.** This bit takes a while, but after a few months you could have enough good Yummy Mummy friends to have a few hours away from baby every week for free.

☆ **You can have girly nights out again soon.** Because you won't manage to see your old, baby-less friends as much as you like any more, cultivating new people to share a bottle of wine with is an essential survival technique. Leave the babies with the daddies, and treat yourselves.

☆ **You can mess up somebody else's house.** There's nothing like getting all the Lego, bricks, farm animals and playdough out, and then leaving somebody else to clear up the mess. Obviously you will *offer* to help, but she will graciously refuse, and do it all when you've gone.

☆ **They will become your best friends for years to come.** Like that special group of girls you grew up with, the friends you will make in the first years of motherhood can stay with you forever.

Sharing these early experiences forges a special bond between you.

☆ **You need somewhere to offload your woes.** This 'somewhere' shouldn't be your partner (who will go *mad* if you continue to tell him about yet another day at home with the baby), your mother (who will tell you how much harder it was when she was young) or your old friends (who will find you very boring, and won't be able to offer any help at all, as they don't have a baby). The best place to unload is onto your new Yummy Mummy friends, who know exactly what you're talking about, and can help.

My Mummy friends have been the most important part of my Mummy life (apart from the actual children, of course). We've been through so many new experiences together, they have taught me masses (even if some of it is how *not* to do things), and we have kept each other company through hours and hours of swing-pushing and tower-building. If you can get over the hurdle of accepting that you are a mother too, then making friends with other Yummy Mummies will be a lot easier.

TOP TIP: *Don't only talk about babies with your Mummy friends. They will find you as boring as you find yourself, and it reinforces your concerns that there is nothing beyond nappies and vomiting. Once you've formed the habit of only being 'mothers', it's impossible to shake. They want to talk about something else too! Setting up a book group, cinema group or organising regular outings together works brilliantly, and you have tons to talk about straight away.*

Competitive Mums

Nightmares. It reminds me of those irritating poeple at university, who would stand outside the exam hall asking everyone if they had learned the most obscure and probably non-existent chapters about this, that or the other in some totally unheard-of textbook. Just to freak the more insecure students out, (like me!) for the fun of it.

Well, there is an element of this present in many Yummy Mummies, who get a kick out of winding other Mums up into a frenzy about whether their child is retarded or not. If Helena claims her four-month-old is walking, she is lying. If Kate asks whether *your* baby also prefers Mozart to Gershwin, she is playing silly mind-games with you. Hit back with a top-spin volley, and say yours is going through a Rachmaninov phase actually, but hasn't had much time to listen lately, due to all the French verbs she's having to learn. Gershwin, my oversized arse.

The most irritating form of this competitive Mumminess is the subtle drop-hint. I don't mind if somebody is just being a prat, and psyching me out overtly. It's the 'Oh, bother, I must have left Hannah's bottle at Baby Algebra. Do you have spare one I could borrow?' No. Fuck off.

Playing them at their own game is fun, but it only brings you down to their petty level. Much better to go the other way, and make your baby look a tad slow on the uptake. That way, when your little Einstein *does* talk three months before anyone else's, it will come as a surprise. Ta da!

A Problem Shared...

3 December 1998.

Huge relief: I met up with Caroline today, and somehow the subject of finding babies really annoying came up. Probably because she got annoyed with Louisa in front of me, and felt she had to apologise. Anyway, I told her I seem to be getting really irritated by Emily these days too, and that I find her constant need for cuddles and attention really debilitating. I can't even go to the loo without taking her in with me, and she follows me absolutely everywhere. It's just so annoying and I sometimes want to lock myself in my room for five minutes just to be able to think. Caroline said she feels exactly the same way about Louisa, and had thought it meant she was a selfish, unloving person . We were both so happy to find that we weren't alone in this, and I don't feel so guilty at all any more. Hurrah!

One of the best things about having good Yummy Mummy friends is to relieve a lot of worry. **We all worry.** We worry SO MUCH: we worry about our babies, our children, our partners and ourselves. We worry about whether we are doing it 'right', whatever that may be, and we convince ourselves that we are getting it wrong, that we're making a total mess of it, and that we are unfit to take on such a responsible role.

Worry about your pregnancy becomes worry about the birth, which then glides seamlessly from worries about your baby's well-being, to your toddler's development, to your marriage's chances of survival through all this worry, to your teenager's catalogue of disasters. (I assume. I'm a long way off that stage, but I can already feel the seeds of 'If I had only *given* her that Barbie scooter, she wouldn't be taking drugs' starting to germinate.)

Worse, even, than all this worrying is that 99% of mothers worry alone. All of us are absolutely certain that *we* are the only ones finding it difficult, that only we lose our tempers with our children, and that no other mums cry themselves to sleep three nights a week. Unfortunately all this self-doubt is just part of being a mother (and a woman generally, I think), but there is a simple way of relieving a huge amount of the worry, which I didn't try until several years of concern had turned me into a nervous wreck:

Talk to other mothers about your concerns.

'Like, duh!' I hear you scoff. '*Obviously* you talk to other mothers. That's what friends do, right?'

Wrong. Sharing problems about love-lives, wobbly thighs or recent hair disasters with friends at work is one thing, but admitting that you are having trouble being a MOTHER, even to yourself, never mind to a perfectly turned-out Yummy Mummy, is completely different. There is something so personal, so almost *untouchable* about the way we cope with motherhood, that telling *anyone* about troubles in the newly re-decorated nest feels like self-crucifixion.

Paradoxically, it's the not-telling-anyone-and-bottling-it-all-up that causes far more damage, not only to yourself, but also to your baby and your partner. Mothers are very proud, and they like to give the impression that raising kids is as natural to them as achieving a glowing complexion and making toddler-sushi. Even though you *know* it's not that simple, it's sometimes hard to remember that behind the façade is another confused mother, just like you, desperately trying to work it all out.

Every time I have opened up to another mother about something that worries or upsets me concerning my kids, several things have happened:

☆ I was offered fantastic advice and helpful tips.
☆ I was supported and comforted.
☆ I found out that they also struggle with exactly the same things.
☆ I felt much happier and more confident.

Nervous about turning this into a lengthy 'supporting the sisterhood' lecture, I'll stop there, and leave you with the comforting thought that, whatever your current concern or doubt, somebody you know is in the same smelly, messy, exhausting boat, and will be very relieved to talk about it with you.

What's It Like Becoming a New Dad?

I asked the lovely father of my children to give me a few pointers on this subject two months ago, and then again six weeks, two weeks, four days and one day ago, and I still haven't got much further than 'Ummm, I don't know, really'. He's a man of very few, but very well chosen words...

What I have gleaned, through our years of baby and family talk, and by talking to other dads who have made contact with their feminine side enough to be *able* to talk about such personal things, is that becoming a new dad is almost as scary as becoming a new mum, but without any of the attention or help with the emotional issues involved. (I should bloody well hope there isn't the same level of attention: we're giving birth here, you know, guys, not just loafing around the sidelines offering moral support and tactics.) That said, it's very important not to neglect the needs of Delicious-or-otherwise Daddies, who also need some extra TLC in this tumultuous year of change.

There are three key relationships which change for new daddies: his own with himself (not the sacred bathroom relationship, although that will definitely change, as the amount of sex he's offered declines), his relationship with you, and his new relationship with his baby. For your relationship to survive and thrive, and for your baby to have a great relationship with his dad as well as with you, there are some things you might find it useful to know about New Fatherhood. Not that you care, really, but I think we should at least *try* to understand.

☆ **Dads can feel left out and alone:** This applies mainly to the pregnancy, when all the attention and care is (quite rightly) lavished on *you* and your bump, body and mind, while he is meant to just stand there, nodding and heaping on more praise. But he is probably getting scared of all the imminent changes too, feeling a tad excluded and jealous of your bond with his baby, and is desperate for an 'And how are *you* doing?'

☆ **Dads aren't just glorified sperm-donors:** If all you want is the sperm, then there are plenty of places which will provide some. If you want a father for your child, and a partner for life (or at least a large chunk of it), then Daddy will need some care and attention, and a defined role in your family, which is separate from any money-earning or toilet-seat-raising responsibilities. If you can offer any words of encouragement and comfort on the daddy front, it will help him to *feel* more like a Daddy.

☆ **Dads miss sex:** From the embarrassing conversations I have had with many a Mum, I have concluded that this must sadly be true of 95% of the male population when they become fathers. Men really like having sex, and when it suddenly becomes as likely as a good song winning Eurovision, their levels of frustration and neglect can reach bursting point. Literally. If your partner isn't getting any from *you*, but he doesn't seem to be at all tetchy or frustrated after two months, then you had better find out about his sudden increased working hours. Either he's getting some somewhere else, or he has stopped functioning normally as a man, which is very serious indeed.

Marcus Brigstocke, comedian

Wait until you are invited to try sex again, don't whatever else you do attempt it too soon after the event. I'm sure there are certain fetishists who would find that sort of thing very pleasing but for your average new parents my advice would be let it all settle; and then when you think everything is about ready again, wait another fortnight. After that do it as much as you can (roughly once every six weeks but less often if you really are very tired) before your children learn to walk and talk and come to discover exactly why Daddy is trying push Mummy through the headboard and why Mummy is asking for God, oh God, oh God.

☆ **Dads miss their mates:** I feel nervous about mentioning this, because it's not as though *we* don't miss going out with our friends as well. But men like their nights out with the lads as much as we like our nights out with the girls, and when a colicky baby and a moody wife keep him home night after night, he can become very grumpy indeed. The temptation to say 'I really don't care at all – I'm having a much worse time than you, so how about a shoulder massage?' is very strong, but you will get on a lot better if he goes for the occasional bender down the Frog and Whistle with his mates. Occasional, mind you, not frequent: just enough to make him feel his own self, but not enough to be living the life of Reilly is about right. (I assume Reilly had a fun life?)

☆ **Let him have a go:** I fell into this trap immediately, being the controlling sort of person I was before three children sorted me out. Most New Dads really want to have a go at changing, bathing, dressing and playing with their new progeny. It's the only way they can bond with their baby and feel that they have a role. If you jump in with a 'No, not like *that* – she likes her socks to go on *before* her dress' every time he tries to help, he will feel as rejected as your non-maternity bras. Let him have a go, mess it up a few times, and then develop his own methods. Half of the time they are more efficient and effective anyway, and I have had to choke on my Very Knowledgeable Words many times.

☆ **Daddy Time:** Being pregnant has one enormous benefit: we feel much closer to our babies than men do by the time they are born. Men miss out on all of this antenatal bonding and this can leave them feeling somewhat out in the cold when the baby comes. I'm not saying I actually feel *sorry* for them (the memory of the births is still too fresh for any sympathy), but it does sound quite sad from the stories my Daddy friends have told me.

They all seem to agree that the only way to catch up to the maternal level of affection and love, is to spend as much time alone with the baby as possible. This tends to be in the evenings or at weekends, and many dads have started to have special 'baby time' scheduled into the normal family week. While he and your baby bond with each other, you can go to the gym, pamper yourself, or just dash around the supermarket without all the baby clobber in tow. It's also a great way for him to learn how tricky the simplest baby tasks can be, so you get more appreciation for what you do. A perfect solution all round. **WARNING:** a man's idea of looking after his baby for a day, involves *only* that. Just him and his baby. It does *not* include putting any toys away or clearing up any of the paint/playdough/sticking mess they have made together, making sure there is anything edible in the house, feeding the baby, taking the washing in if it rains, sticking to any of your hard-established baby routines, going to the bank, or any of the other fun things you do every day, *as well as* looking after your baby. *Every* couple has rows about this, so be prepared and work out a strategy for changing it.

☆ **Daddies get jealous:** It may sound strange that anybody could be jealous of what we have to go through, but after the birth it is very common for dads to become jealous of your baby, who gets a whole load more kisses, cuddles and affection than he does. It's also common for Daddy to become jealous of you, because you have such a special bond with your baby, and it *still* looks to him as though you are sitting at home all day cooing over your baby while he goes off to earn some dough.

If you can try not to be too smoochy with your baby the whole time when Daddy is around, this might help, as would the occasional cuddle and kiss for Mr Yummy Mummy. Tell him he's gorgeous, remind him how much you do still love him, and he will be a much happier daddy indeed.

☆ **Guilt:** Hurray! Men suffer from feelings of guilt and inadequacy too. Many of my Dad friends say they feel terribly guilty when they leave the house every morning to go to work, and worse still when it's a business trip away for a few days. Personally I think we should milk this as much as possible, and I always treat myself to an extra something special when he gets back. Just a walk into town on my own is enough, after a week looking after the children day and night. Oh, I know he's been working too, but I've done that kind of work as well, and I know which is harder! Most importantly, so does he…

Bill Amberg, designer

Becoming a dad has been a fantastically uplifting experience. It has calmed me down, and has introduced new realities, putting everything into perspective. I still have a very active life, and I love having more things to think about – it's the best fun, really.

Sharing the Load

I am writing this book at the beginning of the twenty-first century. The only reason I mention this is to give any readers in the future an understanding of the social set-up I'm talking about. At the beginning of the twenty-first century it is no longer considered acceptable for a man to assume that only a woman will do all the household chores, while he brings in all the money during the day and drinks lager in the evenings. It is also considered to be somewhat out-of-date to believe women who work to be Evil, Rotten Mothers, and for fathers who look after their children to be simple-minded, weak men. Rather, it is the people who still think that way who are simple-minded and weak, *à mon avis*.

Sharing the work at home is crucial if daddies are to understand what it is you *do* all day, and for him to be a part of the family, as opposed to a sexually repressed cash-machine. It's just not good enough to say 'I've been at work all day – I don't want to come home and do the washing-up or feed a baby her bottle.' Any daddy who says this is a complete bastard, and should have his balls pulled off. Seriously.

This sharing applies even more so if you go back to work. I am regularly shocked when women I know go back to work, but are still expected to do all the housework and childcare when they get home. And they obediently get on with it, too, without so much as an 'Are you taking the piss, mate?' It's utter madness, and they have some serious talking to do with the man in the house, and with themselves.

Another complete fallacy is that men can't multi-task. Yes they absolutely can. I know plenty of men who used to find holding more than half a concept in their office-mode brains well beyond their ability, but who have become the meanest multi-taskers in the West of Cambridge since taking over more of the childcare responsibilities. It's all a question of practice, and to diss all men as useless puppets with two left feet and a half a brain is ridiculous. Give them more to do, and they manage brilliantly – after a few major screw-ups involving burning the dinner and forgetting to take the library books back because a Lego tower was being constructed. Practise, practise…

The Family Man

Some guys are, and some just aren't, and that seems to be the end of it. The assumption that women find all the chit-chat and social change associated with being a family easier than men, who simply retreat into a macho shell and need to talk about breasts and football more, is completely false: I know just as many Yummy Mummies as men who struggle with their new roles.

That said, I do know a lot of dads who have found it very difficult to get into the Sunday-afternoon playground sessions, kids' birthday parties and general baby talk. It doesn't feel right, and some even seem to find it embarrassing, which is odd. What's so embarrassing about being a dad who takes an interest in his baby? These fathers would far rather spend a couple of hours filling in their tax return than putting on their New Dad hats and facing the baby music. It's very sad, but it's very common. I think a lot of it has to do with practice: men get less opportunity to work on their small-talk skills than women do, and find it hard when they are thrown in the deep end down at the swings, just as we clam up when we first go back to work after a long maternity leave.

Rory McGrath, comedian and writer

Before you have a child you are a normal, happy couple. As soon as the baby arrives you become a Mum and a Dad, and quite often the Mums are assumed to be getting everything right, while the Dads are getting it all hopelessly wrong. This is generally untrue, and it really doesn't help a new father to be made to feel that he is at best useless, and at worst unhelpful. Men do things differently, but that doesn't make them wrong.

The more you can try to talk with him about his feelings, and how he is dealing with his new family role, the easier it will be for him, and therefore for all of you. I spend hours talking with Yummy Mummy friends about our partners, and there seem to be as many ways of handling a family, and all the juggling, sharing, helping, rowing, laughing and crying that goes with it, as there are of raising the source of all this juggling. Most agree that Daddy is less able to talk about his feelings than Mummy is, but those that keep the communication going seem to be happier than those who don't.

And that's more than enough family counselling for this lovely book!

PART THIRTEEN

Going Back to Work

As I mentioned way back at the beginning of our long journey, there is absolutely no point deciding for certain whether you will go back to work after you have a baby before you have it, because you have no idea how you will feel. Some mothers-to-be intend to go straight back to the office as soon as they can, but suddenly find themselves so deeply in love with their puking, shitting, gorgeous baby that they burn their briefcases and settle down to a happy life at home. Others swear they will never work again, but find themselves banging on their boss's door within a month, desperate for some mental stimulation and a hole-punch. Still others have some kind of epiphany while they are pregnant, and realise that they never really wanted to work in advertising, and that re-training to become a potter is what they were destined to do. You don't know how you'll feel, so prepare to improvise.

When you are facing the Big Work Question, many frightening things will whiz through your mind: *Should I? Shouldn't I? What will my mum say? What will my baby say? What can I wear? Will I regret it? Am I copping out? Can I handle talking to so many adults in one day?* Making the decision is one of the hardest moments in your first year, unless you either have no choice financially (as is the case for most working mums), or you are remarkably good at knowing what you want. Being a smart woman, I suspect you *are* remarkably good at knowing what you want, but are equally rubbish at getting it without wallowing in guilt and self-doubt. I can't really make it much easier, but I can tell you what it was like for me, and how other working Yummy Mummies I know have coped.

I Need a Job: Part One

No you don't. You have a job. You have a full-time, full-on job called 'looking after your baby'.

Yes, but I want to earn some money.

You are earning money, by not spending money.

What?

It's true. You are earning a small fortune by doing all the hard work that you do. It just doesn't feel like it, because nobody gives you a pay cheque at the end of the month.

This sounds good. More details please.

OK, let's break your parenting job down, and see how much you would cost to replace:

☆ **First-rate, full-time childcare, 24 hours a day, every day:** There is no figure you could put on this kind of dedicated love and care, but let's say, as a very mean estimate, £20 per hour, plus bonuses. That's about £200K per year. Yikes!
☆ **Cleaning:** Three hours per day (at least – you just wait) at £10 per hour: £11K per year.
☆ **Cooking:** I've never had one, but my friend is a personal chef, and she can earn up to £45K in a culinary year. (What are they *eating*? Gold?)
☆ **Personal shopper:** I've read of quotes up to £120 per hour, but let's just say £200 per week for food, toiletries and basic clothing, which is another £10K every year.

Now, even if we ignore all the other housekeeping duties, and the fact that you are the best PA your husband could ever afford (who else would make sure he leaves the house on time every morning with his glasses, a clean-ish shirt, and no sick on his shoulder? Who else will pick up his dirty pants, rinse his toenail clippings down the drain, and will still have sex with him occasionally, which must save a fair whack on expensive visits to ladies who charge for that sort of thing), we are looking at a pretty hefty salary you're bringing in here. In fact, about £266,000 a year, going by the above estimates.

I see.

Good, because put like this you quickly realise that you're quite the little earner really, and it makes you feel a whole lot better when the laundry needs folding for the sixth time in a week. In fact, I'd say you probably deserve a bonus for the extra hours you put in over the weekend while Daddy was away on business, wouldn't you? How about a nice mosey around the nearest bookshop, followed by a relaxing facial and lunch with friends? Oh, and you'll probably be needing a new pair of shoes: all that buggy-pushing can be murder on the soles... Only after all this will you be ready to go back to the real world of motherhood.

You are, after all, well worth it, as we've just proved.

I Need a Job: Part Two

Yes, you do.

But I feel so guilty. I should be spending all my time with my baby.

Why? Is that the only thing you want to be doing? Do you feel wholly fulfilled and satisfied when you have nothing else in your head other than thoughts about your baby? Are you a better parent for giving up the work you used to enjoy doing?

No, but other people (i.e. my mother, very rich Yummy Mummies with full-time au-pairs, and childless, smart ladies in town) will pour scorn on me for neglecting my baby.

If you truthfully answered 'yes' to the questions above, then skip forward to the next chapter, but book yourself an appointment with your doctor just to check you really are human. For everyone else, stop right there!

Being a full-time parent is just that: FULL TIME.

Anyone lucky enough to have a job involving an employer, a water-cooler and a lunch break (the word '*break*' kind of implies a *pause* in the work) thinks that 'full time' means 'until I have finished my work for today, or I can't be bothered any more'.

'Full time' for you, on the other hand, is the real McCoy. FULL. There is NO BREAK. There are no lunch breaks, weekends off, holidays or long lie-ins. There's no sick leave, no office parties or flexi-time. Even when your baby is not *physically* present, he exists somewhere in the world and in your subconscious, and that is enough to make you, even at the lowest level, on duty. From the second he wakes you up two hours too early to the moment his squidgy hands flop down to the sides of his hot head at night, your mind and body belong to your baby. There is no let-up.

The result of this omnipresence is that you have absolutely no time to be, or to do anything for yourself.

☆ **You can't go to the loo** when you need to, because you're usually in the middle of finger-painting or feeding your baby when you need to go, and you can't leave her alone in case she swallows the paintbrush or does a stage-dive out of the high-chair. Even when a small window arises for you to relieve yourself, this is hardly a moment for quiet reflection: there is almost always a small person present to hand you the paper, ask what you're doing or just want to sit on your lap.

☆ **You can't phone anyone.** At least, not anyone to whom you actually wish to speak. If it's just a 'Hi, how are you? Bye' kind of call, then it's fine, but any more than that is just asking for trouble. And *work* phone calls?? God, woman, are you *mad*? No, no and no. (See **Simply the Bes**t, below.)

☆ **Your personal grooming will take a battering unless** you develop very clever strategies. Just finding a moment to wash your face can be tricky, and applying make-up with a baby on one hip is a skill which you *can* develop, but it never has quite the desired effect: i.e. to cover up the enormous bags under your eyes, and to make you feel just a teeny-weeny bit attractive again.

☆ **You can't think**. This is the hardest one for me, because I need to think *a lot* (there is a lot going on in this head of mine), and putting all of my thoughts on hold until the baby goes to sleep leaves me completely frustrated, confused and badly distracted from the task at hand, i.e. being a good Mum.

Clearly, I am exaggerating, and you *can* still do all of these things. They just become a lot more difficult and stressful, or even impossible, unless Junior is either asleep or somewhere else. From the moment of birth, *everything* you do, *everything* you think, and *everything* you talk about becomes, in some way, child-related, whether you realise it or not, and this may not be very healthy for you.

And what happens to YOU? Where do you, the 'person' and not the 'parent', go?

Where is that girl full of thoughts, ideas, interests and passions? Where is the woman who used to be a lawyer, a teacher, a journalist or a scientist?

Where are YOU?

Well, the good news is that **you are still there**, somewhere, albeit it in a slightly stretched and haggard form for now. But if you previously had a job, an active social life and numerous hobbies and interests, then a huge part of you gets locked away in a cupboard when your baby is born, and the chances are that it doesn't like it.

This independent, thinking part of you wants to come out, and if you feel it knocking on the cupboard door then you should let it out.

By getting a job.

Even the smallest, most part-time, mundane kind of a job will do, if you are desperate. It is just something which allows you to stop being a mummy for a few hours and lets you be someone else again. Obviously, not everyone feels this way. Lots of my Yummy Mummy friends stopped working (out of the house) for the first four years, until their children went to school, and for some of them it seemed to work very well. I take my rather nice new floppy sunhat off to them: they have done an enormous job very well, and they should feel a huge sense of pride in what they have achieved.

Some job-related things to consider:

☆ **Everyone is different**, and has different priorities and needs. You shouldn't feel under any pressure to do something that doesn't feel right to you. Not to me, or your mother, or your partner: **to you**.

☆ **Don't make any fixed plans until after you have your baby:** You have no idea how you will feel about your baby until a good few weeks, and probably months, after the birth, and a massive number of women have a complete change of heart and realise they want to change their work plans.

☆ **Having a job relieves any guilt about spending money.** If you are lucky enough not to feel guilty at all about spending someone else's cash, then you just go for it! But I found every cappuccino, every train fare, every book and every haircut became tinged with guilt, and I was constantly justifying my purchases, which annoyed the Hell out of my husband, who couldn't have cared less. Getting my own pay cheques means I can spoil myself rotten, knowing *I* earned it and deserve it, and it feels so much better.

☆ **You might not earn much more than the extortionate cost of the childcare**, but if it gives you some personal satisfaction, and a chance to be an adult for a time, then the lack of financial gain is offset by the freedom you get.

☆ **Having a job keeps your foot in the door:** One day your baby will be a Big Person, and will disappear off to school for six hours a day. Unless you are happy to do nothing but cook dinner and water the house plants every day during that time, you'd better have a strategy for getting some mental stimulation, in the form of work, lined up.

☆ **Keeping in work means you don't lose your nerve:** It's very common for women who stay at home with children for a large number of years to be absolutely terrified of going back into a 'work' environment. Job interviews scare the bejesus out of them, and when they get into the office it's hard to know what 'normal people' talk about.

I have tried all of the options available: I have been a full-time, stay-at-home mum and wife; I have worked full-time (for a couple of weeks only) and I have mixed part-time work with part-time parenting. Giving up work just didn't suit me at all, and it was very difficult to admit it. I thought that if I didn't want to look after my kids all the time there must be something wrong with me. I must be a bad mother, or a horribly selfish person. And I felt so pathetic and ridiculous: how hard could it be to just play with your kids all day? What was the big problem there? As most people who have only ever done it for a day or two at a time are quick to point out, childcare is great fun! Anyone would jump at the chance: playing, drawing, going to the playground, feeding the ducks, stopping for a coffee and cake at a café, reading books: not exactly hard work, is it? No deadlines, meetings, bosses breathing down your neck, hellish commutes or irritating colleagues. Just you, your lovely baby, and a whole day of playing.

Bummer.

Well, actually, it is a huge bummer, after a while. Before my first baby was born I was quite sure that I would stay at home for the first year or so and look after her. But after a few months of playing, singing, swing-pushing and duck-feeding, I craved mental stimulation like reality TV contestants crave attention. I *wanted* irritating colleagues. I would have sacrificed a year's worth of hair cuts for a hellish commute or two, or a boss who would breathe down my neck.

I have stood in playgrounds staring at the slide, the roundabout and the 'wibble-wobble' thing, just aching and longing for the chance to put some of the ideas flying around my head to some use again, to talk to some adults about PDF files and final edits, to walk from A to B without pushing a buggy, and to wear something expensive which shouldn't go within a mile of any young child.

Here is an extract from my diary a year after I had decided to stop working part-time as a television presenter, in order to look after my two children full-time:

I am so, so, so UNHAPPY. I am so bored and angry and frustrated. I want to write, to read, to do something, ANYTHING which makes me think and use my brain. I'm going mad. I keep snapping at Emily, and I am horrid to H, and I can't stand it any more. I just want a break. I need somewhere for all my energy and ideas to go, which is just for me. To achieve something which is separate from babies and being a mum. I have book ideas, scripts, TV series ideas, photography projects, whole scenes from films, feature articles and columns all in my head, just piling up, building up and exploding my head. They need to get out or I will go MAD. I can't concentrate on anything. My mind just buzzes from idea to idea and thought to thought and I can't think about any of them for more than a second or two before I have to go back to pushing the swing or whatever. I can't get anything done. I hate everything right now, and then I feel so bad about that. I love my kids. I adore them, and couldn't live without them. I should be so happy, but I am just miserable and frustrated. I hate myself. I don't know what to do.

Luckily, I figured out what to do: I booked my kids into a nice nursery for two days a week, and I went back to work part-time, as a freelance writer and broadcaster. I had no terrible feelings of guilt and failure: I had given the alternative a good chance, but it just wasn't working for me, for my children or for our family.

It was an immediate cure, even before I'd started work:

☆ As soon as I knew I would have some regular time away from my kids, I relished every moment with them: instead of counting the hours until bedtime, I wanted to be with them as much as possible on my 'childcare' days, because I knew there was a break just a few days away.

☆ Even the smallest bits of work here and there were enough to give me back my self-confidence, and allow me to become my own person again, at least for two days out of seven. I even started to smile again, which was a definite improvement on the permascowl.

☆ Another plus-point for going back to work is collecting your baby at the end of the day. Almost nothing beats a hard day's work, getting off a smelly train, exchanging smart work-clothes for some slouchy jeans and a comfy (but stylish – careful!) T-shirt, and going to see your baby. I still break into a sprint on the way to nursery *every* time, and when I see my beautiful little boy I cuddle and kiss and hug him to bits. It's very embarrassing for him, but I can't help it.

☆ On 'work' days I can hardly bring myself to put my kids to bed: I want to stay up and play with them all for hours. Contrast this with the end of a long childcare day, when I am often so exhausted and fed up with the lot of them that the only thought in my head is to get them all to bed and asleep as soon as possible, leaving me free to cook my own dinner, clean the kitchen and put all the toys away. In peace. On my own.

So I guess my conclusion, and my advice to you, my worried friend, is to know yourself and know your limitations. Do whatever works for YOU and makes you happiest, because if YOU are fulfilled and happy your family will be happier too.

Tamara Mellon, president, Jimmy Choo
Being a working mum is an extremely difficult balance because the day doesn't stop when you leave work. It starts again when you get home! I am always feeling guilty that I can't pick my daughter up from school every day whilst other mothers do. Nobody ever feels prepared. I certainly didn't feel ready but I don't think I could find one woman who regrets having children.

Potential Work-related Disasters

Kipling didn't quite write 'Babies are Babies and Work is Work, but never the twain shall meet', but if he had, he would have been equally astute.

When you go back to work, you will need to adopt some cunning methods of ensuring that no traces of Baby enter your world of Work. Any crossover between the two results in some very pissed-off work colleagues, or a very neglected baby. It also means that you risk going to work looking somewhat below office par (sick on the shoulder is only *one* of the many common outfit disasters you will encounter, unless you stick to your prevention strategy like glue).

The easiest way to separate work and motherhood is to make sure that your baby doesn't come to work with you. This is a good deal less obvious than you are thinking: with ever more Yummy Mummies working from home these days, it's easy to be caught out, and conference calls run the risk of being jeopardised by a very junior fifth party who wants Mummy to come back and play with the trains again. I remember an unscheduled phone conversation with my executive producer at *Live and Kicking*, which eventually ended with him saying, very curtly, 'Why don't you call me back when you've stopped your baby from crying, hmmm?' Crushing.

To make the transition back into the stress-free world of paid work easier, here is the Yummy Mummy's guide to avoiding work catastrophes:

☆ **Never bring your baby to the office.** In the very early days I used to take my newborn daughter into the television studios with me, and there must be cupboards full of recordings of me talking to camera to the background accompaniment of a very vocal baby making her dislike of my absence known from the adjoining room. This was the clearest example of how *not* to combine work and motherhood, and I gave up very quickly in favour of a part-time nursery place.

☆ **Never wear your work clothes at home.** Obviously there will be an unavoidable few minutes, just before you leave the house, and then just after you get in the door again, when you will have to wear your best stuff in front of your baby, but if it's any more than three minutes your favourite Zara shirt will be ruined by apple and blueberry dessert, blue paint, or whatever indelible goo is in your baby's hand.

☆ **Leave tons of extra time for getting to work.** The very fact that you are a Mother Who Works will put you under the spotlight for even the smallest gaff on your part. Being late gets the day off to a flying start, and every incident of this kind will be mentally logged by petty colleagues who are too small-minded to know any better. This is even more annoying because you just *know* they are having sex more frequently than you, dammit.

☆ **Have emergency childcare sorted out.** Your baby will be ill from time to time, and most nurseries have a very strict policy on when they don't want your spotty, snotty sneezer on the premises. As luck will have it, 'ill' days always fall on 'big presentation' days at work, so you'd better have at least one other person on 'holding-the-baby' standby, if you want to keep your job for longer than the time it takes to conceive a sibling.

☆ **Wear two hats: symbolically, not as a fashion statement.** At home you are Mummy, but at work you have to transform into

Work Lady. Don't talk about your baby at work: nobody cares. Honestly.

☆ **Keep the photos for the photo album**, and resist the temptation to use 'Freddie's first smile' as a screensaver. You are at work, so *be* at work. The only thing cutesy photos will do is make your boobs start tingling, and we all know what *that* can lead to. A photo in the wallet is worth ten on the desktop, in my experience.

☆ **Try not to phone the childcarer to find out how your baby is getting on.** I used to do this a lot, and all it did was distract me from my work, upset me, and make me feel guilty again, just as the guilt was beginning to wear off. If there's a problem, they will call.

☆ **Keep an emergency make-up kit in your desk**, for any 'I didn't realise I only put foundation on my *left* cheek' disasters. Foundation, concealer, multi-purpose colour for cheeks, eyes and lips, perfume, deodorant, and some make-up remover to wipe away smudged mascara after a tear is shed should see you immaculately through a busy day.

☆ **Stop breastfeeding well before you go back to work.** This will prevent embarrassing leakages, and also mean you won't have to express breast milk in the toilets during your lunch break when you could be shopping instead. Many women I know did this and while their dedication is very commendable, I think it's easier all round to switch bottle feeding before hitting the office.

☆ **Leave a clean change of clothes at work.** That way, if you do fall foul of the 'last-second posset' as you leave the house, you can still go to your 9.30 board meeting looking spotless. Some spare breast pads are also essential, but hide them well!

☆ **Check your bag for hidden evidence.** It's not cool to turn up with a nappy and a plastic teat poking out of your Chloe briefcase. Work bag is for work stuff only.

At some point you will be caught out, and your family life will stray into your work territory. If it's a one-off, nobody will mind too much: it's part of who you are now, and it shows a more human side of your character. Turning up an hour late with baby porridge on your crotch on a regular basis is not OK at all, and you will be doing all working mothers a huge disservice. Sort yourself out, and try again tomorrow.

Simply the Best

This is what you will have to be at work from now on. The Best. Being a mother leaves you wide open to criticism about having a fuzzy, distracted brain, being too tired to think, arriving late because the baby needed changing, leaving early to collect a child who has developed a temperature, having far-too-droopy boobs and so on, which all mean that you need to prove yourself more than ever. You have to out-perform every other member of staff or competitor, look better than they do, work faster, and appear to be taking everything well within your maternal stride, because any less than this will immediately be blamed on the fact that you now have a baby, and can therefore only handle talk about nappies and nipple cream.

You will, of course, cry in the toilets, but so long as you have your emergency make-up kit with you, nobody at the 3 p.m. team meeting will know.

If you are lucky enough to work for people who are sympathetic to the needs and commitments of working mothers, then you will find the return to work a lot easier. If all of this sounds somewhat offputting, then just remember how fantastic it will feel when you are reunited with your lovely, lovely, *lovely* baby, and how much you will enjoy feeding the ducks tomorrow after the break at work. And it *is* a break...

Who's Holding My Baby?
Childcare Options to Worry About...

Before we even start, here's a word of warning (actually 72 words of warning): If you are even thinking about going back to work within a year or two of having your baby, start looking into child-care *now*, unless you are happy to take whatever you can get when the time comes. Most nurseries are booked up many months and even years in advance, especially for younger babies, and finding a good nanny requires good word of mouth, which means working on that Yummy Mummy network…

I am not Madonna. Nor am I Kate Winslet (damn!) or any other of the lucky group of women who can bring their children to work with them because they have a full-time nanny on hand during takes. They are the lucky few, and we should not kid ourselves into thinking we can do the same despite our obvious lack of 'full-time nanny on hand'.

What this lack of extra pairs of manicured hands means is that you need to find somewhere else for your baby to be while you bring in the dough. Preferably somewhere safe, happy, clean and in the presence of a qualified childcarer. Not the ball pit in your local shopping centre, in other words.

I *Can't* Leave My Baby, Can I?

It's possible that you can't, because you find it all too upsetting, but for the majority of Yummy Mummies who need a bit of independence, getting used to the idea of leaving their baby in the capable hands of a qualified Yummy childcarer is just something they have to do. Millions of very happy babies are spending time with gorgeous nannies or in bright, beautiful nurseries, and you can leave them there perfectly happily without opening a trust fund to pay for their therapy in years to come. I think.

So What *are* the Options?

Choosing which *type* of care is best for you and your baby is a very tricky one. You and your partner may disagree on what's best for your baby (this is a nightmare, and cannot be solved by tossing coins or promising blow jobs), and when you do come up with the ideal solution for all of you, this is bound to be unmanageable, because your area only seems to have really ugly nannies, or all the nursery places are filled with other Yummy babies.

To get you started on the arguing and decision-making, here is a guide to the main options available, and some facts about each one:

☆ **Nanny:** Forget the Nanny McPhee image, most nannies I know are leggy East European beauties who love the children they care for almost as much as their parents do. This is a great option if you want more one-to-one attention for your baby, or you could go for a nanny-share with another Yummy Mummy, to allow for some baby socialising. A huge advantage is that you get to hand-pick the one you want, and your nanny will form a very strong bond with your baby. It's also handy that they can stay on a little longer (for a huge fee) if your meetings overrun, or there's a sudden vacancy for a much-needed cut and blow-dry. You can give clear instructions as to how you want your baby to be looked after, and you should feel very confident that this is happening while you're off earning some dough.

The bad news is that you might feel jealous of the bond between your baby and her nanny, and there is the problem of leggy East European beauties hanging around the house. Risky…

Baukjen, co-founder Isabella Oliver

Our nanny doesn't do everything the way I would do it but this is good because it means I learn from her, and that can be very helpful.

☆ **Day Nursery:** This is the option we chose, but, as with every other option I considered, it's not ideal. The best thing about nurseries, in my experience, is that there are lots of other little dudes to mingle with, and it teaches your little dude how to socialise, and how to be patient while one of these other little dudes is being sorted out. When our children went to school it was very clear which of their peers had gone to a nursery, because they were more confident in the classroom, and found a long day at school less exhausting.

Other advantages are the fact that they are usually open from 8 a.m. until 6 p.m., should you ever need such horribly long hours away from your baby, plus they don't close during school holidays and there is no problem with staff illness, because there are always extra employees on hand. If you are uneasy about leaving your baby alone with only one person, then this is a great option for you.

What I've found hardest to cope with is the thought that my baby can't have somebody's full attention all the time, and there are probably longish periods when he is playing on his own. If you can see this as a valuable lesson in independence, you'll cope better than I did. There is also the risk of staff turnover, and we have had some awful periods of staff leaving every time our baby starts to like them. It's very upsetting, but babies seem to adjust again quite quickly. Here's hoping for no permanent scarring.

☆ **Childminder:** Childminders do what nannies do, except in their own home, rather than yours, and usually with several other children as well as yours. This means it's a great way for your baby to meet other, like-minded small people without committing to a full nursery experience. Finding a good childminder can be tricky, and word of mouth is invaluable. That means getting some Yummy friends, and putting your feelers out soon...

☆ **Au Pair:** Most au pairs I know are of the same gorgeous stock as the nannies, except that they live with the family all the time. If you need your privacy and don't like the idea of six-foot Stunninga Modellova sharing your bathroom then don't even consider it. If you happen to have a fully-furnished annex then you are sorted, and an au pair will be the most useful thing you invest in. All the Yummy Mummies I know who employ au pairs use their household help to the max, and seem to have more free time on their hands than any of us lowly nursery types. I am insanely jealous, but value being able to walk around my house stark-naked singing, while Robbie Williams offers to entertain me, too highly.

☆ **Family member:** I would never consider this as a long-term option (can you imagine the potential for enormous bust-ups?) but if you are lucky enough to live near either set of grandparents it can be a fantastic gap-bridger in emergencies. We are in the process of trying to move closer to my parents partly for this reason. Oh, and because I like them very, very much and think they are wonderful, kind, perfect grandparents, of course. (That weekend in July still OK for you guys, then…?)

These are the main options you'll have to choose between. (There are others, like doulas and maternity nurses, but I've never met anyone with either of these, so I wouldn't like to comment.) What you end up going for will depend on what you feel most comfortable with, what's available, and what seems to suit your child best. Not all babies are happy in a nursery environment, while others need the company and stimulation of friends. Similarly, a desperately shy baby might benefit from the one-to-one attention of a nanny, or you might feel that mixing with other babies will loosen her up a bit. It's a tough one.

Settling a baby into childcare takes time, so try not to give up at the first sign of tears. (Your baby's, not yours.) We did lots of visits together for a few weeks before the Big Day, which seemed to settle them all in gently. The most important things to remember when choosing childcare for you baby are that you will always feel guilty about leaving your baby, however perfect the temporary alternative is, and that you must choose something you are happy with, not what other people advise you to choose. Just because Francesca Thompkinson-Smythe has an au pair and is going to Gstaad in February does not mean you need to extend the loft and move your own au pair in before Christmas.

And, lastly, one of the most important things for your baby is consistency. Once you choose a nanny, nursery or whatever, try to stick with it as long as possible. Babies are rather unadventurous, and don't like change. All types of childcare will go through good and bad phases but things generally settle down again soon, and the fewer changes the better.

'Well *I* Didn't Work When You Were Little'

If your mother ever says this to you when the 'I'm thinking of going back to work' conversation arises, it's worth pointing out how totally unhelpful and unfair such a statement is. Yes, she did stay at home and look after all her six children, and she did sacrifice everything and dedicate herself to you all. Such personal sacrifice should never, ever go unthanked and unappreciated, but thirty-whatever years ago things were a little different. Thirty years ago, women didn't run multi-million-pound businesses. (Well, hardly.) Thirty years ago most women didn't *expect* to have a well-paid, well-respected job in advertising, merchant banking or fashion design. There was, quite simply, less *CHOICE*.

Choice is a dangerous thing. As soon as we have a choice, it means we have to make a decision, and human beings find personal decision-making very, very difficult, even without all the gorgeous things we can now have clouding our judgement. Don't get me wrong, *I'd rather have the choice*. But it doesn't make things a whole lot easier, because choices bring all the stress and worry that we might have made the wrong choice, that we could be doing something else, or that we are missing out on something. It makes accepting the status quo much harder.

So don't feel pressured into doing what your mother did. Maybe she didn't have ten years of a career behind her when she started to have kids. Maybe she wishes she had. Maybe she did, and wishes she had gone back to her work when you were young, but chose to stay at home instead. Maybe you have different needs and personal goals and expectations. Do what feels right for you.

You'll probably make the wrong decision, but that only shows how human you are. Life, eh? Bloody nightmare!

Guilt

I'm really good at this bit: I feel guilty about feeling guilty. I am the only person I've ever heard of who apologises throughout her labour to anyone entering the room for being so annoying as to be having a baby and for making such a lot of noise. If someone bumps into me, my immediate reaction is to apologise to them.

But even if you don't live off guilt quite as much as I do, you can be sure that you will feel pretty rotten every time you leave your baby in childcare and go off to work. It just comes with the territory, and you had better learn how to deal with it.

Here are some things to remember, which help me:

☆ If working makes you happier, this will be better for your baby when you are together.

☆ Babies play the Guilt Game very skilfully, and can put on an amazing show to make you feel bad. Within two minutes of your leaving, your baby will be perfectly happy again. Devious little thing.

☆ Your baby will learn different things, play with different toys, and learn how to get on with others while you are away. All positives.

☆ In my experience, babies who have some childcare in their lives are just as happy as those who don't, they do well at school and have more relaxed and fulfilled mummies.

☆ All children behave differently with others than with you, and babies do this too. It's really interesting to hear what they are like when you are not around.

☆ A fresh pair of eyes can point out lots of traits that your maternal eye never sees.

If you are finding leaving your baby too traumatic, then maybe you need to look for an alternative. It's worth remembering, though, that babies go through phases, and you can go for weeks with no problem at all and then suddenly find yourself leaving a crying baby every morning. It's horrible, but it will pass.

More Information
☆ **National Childbirth Trust.**
☆ **The Daycare Trust.** National charity providing childcare information.
☆ **Ofsted.** In case you want to check out a nursery.

☆ **ChildcareLink.** Government website with details of local childcare services.

The Yummy Mummy's Work Wardrobe

One of the biggest stresses of going back to work is knowing what to wear. Or rather not knowing – that being the stressful part. Before your baby, you may have used workwear to express your personality, or to fit in with the work environment. Nine months of an enlarged tummy and breasts can leave you with no sense of who you used to be, let alone what you used to wear, and getting back into a work role can test the most proficient chameleons among you.

In a way, though, this is one of the most useful things about returning to work: it forces you to address this potentially catastrophic personality loss, and work out how you will go back to looking sharp in the workplace (unless you are a landscape gardener or something which allows roughing it big-time). Without this enforcement, I think most of us would disappear into the fleecy, safe, boring uniforms seen in playgrounds the length and breadth of the country. And this would be a tragedy on a national level, as I'm sure all serious politicians would agree.

Here are some very useful tips to make your work wardrobe workable and practical for your new dual Yummy Mummy/Professional Woman roles. It's very office-orientated, but the same general rules apply for most places of work or jobs, where looking nice is preferable to looking dreadful. Adjust as required:

☆ **Forget anything which needs dry cleaning or special care and attention** unless you are a complete glutton for punishment, (my daughter was five before she laid eyes on an iron – a fact I am still proud of). You need work clothes which can also withstand all the goo your baby will splatter on them before you manage to leave the house, but they still need to look smart. If you team machine-washable suits with good shoes and a decent hairstyle, you will manage to pull off a smart look without too many letters to your bank manager. Armani tailoring does look fantastic, but he wasn't thinking about babies when he designed his best suits, alas.

☆ **Prints and patterns are great for disguising** the aforementioned goo. Just because you are a mummy does not mean you have to resort to Plain Jane white shirts every day. (Although a good white shirt is still the staple of every working woman's wardrobe.) Go to Zara or Top Shop and get something colourful and clever. Pureed carrot on my sleeve? Where?

☆ **Your basics should remain simple**, having said that, with any colour coming as shirts or accessories. **Buy plenty of core black** vests, long-sleeved tops with pretty neck-lines (your décolletage is one of your assets at the moment), cardies and, of course, trousers and skirts: by Friday you will be desperate to find any two clean items which go well together, and the more simple, co-ordinated items you have, the higher the chances of success.

☆ **Invest in some killer shoes.** Not high, necessarily (can *you* get your baby to nursery on the back of your bicycle wearing four-inch heels?) but very, very good ones. Shoes are the item which will set off the rest of your work outfit, and they can outshine a multitude of baby sins elsewhere. I only ever wear flats, because of all the buggy-pushing and bike-riding, but they are beautiful flats, and they make me feel all woman and no mummy for the day.

☆ **Buy multiple copies** if you find something which works. Again, this is where high-street wins over designer luxury. I'd rather have five tops from Mango than one Prada one. Actually, that's a lie: I'd rather have one Prada anything, but given the circumstances I'll take the cheaper lot. Such a shame, but that's the reality. Boo.

☆ **Avoid lots of buttons:** Quite apart from the fact that they take ages to do up in the morning – and you don't have ages any more – your baby will love pulling them off while you brush your teeth.

☆ **Get a clothes brush.** The moment you do, you'll realise why.

If you can find something which works for the first few weeks, that's a great start, and everything else can just develop from there.

Everyone's first day back at work after maternity leave is terrifying, and you will probably make at least one major cock-up. Mine was a once-white-now-grey maternity bra, for example, which unfortunately showed up beautifully under the studio lights. I learned that lesson and got a new, clean one as soon as I had the chance – which was probably several weeks later but I did get eventually around to it.

If you think you are failing hopelessly, then take heart from the fact that most working mothers feel exactly the same most mornings, as do most working *non*-Mummies, and they have no such excuses. Knowing what to wear is just a permanent dilemma for almost all women – praise be for that second X-chromosome once again! – and the fact that you are managing to throw anything together which feels un-Mummy-ish is a step in the right direction. You'll get there – it just feels dreadful to start with.

And Finally . . .

Where does all of this leave us? What have the six months of trying, nine months of growing, twelve hours (if you're lucky) of delivering and twelve months of nurturing actually achieved?

Well, they have produced a baby, for one; a Mummy for another; and a Daddy for another. And that's probably slightly more impressive than a hundred nights in the pub, twenty-five visits to the cinema, three short holidays and a promotion. In fact, it's the biggest achievement of your life.

There may have been many times throughout the reading of this book when you have wondered: Is it really worth it? The pain, the physical and mental hammering, the emotional upheaval, the relationship strain, the sagging, the crying, the house-trashing, the career-hampering and the messy bathroom. Is it really worth all that?

Of course it bloody is! It's worth it a thousand times over, because if it weren't the human race would die out before Steven Soderbergh could finish the final edit on *Ocean's 57*.

If you still need reassurance and encouragement, then think about the future. It seems ridiculous to think of it now, but very, very soon your baby will be a child – a child who thinks, talks, makes you presents, argues with you, has friends round to play, has fights with his friends, brings you Mother's Day cards from school, writes stories, learns the violin, invents games, plays tennis, paints wonderful pictures, gives you cuddles, helps you cook, develops unique talents, and says 'I love you, Mummy'.

This last one is the clincher. When everything is falling apart, and you can't see the end of the day for the washing up, tidying, negotiating bedtime with a stubborn toddler, paying the bills, watering the plants and finding out where your husband was until 10 p.m., your sticky, argumentative, wilful, beautiful child will tell you that she loves you. And everything is put back into perspective.

I know that's a little way off yet, but it's worth remembering when the baby phase starts to drag on a bit.

Good luck, good luck! Try to enjoy it. Love your baby, and look after him or her as well as you possibly can. Try not to make as many mistakes as I did (that's what this book is for, silly!), try to remember that you are a woman as well as a Yummy Mummy, and don't forget to smile, just occasionally. You look much prettier when you smile, and that's a good start!

Liz xxx.

Acknowledgements

Like most authors I've ever heard of, I have been blessed with a more than generous helping of self-doubt, paranoia and a propensity to throw my hands in the air and sigh, 'Oh, what's the point? It's crap. A glass of wine is what I need.' Luckily, like most authors who have ever been published, I have been kept on the bumpy route to completion by a group of wonderful people who have just as much doubt in my abilities as I do, but who are fantastic liars. And so I would like to say 'thank you' to as many of them as I can remember in my sleep-deprived state.

Straight in at number one is you, dear Harry: firstly for providing the essential sperm without which none of this would have been possible, secondly for your unwavering support (sorry, lies) through the strops, crises and 'what's the point's, and thirdly for being the loveliest man I have ever met who let me, for the first time in my life, feel that there is a point and that I could have my own opinion about things. That backfired, didn't it? Yes it did – don't argue.

To my brother Andrew for reading my early scribbles and making positive noises about them: yours is literary criticism I value very highly, and which really encouraged me to keep practising.

To my agent Euan, for agreeing to meet me in the first place, and then for understanding what I wanted to write. I am very sorry for making you read so much about grim 'lady things', but just think how eligible you are now: you will sail through fatherhood saying and doing all the right things and knowing that your place is in the wrong 90% of the time.

A huge 'thank you' to my lovely, lovely editor Maxine: your patience, extreme care and wicked sense of humour have made the cruel process of picking apart every line and condemning large chunks of waffle to the waste bin almost painless.

To Livia, for the toast and coffee, over which you promised to kill me if I didn't finally write the book I kept muttering about. It would never have progressed beyond mutterings without your threat.

To Camilla for sitting through hours of boring book talk and worry when you surely have much better things to think about, and for all your helpful advice. Your jeans are still great!

And finally, the biggest thank you goes to my three children. For once, I am completely lost for adequate words, but hopefully my love for you shows itself so strongly every day that I don't need to spell it out. You are the reason this book exists, the reason I want to get up every day, and my greatest source of happiness. If you could just tidy your rooms occasionally that would just about nail it, I think.

Details of Stockists, Services, Manufacturers, Organisations

Agent Provocateur –
www.agentprovocateur.com
Apotheke's Jurlique Day Spa and
Sanctuary –
www.apotheke20-20.co.uk
Arabella B – www.arabellab.com
Arco – www.arcocandles.com
Argos – www.argos.co.uk
Asda: George at Asda –
www.asda.co.uk/www.george.com

Baby-O – www.baby-o.co.uk
Bach's Herbal Remedies –
www.bachshop.com
Beaming Baby –
www.beamingbaby.co.uk
Berkeley Hotel, London –
www.berkeleyhotel.com
Bill Amberg – www.billamberg.com
Bliss; Bliss Spa – www.blissworld.com
Blooming Marvellous –
www.bloomingmarvellous.co.uk
Blossom Mother and Child –
www.blossommotherandchild.com
Bobbi Brown –
www.bobbibrowncosmetics.com
Boden; Mini Boden –
www.boden.co.uk
The Body Shop –
www.uk.thebodyshop.com
Bombay Duck –
www.bombayduck.co.uk
Boots – www.boots.com
Brown's –
www.browns-restaurants.com
British Airways –
www.britishairways.com

Bumps Maternity Wear –
www.bumpsmaternity.com
Bumpsville – www.bumpsville.com
Burberry – www.burberry.com
Burt's Bees – www.burtsbees.com

Caramel – Tel 0207 589 7001
ChildcareLink –
www.childcarelink.gov.uk/ Tel: 0800
096 0296
Christian Lacroix –
www.christian-lacroix.com
Clarins – www.uk.clarins.com
Clinique – www.clinique.co.uk
Cotton Bottoms –
www.cottonbottoms.co.uk/
Tel: 08707 778 899
Crabtree & Evelyn –
www.crabtree-evelyn.com
Cutex – www.cutexnails.com

Daniel Galvin –
www.daniel-galvin.co.uk
The Daycare Trust –
www.daycaretrust.org.uk/ Tel: 020
7840 3350
Dermalogica –
www.dermalogica.co.uk
Diane Von Furstenberg Maternity –
www.dvflondon.com
Dior; Baby Dior – www.dior.com
Diptyque – www.diptyque.tm.fr
Doctor Burt – www.burtsbees.com
Dolce & Gabbana –
www.dolcegabbana.com
Dorothy Perkins –
www.dorothyperkins.co.uk

Dove – www.dove.co.uk
Dr Hauschka – www.drhauschka.co.uk

Earl Jean maternity wear –
  www.earljean.com
Eco-Babes – www.eco-babes.co.uk/
  Tel: 01366 387851
Eco Clothworks –
  www.clothworks.co.uk/ Tel: 01225
  309218
Elemis – www.elemis.com
Elizabeth Arden –
  www.elizabetharden.com
Elle MacPherson –
  www.ellemacphersonintimates.co.nz

Formes – www.formes.fr

Gap; Baby Gap – www.gap.com
Graziella; Baby Graziella –
  www.babygraziella.it
Greenfibres – www.greenfibres.com/
  Tel: 01803 868001
Grove Hotel, Hertfordshire –
  www.thegrove.co.uk
Guinot – www.guinotusa.com
Gulf Pacific – www.gulfairco.com
Gymboree – www.gymboree.com

H&M Mama – www.hm.com
Homme Mummy –
  www.hommemummy.co.uk

Ickworth Hotel, Suffolk –
  www.ickworthhotel.com
Ikea – www.ikea.com
Isabella Oliver –
  www.isabellaoliver.com

Jigsaw; Junior Jigsaw –
  www.jigsaw-online.com
John Frieda – www.johnfrieda.com
John Lewis – www.johnlewis.com
JoJo Maman Bébé –
  www.jojomamanbebe.co.uk
Jo Malone – www.jomalone.co.uk
Joseph Baby – www.joseph.co.uk

Juicy Couture –
  www.juicycouture.com

Kenzo – www.kenzo.com

Lancome – www.lancome.com
Little Chicks Nappies –
  www.littlechicksnappies.com/
  Tel 07958 649 420
Little Darlings –
  www.littledarlingsfashion.com
Little Green Earthlets –
  www.earthlets.co.uk/ Tel: 0845 072
  4462
Little Me Baby Organics –
  www.littlemebabyorganics.co.uk
L'Occitane – www.loccitane.com

Mama Mio – www.mamamio.com
Marks and Spencer –
  www.marksandspencer.com
Maternity Exchange –
  www.maternityexchange.co.uk
Molton Brown –
  www.moltonbrown.co.uk
Monsoon Baby –
  www.monsoon.co.uk
Mothercare – www.mothercare.com

Nappy Nation –
  www.nappy-nation.co.uk/
  Tel 07930 964 582
National Childbirth Trust –
  www.nctpregnancyandbabycare.com/
  Tel: 0870 444 8707
Natural Mat Company –
  www.naturalmat.com
Nature Boy and Girl – www.naty.se
Neal's Yard –
  www.nealsyardremedies.com
Next – www.next.co.uk
The Nice Nappy Company –
  www.nicenappy.co.uk
9London – www.9london.co.uk
Nivea – www.nivea.com
Nuxe – www.nuxe.com

Ofsted – www.ofsted.gov.uk/ Tel: 020 7421 6744
Olay – www.olay.com
Origins – www.origins.com

The Parlour – www.theparlouruk.com
Paul & Joe – www.paulandjoe.com
Paul Smith – www.paulsmith.co.uk
Petit Bateau – www.petit-bateau.com
Petit Planet – www.planet21group.com
Philip Kingsley Post Partum Hair Management – www.philipkingsley.co.uk
Pizza Express – www.pizzaexpress.co.uk
Posh Baby – www.poshbaby.com
Prada – www.prada.com
Precious Earth – www.preciousearth.co.uk/ Tel: 01584 878633
Push – www.pushmaternity.com

Ralph Lauren – www.polo.com
Roberts – www.roberts-radios-online.co.uk

St Tropez – www.sttropeztan.com
The Sanctuary – www.thesanctuary.co.uk
Schmidt Natural Clothing – www.naturalclothing.co.uk
Séraphine – www.seraphine.com
Serendipity – www.serendipity-online.com
Simonetta Tiny – www.simonetta.it

Smythson – www.smythson.com
Space NK – www.spacenk.co.uk
Spirit of Nature – www.spiritofnature.co.uk/ Tel: 0870 725 9885
Stila Cosmetics – www.stilacosmetics.com
Storksak – www.storksak.co.uk

Temperley for Little People – www.temperleylondon.com
Tesco – www.tesco.com
Tête-à-Tête – try maternityexchange.co.uk
Tigerlilly – try ebay.co.uk
Top Shop – www.topshop.co.uk
Tot Bots – www.totsbots.com/ Tel 0141 550 1514
Tushies – www.tushies.co.uk

UK Nappy Line – www.nappyline.co.uk
Upfront – www.upfrontmaternity.com

Versace – www.versace.com
Vichy – www.vichy.com
Virgin Atlantic – www.virgin-atlantic.com
Vital Touch – www.vitaltouch.com

Waitrose – www.waitrose.com
WH Smith – www.whsmith.co.uk
The White Company – www.thewhitecompany.com
Woolley Grange hotel - www.woolleygrange.com

Index